THE
SYNERGY TRAP

How Companies Lose the Acquisition Game

MARK L. SIROWER

THE FREE PRESS

THE FREE PRESS
A Division of Simon & Schuster Inc.
1230 Avenue of the Americas
New York, NY 10020

Manufactured in the United States of America

10   9   8   7

Library of Congress Cataloging-in-Publication Data
Sirower, Mark L., 1962–
    The synergy trap: how companies lose the acquisition game /
Mark L. Sirower.
        p.   cm.
    Includes index.
    1. Consolidation and merger of corporations—United States.
2. Tender offers (Securities)—United States.   3. Management
buyouts—United States.   4. Competition—United States.
5. Risk—United States.   I. Title.
    HD2746.55.U5S57   1997
    338.8'3'0973—dc20   96-44862
                                                         CIP

ISBN 0-684-83255-0 (alk. paper)

To Mom and Dad

You will always be my greatest teachers

Contents

Appendix A: Review and Critique of Prior Research on
Mergers and Acquisitions   145

Appendix B: Detailed Results of the Analysis in Part 2   167

Appendix C: Sample and Descriptions of Targets and Acquirers
Used in the Analysis   201

Preface

The M&A wave of the 1980s has become the tidal wave of the 1990s. In 1996 alone, merger and acquisition announcements totaled over $500 billion. Although much has been written over the past three decades about these major corporate investment decisions, the fundamentals of acquisition performance have remained a mystery.

This book grew out of my doctoral research and through a course I developed, called "The Management of Corporate Merger and Acquisition Strategies," for MBAs and executives at Columbia Business School. The objective of the book is to break down the walls between finance and strategic management—and to expose the foundations of performance—in the vitally important area of acquisitions. Indeed, it is precisely the walls dividing the two fields that have given rise to unexamined and misleading folklore about the so-called "keys" to acquisition success.

Most prior research on mergers and acquisitions has reflected the divisionalized nature of business schools. Financial perspectives have ignored the competitive and organizational realities, and strategic management perspectives have been devoid of the finance so essential for an understanding of the value of investment decisions. A major result is that *synergy* has remained a vague and even mysterious concept—with little financial *or* strategic meaning. Unfortunately, in practice the use of "sophisticated" valuation models, combined with a poor understanding of what, exactly, synergy *is,* has caused the justification of many predictably bad acquisitions and the destruction of billions of dollars of shareholder value in acquiring firms.

Amid all the excitement surrounding M&A activity, it is easy to forget that acquisitions are strategic *alternatives*. CEOs, executive teams, and boards of directors readily choose acquisitions over other investment alternatives, paying substantial premiums in the process. They often fail to consider that it is incorrect to judge the soundness of an acquisition decision on the basis of what it would cost the company to develop that particular business from scratch—an idea that may have been a value-destroying decision on its own. In fact, acquisitions are unique alternatives and the success of these *strategic* decisions must be judged by their effects on the wealth of the owners—the shareholders—of the acquiring company.

It is the payment of an acquisition premium that sets up the unique business gamble that acquisitions represent. The premium forces a consideration of the performance already embedded in pre-acquisition share prices and the *improvements* in performance that will be required. In turn, these considerations give rise to the precise meaning and the *competitive* nature of synergy itself—a major component of this book.

When I first became interested in studying the managerial significance of the acquisition premium as a doctoral student at Columbia over seven years ago, a senior strategy professor challenged my ideas by saying, "Acquisition premiums are not a management issue—that's a finance topic." Although I knew this meant there would be a struggle ahead, the statement assured me there was an important opportunity to get to the heart of acquisition performance. The book is the result of a long journey. I hope the fundamentals of the acquisition game developed herein will set the stage for more thoughtful acquisition decisions and for future scholarly work on acquisition strategies.

The book is divided into two parts, beginning in rather shallow water and getting deeper as the book progresses. Part 1 presents the elements of acquisition performance, developing the competitive principles behind synergy and the economics of the acquisition premium. In particular, Chapter 4 integrates and extends the financial and strategic concepts presented in Part 1 and gives useful tools and lessons for anyone involved in acquisition decisions. This chapter is essentially a short course for managers, directors, investment bankers, and consultants involved in acquisitions.

Part 2 presents an extensive analysis of the performance of corporate acquisition strategies, incorporating and examining the elements of Part 1. Chapter 6, which details the methodology behind the study, can be bypassed by the manager who wants to get right to the discussion of the results in Chapter 7. Finally, Chapter 8 discusses the implications and contributions of the two parts of the book.

There are a number of people I would like to acknowledge for their contributions and support while I completed the book and the research behind it. First, I owe a very special thanks and an intellectual debt of gratitude to industrial-organization economist Dennis C. Mueller and the legendary chairman and CEO of Cooper Industries, Robert Cizik. Their contributions, over the past thirty years, to the academic literature and to the practice of acquisitions, respectively, have had a major impact on my thinking on acquisitions. In addition, I benefited greatly from their comments, advice, and encouragement during the process of writing the book.

I must thank my professors at Columbia University who allowed me the opportunity to pursue interdisciplinary work during my years in the business school. Ellen Auster, Warren Boeker, James Freeman, Kathryn Harrigan, Gailen Hite, and Boris Yavitz gave encouragement when this book was only ideas. Gailen Hite, my mentor and friend, guided me through the demands of the research on which this book is based. It will always be an honor to have worked with a scholar of his integrity. I am grateful to Kathryn Harrigan for encouraging me to transform this research into a book and, particularly, to publish with The Free Press. On both counts, it was truly a rewarding experience.

I also must thank my colleagues in the management department at the Stern School of Business at NYU for their support for the writing of this book. In particular, I must thank William Guth, Robert Lamb, and William Starbuck for convincing me to take the underlying research and open the ideas to managers. I am also grateful to my colleagues Rikki Abzug and Joseph Lampel for countless hours of helpful advice during the project. Karen Angelillo and Li Yang provided invaluable administrative support throughout.

In the process of presenting pieces of this work in various stages of development at universities and to executives, several people gave many insightful comments and suggestions. As with so many things in life, it is those little things here and there that add up over time. These people include: Bernard Black (Columbia Law School), Glynn Bolar (AT&T), David Collis (Harvard Business School), Bruce Greenwald (Columbia Business School), Philippe Haspeslagh (IN-SEAD), Robert Klemkosky (Indiana), Keith Kostuch (The Boston Consulting Group), Stephen O'Byrne (Stern Stewart & Co.), Jeff Phillips (Coopers & Lybrand), Mark Shanley (Northwestern), L. G. Thomas (Emory), Sheridan Titman (Boston College), Jeff Salzman (CS First Boston), Harbir Singh (Wharton), Nikhil Varaiya (San Diego State), Theo Vermaelen (INSEAD), and Feng Ye (Deutche Morgan Grenfell).

The professionals at The Free Press deserve extensive credit. I owe a large debt of gratitude to my editor, Robert Wallace, for his confidence in this project and for pushing its timely completion. Fortunately, he is surrounded by first-rate professionals. Dewey Brinkley, Iris Cohen, and Loretta Denner were instrumental in improving the quality of this work and seeing it through to completion. Loretta, in particular, was practically part of the family during the final months of production. Her patience and attention will always be remembered.

To my wife, Yaru: Although I do not know if I can stop talking about M&A, I will try to use the words *synergy* and *premium* less often. This book could never have happened without your love and support. I promise to get a much bigger up-front advance next time. Finally, this book is dedicated to the memory of my parents, who lovingly preached the values of integrity, honesty, determination, and perseverance. I hope this book reflects their teachings.

Mark L. Sirower
New York, New York

PART 1

UNCOVERING THE RULES OF THE GAME

1

Introduction:
The Acquisition Game

Many managers were apparently over-exposed in impressionable childhood years to the story in which the imprisoned, handsome prince is released from the toad's body by a kiss from the beautiful princess. Consequently they are certain that the managerial kiss will do wonders for the profitability of the target company. Such optimism is essential. Absent that rosy view, why else should the shareholders of company A want to own an interest in B at a takeover cost that is two times the market price they'd pay if they made direct purchases on their own? In other words investors can always buy toads at the going price for toads. If investors instead bankroll princesses who wish to pay double for the right to kiss the toad, those kisses better pack some real dynamite. We've observed many kisses, but very few miracles. Nevertheless, many managerial princesses remain serenely confident about the future potency of their kisses, even after their corporate backyards are knee-deep in unresponsive toads.

—Warren Buffett, 1981 *Berkshire Hathaway Annual Report*

The 1990s will go down in history as the time of the biggest merger and acquisition (M&A) wave of the century. Few, if any, corporate resource decisions can change the value of a company as quickly or dramatically as a major acquisition.

Yet the change is usually for the worse.

Shareholders of acquiring firms routinely lose money right *on announcement* of acquisitions. They rarely recover their losses. But share-

3

holders of the target firms, who receive a substantial premium for their shares, usually gain.

Here's a puzzle. Why do corporate executives, investment bankers, and consultants so often recommend that acquiring firms pay more for a target company than anybody else in the world is willing to pay? It cannot be because so many acquisitions turn out to be a blessing in disguise. In fact, when asked recently to name just one big merger that has lived up to expectations, Leon Cooperman, the former cochairman of Goldman Sachs's investment policy committee, answered, "I'm sure that there are success stories out there, but at this moment I draw a blank."[1]

It doesn't make sense. For over thirty years, academics and practitioners have been writing books and articles on managing mergers and acquisitions. Corporations have spent billions of dollars on advisory fees. The platitudes are well known. Everyone knows that you should not pay "too much" for an acquisition, that acquisitions should make "strategic sense," and that corporate cultures need to be "managed carefully." But do these nostrums have any practical value?

Consider. You know you've paid too much only if the acquisition fails. Then, *by definition,* you have overpaid.

But how do we predict *up front* whether a company is overpaying for an acquisition—in order to prevent costly failures? What exactly does the acquisition premium represent, and when is it too big? What is the acquirer paying for? These are the details, and the devil is in them.

This book returns to first principles and precisely describes the basics of what I call *the acquisition game.* Losing the game is almost guaranteed when acquirers do not realize that acquisitions are a special type of business gamble.

Like a major R&D project or plant expansion, acquisitions are a capital budgeting decision. Stripped to the essentials, an acquisition is a purchase of assets and technologies. But acquirers often pay a premium over the stand-alone market value of these assets and technologies. They pay the premium for something called *synergy.*

Dreams of synergy lead to lofty acquisition premiums. Yet virtually no attention has been paid to how these acquisition premiums affect performance. Perhaps this is because the concept of synergy itself has been poorly defined.

The common definition of synergy is $2 + 2 = 5$. This book will show just how dangerous that definition is. Pay attention to the math. The easiest way to lose the acquisition game is by failing to define synergy in terms of real, measurable improvements in competitive advantage.

A quantifiable post-merger challenge is embedded in the price of each acquisition. Using the acquisition premium, we can calculate what the required synergies must be. Often this calculation shows that the required performance improvements are far greater than what any business in a competitive industry can reasonably expect.

By analyzing the acquisition premium, we can determine in advance when the price is far above the potential value of an acquisition. We can also show why most purported synergies are like the colorful petals of the Venus flytrap—dangerous deceivers. But managers who analyze the acquisition premium and understand the concept of synergy will not get caught. They can predict the probability and the amount of shareholder losses or gains.

My claim is that most major acquisitions are *predictably* dead on arrival—no matter how well they are "managed" after the deal is done.

The M&A Phenomenon

Mergers and acquisitions are arguably the most popular and influential form of discretionary business investment. On the single day of April 22, 1996, with the announcement of the Bell Atlantic–NYNEX merger and Cisco Systems' acquisition of Stratacom, over $27 billion of acquisitions were announced. For 1995, the total value of acquisition activity was over $400 billion—for 1997, over $1 trillion.[2] By comparison, in the aggregate managers spent only $500 billion, on average, over the past several years on new plant and equipment purchases and a mere $130 billion on R&D.[3]

Acquisition premiums can exceed 100 percent of the market value of target firms. Evidence for acquisitions between 1993 and 1995 shows that shareholders of acquiring firms lose an average of 10 percent of their investment on announcement.[4] And over time, perhaps waiting for synergies, they lose even more.[5] A major McKinsey & Company study found that 61 percent of acquisition programs were failures because the acquisition strategies did not earn a sufficient return (cost of capital) on the funds invested.[6] Under the circumstances, it should be natural to question whether it is economically productive to pay premiums at all.

Logically, we should expect that managers choose an acquisition strategy only when it offers a better payoff than other strategic alternatives. But there are several pitfalls inherent in acquisitions because they are, in fact, a very unique investment.

First, since acquirers pay a premium for the business, they actually have two business problems to solve: (1) to meet the performance targets the market already expects, and (2) to meet the even higher targets implied by the acquisition premium. This situation is analogous to emerging technology investments where investors pay for breakthroughs that have not yet occurred, knowing that competitors are chasing the same breakthroughs. However, in acquisitions, the breakthroughs are called "synergies."

I define synergy as *increases in competitiveness and resulting cash flows beyond what the two companies are expected to accomplish independently.* In other words, managers who pay acquisition premiums commit themselves to delivering more than the market already expects from current strategic plans. The premium represents the value of the additional performance requirements.

Second, major acquisitions, unlike major R&D projects, allow no test runs, no trial and error, and, other than divesting, no way to stop funding during the project. Acquirers must pay up front just for the right to "touch the wheel."

Finally, once companies begin intensive integration, the costs of exiting a failing acquisition strategy can become very high. The integration of sales forces, information and control systems, and distribution systems, for example, is often very difficult to reverse in the short term. And in the process, acquirers may run the risk of taking their eyes off competitors or losing their ability to respond to changes in the competitive environment.

Legendary and successful acquirers such as Bestfoods, Cooper Industries, and Emerson Electric have learned over time and implicitly understand the fundamentals of the game.[7] But most companies make very few major acquisitions and often hire outside advisers to do the acquisition valuations (called *fairness opinions*). A Boston Consulting Group study found that during the pre-merger stage, eight of ten companies did not even consider how the acquired company would be integrated into operations following the acquisition.[8] It is no wonder that often the acquirer loses the entire premium—and more. Escalating the commitment by pouring more money into a doomed acquisition just makes things worse, perhaps even destroying the acquirer's preexisting business.

The objective of management is to employ corporate resources at their highest-value uses. When these resources are committed to acquisitions, the result is not simply failure or not failure. Instead there is a whole range of performance outcomes.

Shareholders can easily diversify themselves at existing market prices without having to pay an acquisition premium. My analysis in this book shows that acquisition premiums have little relation to potential value and that the losses we observe in the markets to acquisition announcements are predictable. What do acquiring firm executive teams and advisers see that markets do not?

The most obvious answer to this question is synergy, yet anecdotal evidence suggests that managers are somewhat reluctant to admit that they expect synergy from acquisitions. In the battle for Paramount, synergy became the embarrassing unspoken word. And Michael Eisner has stated that he does not like to use the "s" word regarding Disney's acquisition of CapCities/ABC.[9] So why do these executives pay premiums? Is it that those who do not remember the past are thoughtlessly repeating it?

The 1980s set all-time records for the number and dollar value of corporate mergers and takeovers in the United States, firmly displacing the famous merger wave of the 1960s. More than 35,000 deals worth almost $2 trillion were completed during the 1980s, with the average size of a deal reaching over $200 million in 1988 and 1989.[10] Advisory fees alone totaled over $3.5 billion in the peak years, 1988 and 1989.[11]

The merger and acquisition field is well established. Since 1980, managers have allocated over $20 billion to investment banking and other advisory fees to help formulate and ensure the success of their acquisition strategies. In addition to professional advisers, there are academic courses: leading universities give week-long seminars to packed houses all over the world, and the American Management Association has an extensive program on M&A. Yet despite all of this advice, many fail.

As Bruce Greenwald, a professor at Columbia Business School has said: "Once you see the truth about something it is obvious, but there are many seemingly obvious things that simply are not true." Obvious but untrue advice and folklore about acquisitions has led to bad business decisions. Why in fact do some acquisitions lose more money than others?

Back to First Principles: The Acquisition Game

A bad acquisition is one that does not earn back its cost of capital. Stock market reactions to mergers and acquisitions are the aggregate forecasts of investors and analysts around the world of the expectations of the value of the investment. What does it mean when these sophisticated capitalists bid down the stock of acquiring firms and bid up the stock of targets?

The theory of the acquisition game and the synergy trap is rooted in the Nobel Prize–winning research of Professors Franco Modigliani and Merton Miller (M&M). The M&M propositions and their pathbreaking research on valuation begin with the assumption that the value of a firm (V) is equal to the market value of the debt (D) plus the market value of the equity (E):[12]

$$V = D + E.$$

Think of this as an economic balance sheet where the market value of claims (the debt and equity) is a function of the expected earnings stream coming from the assets. You can divide the claims any way you like, but the value of the firm will remain the same. In the words of Merton Miller, "Think of the firm as a gigantic pizza, divided into quarters. If now you cut each quarter in half or in eighths, the M and

M proposition says that you will have more pieces but not more pizza."[13]

The application of this principle is crucial to understanding what it means for acquiring firms to lose huge chunks of market value following acquisition announcements. When you make a bid for the equity of another company (we will call this the *target* company), you are issuing claims or cash to the shareholders of that company. If you issue claims or cash in an amount greater than the economic value of the assets you purchase, you have merely transferred value from the shareholders of your firm to the shareholders of the target—right from the beginning. This is the way the economic balance sheet of your company stays balanced.

Markets give estimates of this range of value transfer through changes in share prices. The idea of the transfer of value is the stepping-off point for the development of the acquisition game. In short, playing the acquisition game is a business gamble where you pay up front for the right to control the assets of the target firm, and earn, you hope, a future stream of payoffs. But while the acquisition premium is known with certainty, the payoffs are not. What, then, is synergy?

Investors around the world have already valued the future expected performance of the target firm. That value equals the pre-acquisition share price. These investors' livelihoods are based on paying what the performance is worth. So synergy must translate into performance gains beyond those that are already expected. Simply put, achieving synergy means competing better. But in current hypercompetitive markets, it is a difficult challenge just to achieve the expected performance that is already built into existing share prices—at a zero premium. *What happens when we raise the bar?*

Because markets have already priced what is expected from the stand-alone firms, the net present value (NPV) of playing the acquisition game can be simply modeled as follows:

NPV = Synergy − Premium.

Companies that do not understand this fundamental equation risk falling into the synergy trap. To quote G. Bennett Stewart of Stern Stewart & Co., "Paying unjustified premiums is tantamount to making charitable contributions to random passersby, never to be re-couped by the buying company no matter how long the acquisition is held."[14]

It is the NPV of the acquisition decision—the expected benefits less the premium paid—that markets attempt to assess. The more negative the assessment is, the worse the damage is to the economic balance sheet and to the share price. Folklore says that the share price of acquirers inevitably drops on the announcement of acquisitions—but in a properly valued acquisition, that does not have to be true.

To visualize what synergy is and what exactly the premium represents in performance terms, imagine being on a treadmill. Suppose you are running at 3 mph but are required to run at 4 mph next year and 5 mph the year after. Synergy would mean running even harder than this expectation while competitors supply a head wind. Paying a premium for synergy—that is, for the right to run harder—is like putting on a heavy pack. Meanwhile, the more you delay running harder, the higher the incline is set. *This is the acquisition game.*

For most acquisitions, achieving significant synergy is not likely. When it does occur, it usually falls far short of the required performance improvements priced into the acquisition premium. Putting together two businesses that are profitable, well managed, and even related in every way is not enough to create synergy. After all, competitors are ever present.

What can a manager do with the new business that will make it more efficient for the new business to compete or harder for competitors to contest their markets? When the managers of Novell acquired WordPerfect for $1.4 billion, did they calculate what Word-Perfect was already required to accomplish given the first bid for WordPerfect by Lotus for $700 million? Did they ask what Novell, the parent, could do to make it more competitive against the office suite products of Microsoft or Lotus? If they asked, their answers apparently left something out. Novell lost $550 million of market value on announcement of the acquisition. Since then, Microsoft has continued to gain market share and Novell recently sold WordPerfect, less than two years later, to Corel for less than $200 million—a loss of over $1.2 billion.[15]

A Brief History of the Research on Acquisitions

Faced with the facts of acquisition performance, academics have struggled to explain them. The explanations fall into two broad categories: (1) managers attempt to maximize shareholder value by either replacing inefficient management in the target firm or achieving synergies between the two firms, or (2) managers pursue their own objectives such as growth or empire building at the expense of shareholder value. These hypotheses are an attempt to understand the average results of acquisitions and can be of use to policymakers.

Interestingly, there were good old days in the acquisition business. Research examining mergers from the 1960s and 1970s found that target firm shareholders on average experienced significant gains and acquirers either gained or, at worst, broke even.[16] These results were consistent with the reasonable economic expectation that buyers would bid up asset prices to their fair value.

Then something went wrong. The evidence from the merger wave of the 1980s shows significantly negative results to the shareholders of acquiring firms upon announcement of the acquisition.[17] These negative results extended beyond the initial announcement; shareholder returns declined as much as 16 percent over the three years following the acquisition.[18]

The evidence documenting the destruction of value to the shareholders of acquiring firms came as no surprise to industrial-organization economists who for more than thirty years have studied the effects of mergers on issues such as accounting profitability, market share, and growth. The overwhelming evidence is that mergers do not improve profitability. Indeed, many studies show decreases in profitability at the line-of-business level. And these disappointing results hold also for market share and growth.[19] These results are consistent with the hypothesis that managers are pursuing objectives other than wealth maximization for their shareholders.

Richard Roll, a finance professor at UCLA, explained value-destructive acquisitions with a dramatic template, suggesting that managers actually believe there are synergies that can be achieved from acquisitions but that they are infected with a classic tragic flaw—hubris.[20] They are overconfident and thus pay too much when they win a bidding contest. In this scenario, overinflated egos cause acquisitions to fail.

This type of proposition can generate great notoriety for an academic and is exactly what the popular press looks for: the chance to pin a big failed decision on the ego of a CEO. How do you explain the difference between a failed acquisition and a successful one? The CEO had a bigger ego. Yet the hypothesis fails to explain why the premiums paid over the past ten to fifteen years are as much as five times the premiums paid during the 1960s and early 1970s when acquisitions on average created value for shareholders. Are we to understand that managers today are five times more confident or have an ego five times bigger than it was during the conglomerate era of the 1960s? And what about big-ego executives who do not make acquisitions?

In the end it is impossible to test whether the hubris hypothesis or the hypothesis that managers simply pursue their own objectives is the true explanation. As Dennis Mueller of the University of Vienna so insightfully states, "Whether the premium paid actually represents the underlying beliefs of managers is inherently unanswerable in the absence of testimony at the time of the acquisition by managers under the influence of *truth serum*."[21]

My objective here is to describe thoroughly what senior executives are getting their companies and their shareholders into when they enter the acquisition game, regardless of their motives. Reaching the decision to approve an acquisition is a complex process with a multitude of players, advisers, opinions, and interests. Major acquisitions are actually rare decisions for most companies. The problem is not necessarily hubris or even self-interest but may simply be unfamiliarity with the fundamentals of the problem. Acquisitions must be compared to other strategic alternatives. The real concern for managers is not the personal motivations of the players or the size of their ego but the mechanics of why the acquisition either works or does not work. What does the *range* of outcomes to acquirers mean? There have been many hypotheses, but no explanations.

Students of management strategy have focused on the factors that affect individual corporate performance. Professor Richard Rumelt broke new ground in the early 1970s when he found that firms with a pattern of related diversification had consistently higher accounting profitability than firms that diversified into businesses that had little relation to each other.[22] Before this discovery, folklore held that "professional management" could be applied to any business, from helicopters to men's socks.

Management research in the 1980s wrestled with the question of whether related acquisitions outperform unrelated acquisitions.[23] If Rumelt's hypothesis were true, then it was conjectured that acquirers whose business is more closely related to the business of the target should meet a more favorable stock market reaction than acquirers purchasing unrelated targets.

In fact, the evidence was mixed. Some studies concluded that related acquisitions were better than unrelated acquisitions, others that unrelated acquisitions were better than related acquisitions, and still others that the relationship just did not matter. So despite a decade of research, empirically based academic literature can offer managers no clear understanding of how to maximize the probability of success in acquisition programs.

The intrinsic problem with the literature is a lack of understanding of the meaning of the premium or the meaning of synergy. Instead of examining this problem, the acquisition performance literature in the management field has implicitly assumed the competitive markets' view that prices are bid up to their "fair" value.[24] Within this model, gains may be merely a matter of luck, and losses are a matter of failed potential or mismanagement.[25]

In other words, management researchers simply assumed that acquisition prices are highly correlated with potential value. Given this assumption, they could not consider the acquisition premium's potential as a predictor of post-acquisition performance. Thus, notably absent in all management studies to date is any consideration of the meaning or possible performance effects of the acquisition premium.

Because many researchers have assumed that the premiums represent fair prices in the beginning, a failed acquisition must have been the result of managerial problems such as post-acquisition culture clashes, morale problems, and leadership failures. The practical problem with this approach is that it does not realistically address whether the acquisition strategy could have worked even in the absence of implementation problems. It is wrong to assume that if the management problems were not there, all or any of the synergy promised by the premium would occur.

Whether acquisition premiums are fair values needs to be challenged. Because acquisitions are complex processes involving different levels of management, different political agendas, investment bankers, law firms, and accounting firms, it is altogether too easy for executives to pay too much.[26] Many acquisition premiums require performance improvements that are virtually impossible to realize, even for the best of managers in the best of industry conditions.

The first step in understanding the acquisition game is to admit that price may have nothing at all to do with value. I call this the *synergy limitation view* of acquisition performance. In this view, synergy has a low expected value and, thus, the level of the acquisition premium predicts the level of losses in acquisitions.

For the past two decades, the premiums paid for acquisitions—measured as the additional price paid for an acquired company over its pre-acquisition value—have averaged between 40 and 50 percent, with many regularly surpassing 100 percent (e.g., IBM's acquisition of Lotus). Yet, as I show in Part 2 of this book, the higher the premium is, the greater is the value destruction from the acquisition strategy.

Restating the definition of performance, NPV = Synergy − Premium, we see that if synergies are predictably limited, the premium becomes an up-front predictor of the returns to acquirers. My objective is to explain the range of performance outcomes we observe, no matter how acquisitions perform on average. For example, in the sample of acquisitions from my study, the range of market reactions just on announcement ranges from a positive 30 percent to a negative 22 percent. Since the average size of acquirers in the sample is over $2 billion, we are talking about a significant range of changes in value.

If price represented value, then synergy would generally occur in the amount dictated by the premium. But suppose that price in acquisitions is *not* correlated with potential value. Further, suppose that *potential* is limited even in acquisitions where no post-merger problems occur. Predictions about overpayment up front would then be possible, and integration issues could be considered within a performance context.

In Chapter 2, I discuss the cornerstones of synergy to give a picture of what achieving synergy means and why it would naturally be limited in the absence of detailed post-merger strategies and clearly identified corporate parenting skills. And even then the intensity of the managerial challenge is imposing.

Chapter 3 examines the acquisition premium in detail. I analyze what I call the dynamics of *required performance improvements* (RPIs). The numerical simulations in this chapter give a picture of the actual performance requirements that managers face on a day-to-day basis following an acquisition just to break even. For various levels of the acquisition premium, we consider the "odds" of achieving the RPIs. Unless they consider the odds of payoffs in acquisitions, executives are merely playing craps with shareholder resources (worse—because at least in craps, we know the odds).

Following the fundamentals of the acquisition game and the synergy trap developed in Part 1 of the book, I present a comprehensive cross-sectional study of the determinants of acquiring firm performance. Specifically, I ask four major questions:

1. Do corporate acquisition strategies create value?
2. Can the knowledge of the acquisition premium be used to predict the performance outcomes of an acquisition?
3. How do other factors (such as strategic relatedness, relative size, method of payment, mergers versus tender offers) affect performance in the context of the acquisition premium?
4. Will future risk taking by managers in acquiring firms be affected by the size of the acquisition premium?

Question 4 is posed to probe what may happen to acquirers after predictably falling into the synergy trap. Once they are caught in the trap, do they make matters worse by exhibiting gambling behavior?

This study is based on a sample of major acquisitions during the period 1979 through 1990. Each acquirer and target company was listed on the New York or American Stock Exchange, and the target was required to be at least 10 percent the size of the acquirer since my objective was to examine the effects of major acquisitions on the shareholder value of the acquirer. The average relative size of the acquisitions in the study was nearly 50 percent of the acquirer's value. Finally, the size of the acquisition had to be at least $100 million. Although approximately 80 percent of the number of acquisitions completed across the economy represent deals under $100 million in value, over 80 percent of the dollar value of acquisition activity is driven by acquisitions that are over $100 million in value.

I measure shareholder performance spanning seven different periods of time and using four different models of shareholder returns: (1) total shareholder returns (raw returns, commonly known as TSRs), (2) market-adjusted returns, (3) market- and risk-adjusted returns, and (4) mean-adjusted returns (returns relative to past performance). Past studies have used different measures, so I test my propositions against all of them. Fortunately, the major results are robust to these twenty-eight specifications of performance. Again, the objective is to understand what drives the range of performance no matter how it is measured.

The major results of the study support Michael Eisner's dislike of the "s" word. When other factors are held constant, the level of the premium is a significant up-front predictor of performance across all twenty-eight measures of performance. In other words, armed solely with the knowledge of the premium, any manager can give an estimate of how much money the acquisition strategy will lose and how much value destruction the shareholders of the acquiring firm will experience. From an outsider's perspective, I am offering an explanation of what markets see that managers and investment bankers do not seem to see.

Because the *amount* of losses can be predicted, these results go well beyond the winner's curse where bidders seem to overpay in auctions. And it makes no difference whether multiple bidders exist. (In fact, a potential acquirer should probably worry if no one else is bidding on the company.) I also demonstrate how strategically unrelated acquisitions can create more value than related acquisitions. Once you understand the synergy trap, this makes perfect sense.

There are fewer fairy-tale finishes than expectations out there, as Warren Buffett has related in the opening quotation to this chapter.

The study strongly supports the fundamentals developed in Part 1 of the book. These fundamentals provide real tools for the real world, to enable managers to grapple with real problems.

There *is* a serious problem facing senior executives who choose acquisitions as a corporate growth strategy. *My study reveals that fully 65 percent of major strategic acquisitions have been failures.* And some have been truly major failures resulting in dramatic losses of value for the shareholders of the acquiring company. With market values and acquisition premiums at record highs, it is time to articulate demanding standards for what constitutes informed or prudent decision making. The risks are too great otherwise.

Falling into the synergy trap means losing the acquisition game from the beginning. There are many ways to lose the game, but if you want to better your chances of success, you must understand the components of the game and the underlying fundamentals. The following chapters clearly describe the cornerstones of synergy and show how the seductive simplicity of financial valuation models can spell disaster for the shareholders of an acquirer. And all the implementation and cultural management in the world will not save an acquisition that is DOA.

2

Can You Run Harder? Synergy

There are some [synergies] here for sure. I don't know where they are yet. To say that now would be an idiot's game.

—Barry Diller, *commenting on QVC's proposed "strategic" acquisition of CBS in 1994*

Acquiring firms destroy shareholder value. This is a plain fact. So the size and scope of acquisition activity should be extremely troubling. But here is another puzzle.

Lawsuits and bad press punish other value destroying corporate decisions. When Metallgesellschaft, Barings Bank, and Procter & Gamble lost millions on derivatives transactions, there was a public outcry about the dangers of these decisions and concern whether senior management understood enough about the strategies to effectively control them. But acquirers have lost with impunity even billions of dollars of shareholder value as they have pursued poorly understood acquisition strategies.

"It seemed like a good strategic decision," or "It seemed like a good deal at the time," or "The financials looked good but we just didn't implement it correctly," or "We didn't manage the cultures right." Should we just laugh when hearing these rationalizations? What is synergy, anyway? Can it be achieved? Or is it just a trap? How can an acquirer know whether any value will be gained from an

18

acquisition, *even at a zero premium?* These are the questions that must be answered.

Warren Hellman, former head of Lehman Brothers, has commented, "So many mergers fail to deliver what they promise that there should be a presumption of failure. The burden of proof should be on showing that anything really good is likely to come out of one."[1] The objective here is to describe the intensity of this managerial challenge.

If Value (NPV) = Synergy − Premium, then the first step in understanding synergy is to consider what an acquisition must accomplish to generate value at a *zero* premium. It is hard to achieve synergy even when the acquirer gets the target company at the going market price. Unless certain necessary competitive conditions can be met and the required cornerstones of synergy are in place, there is no chance of performance gains.

The synergy trap opens for the eight out of ten companies involved in major acquisitions that do little pre-acquisition planning. But even for the two out of ten that do plan, performance improvements already required by the pre-acquisition price of the target firm and the certainty of competitor reactions will limit synergies.

Like any other major investment decision, acquisitions represent strategic resource commitments. They must be judged by the same standards as any strategic alternative: Does this commitment of resources, both financial and human, create value for the shareholders of the corporation? The shareholders of the acquirer, after all, can buy the shares of the target firm if they want to, on the market, without paying a premium. So why should executives spend shareholders' money to buy what shareholders can buy more cheaply without help? If the answer to this question is *synergy*, then we have to understand precisely what synergy means.

Synergy and the Acquisition Game

When executives play the acquisition game, they pay, in addition to the current market price, an up-front premium for an uncertain stream of payoffs sometime in the future. Since shareholders do not have to pay a premium to buy the shares of the target on their own, these payoffs, the *synergies,* must represent something that shareholders cannot get on their own. They must mean improvements in performance greater than those *already* expected by the markets. If these synergies are not achieved, the acquisition premium is merely a gift from the shareholders of the acquirer to the shareholders of the target company.

Current share prices at various market multiples already have substantial projected improvements in profitability and growth built into them. Hence, our operational definition of synergy is this: *Synergy is the increase in performance of the combined firm over what the two firms are already expected or required to accomplish as independent firms.*

Where acquirers can achieve the performance that is already expected from the target, the net present value (NPV) of an acquisition strategy then is clearly represented by the following formula:

NPV = Synergy − Premium.

In management terms, synergy means competing better than anyone ever expected. It means gains in competitive advantage over and above what firms already need to survive in their competitive markets.

One reason that synergy is difficult to achieve is that the current strategic plans and resources of the target do have value. The easiest trap to fall into occurs when acquirers forget about this value. Acquirer management must maintain and manage this value while making changes in operations. It may be unrealistic to hope to gain two customers, but it is very easy to lose two customers after an acquisition. As Unisys (the merger of Burroughs and Sperry), Novell (with its acquisition of WordPerfect), and so many other acquirers have learned the hard way, all the cultural management in the world will not generate synergies and will not save an acquisition that reduces the competitiveness of the underlying businesses. Most of the problems that have been considered in managing acquisitions are important with regard to maintaining value rather than creating it. But acquisitions at a premium demand ever more.

Recall that acquisitions are a unique investment decision for some important managerial reasons: (1) there are no dry runs, and all the money is paid up front; (2) the exit costs following integration can be extremely high, in both reputation and dollars; and (3) managing synergy is in many ways like managing a new venture or a new business.

Putting the idea of managing above what is already expected into an earnings per share (EPS) context, we can think of the management challenge of synergy in this way:

$$\text{EPS (tomorrow)} = \text{EPS (today)} + \text{EPS (today)} \times \text{Expected growth} + \textit{Synergy}.$$

The management challenge of any business is the base business today plus the expected growth of the future business. The expected future growth and profitability improvements are already embedded in current share prices. Adding synergy means creating value that not only does not yet exist but is not yet expected. So achieving synergy— improvements above what is already expected or required—is like starting a new business venture. There might be improvements in performance following an acquisition, but if they were already expected, that is not synergy. And if it costs a lot more to run this new venture after the acquisition, funds may be diverted from pre-acquisition strategic plans, and value may be destroyed rather than created.[2]

Let us carefully examine the management challenge already embedded in the pre-acquisition market value of a firm's securities. Before an acquirer can even consider paying a premium, it must understand what is already expected to result from current strategies. This is the base case.

The Performance Requirements of Pre-Acquisition Market Values

The examples presented here are the estimated performance expectations for 1995–2004 given the 1994 performance and year-end total market values for Lotus Development, Scott Paper, Wal-Mart, and Microsoft. The lesson from this analysis is not only the intense management challenge already embedded in the market values of these companies but also the very different *types* of management challenges. Contrary to the common folklore that Wall Street values only short-term performance, market values do reflect long-term expectations of the performance of firms.

The market value of a company (debt plus equity) is equal to the invested capital plus the net present value of this invested capital:

Market value = Invested capital + NPV of investments.

A company resembles a bond. A bond trades at par if the coupon rate is equal to the discount rate; it trades at a premium when the coupon rate is higher than the discount rate. Similarly, if the market value of a company is greater than its invested capital, it reflects the expectations of investors around the world that current and future invested capital has a positive NPV—that is, the return on invested capital is higher than the weighted average cost of capital for the company.

This is the basis for estimating the future expectations of performance embedded in the current market value of a company. Given a current market value, current performance, and the amount of invested capital, what must future performance be in order to justify the current value? Figure 2.1 shows the expected net operating profit (NOP), return on invested capital (ROIC), and the expected spread between the ROIC and weighted average cost of capital (WACC) of each company.[3] This figure presents four different management challenges given the 1994 performance and year-end market values of the four companies.

Lotus and Scott Paper, the targets of two recent acquisitions (IBM and Kimberly-Clark, respectively), are earning negative spreads relative to their costs of capital, but their ROIC is expected to improve dramatically over the coming ten years. Synergies in these acquisitions must be additional performance improvements beyond the already steep expectations. It is not surprising, then, that Wayne Sanders, CEO of Kimberly-Clark, paid a zero premium for Scott Paper, and there were no other bidders. As for IBM's acquisition of Lotus, the market value of IBM dropped by almost the amount of the premium ($1.65 billion) it paid for Lotus right on announcement of the acquisition (NPV = Synergy − Premium).

Contrast this to the performance expectations and challenges for

FIGURE 2.1

Expected Future Performance Embedded in Current Market Values

Year	Lotus			Scott Paper			Wal-Mart			Microsoft		
	NOP	ROIC	ROIC – WACC	NOP	ROIC	ROIC – WACC	NOP	ROIC	ROIC – WACC	NOP	ROIC	ROIC – WACC
1995	$219	15.6%	-2.2%	$277	5.7%	-5.1%	$3515	12.0%	2.3%	$2073	30.9%	16.5%
1996	$249	17.1%	-0.8%	$358	7.3%	-3.5%	$3829	11.8%	2.1%	$2500	32.1%	17.7%
1997	$280	18.5%	0.6%	$439	8.9%	-1.9%	$4177	11.6%	2.0%	$2996	33.1%	18.7%
1998	$312	19.8%	2.0%	$521	10.6%	-0.2%	$4561	11.5%	1.8%	$3572	34.0%	19.6%
1999	$346	21.1%	3.3%	$602	12.2%	1.4%	$4986	11.3%	1.7%	$4240	34.8%	20.4%
2000	$380	22.3%	4.5%	$684	13.8%	3.0%	$5457	11.2%	1.6%	$5016	35.4%	21.1%
2001	$417	23.6%	5.7%	$766	15.4%	4.6%	$5977	11.1%	1.5%	$5916	36.0%	21.6%
2002	$454	24.7%	6.8%	$849	17.0%	6.2%	$6553	11.0%	1.4%	$6961	36.5%	22.1%
2003	$493	25.8%	7.9%	$932	18.6%	7.8%	$7189	10.9%	1.3%	$8175	36.9%	22.6%
2004	$534	26.9%	9.0%	$1015	20.2%	9.4%	$7894	10.8%	1.2%	$9583	37.3%	22.9%

NOP = Earnings (in $ millions) before interest and taxes × (1 − tax rate).

ROIC = NOP/invested capital.

ROIC − WACC = expected spread between ROIC and WACC.

Note: Data courtesy of Stephen O'Byrne, Stern Stewart & Co.

Wal-Mart and Microsoft. For Wal-Mart CEO David Glass, the challenge is *maintaining* the spreads between ROIC and WACC on a huge amount of invested capital. At year end 1992, Wal-Mart's market value was almost $20 billion more than at year end 1994. In other words, the market had expected much higher spreads. When performance did not meet expectations, the market lowered its expectations about the future performance for Wal-Mart.

The picture for Microsoft is truly striking. It illustrates the real dominance that Microsoft has over its competitors. Not only is the company expected to maintain the current spread between its return on capital and its cost of capital of over 15 percent, but this incredible spread is expected to increase.

This is how markets work: they anticipate the future. Synergies exist and add value only if they exceed what is already embedded in market prices. Executives must understand the severity of this management challenge before entering the acquisition game. If they do not understand this picture, as often they do not, then planning for synergy either before or after an acquisition will likely be meaningless.

So where is the new value going to come from? If cultures are managed correctly and all employees receive hats with the new corporate name and logo, will that create synergy? If two large companies are put together that are already operating well above minimum efficient scale and already have to run hard just to stay in place, will cost savings be generated? And if there are cost savings, how much will they be?

The synergy problem must be tackled within a competitive context. At the end of the day, acquirers need to be able to show where additional cash will be available to suppliers of capital. How exactly will they generate higher revenues or lower costs less additional required capital investment in a competitive market?

The Competitive Challenge of Synergy

Certain competitive conditions must be present before synergy can occur in any acquisition, but these necessary conditions are by no means sufficient for performance gains. Recently popular concepts, such as the resource-based view and the core competency view of competitiveness, are really mere descriptions of what has occurred in the past.[4] They give managers little help in formulating expectations about the outcomes of future strategic investments. In these popular views, success derives from private or tacit information and ex post, nontradeable, and specialized resources.[5] Notably lacking is the "how much" quality, so essential for differentiating strategic alternatives.

In acquisitions, managers must show what will be different before they can actually value the strategy. They must be prepared to answer *how* and *in what ways* it will be more difficult for competitors to compete in the businesses of both the target and the acquirer. They must consider whether competitors will be able to challenge successfully— or what I call "contest"—the improvements that the acquirer will attempt in order to generate performance gains. Whether merging firms have valuable resources or competencies as stand-alones reveals little about the ability to create synergy. By contrast, the contestability approach that I present here puts the questions that acquirers must ask in competitive terms.

Using the value chain concept advanced by Michael Porter of the Harvard Business School, we can think of a business as consisting of input markets, processes, and output markets.[6] In any competitive business, competitors are already attempting to contest each other's markets by finding the most efficient means of producing a given set of products and services and/or offering a more attractive set of products and services at a given cost structure.[7] In a competitive environment, the only way to earn economic returns is by preventing rivals (current and potential) from winning along the value chain. At least one of the following conditions is necessary:

1. Acquirers must be able to further limit competitors' ability to contest their or the targets' current input markets, processes, or output markets, and/or

2. Acquirers must be able to open new markets and/or *encroach* on their competitors' markets where these competitors cannot respond.

This is the starting point. Condition 1 involves the ability of the acquirer to sustain advantages or decrease vulnerabilities. Condition 2 involves the ability of the acquirer to engage competitors in current or new markets in ways that were not previously possible. The following examples illustrate these conditions.

Anheuser-Busch/Campbell Taggart/Eagle Snacks

Anheuser-Busch (A-B) is a distribution and marketing giant. In 1979, A-B started Eagle Snacks, and in 1982, A-B paid $560 million (about a 20 percent premium) for Campbell Taggart, a major manufacturer of bread and snacks. What could be more natural than combining the distribution and sales of beer, bread, and salty snacks? After all, they all use yeast. In fact, however, beer and snacks go into different areas of supermarkets and convenience stores, and they have different ordering schedules. Although A-B devised a distribution strategy using Eagle distributors, Campbell Taggert distributors, and its regular beer distributors, it failed to achieve synergy. What's more, A-B's beer distributors refused to detract from their own core business to support A-B's emerging and inevitable fight with snack-food leader Frito-Lay.[8]

Anheuser-Busch's distributors laid the blame for the failure squarely at the feet of Frito-Lay, which did not sit still to watch while A-B generated synergies at its expense. Indeed, as A-B expanded the Eagle product line, Frito-Lay attacked with an array of new products and price cuts on existing products. A-B's snack market share never topped 6 percent, while Frito's increased from 40 percent to 50 percent. For 1995 alone, the Eagle brand lost $25 million on sales of $400 million. After seventeen years of losses, A-B put the Eagle brand to rest. Interestingly, A-B sold its four Eagle Snacks plants to none other than Frito-Lay, and Campbell Taggart was spun off to shareholders. The lesson is that if the strategic moves of an acquirer are easily contestable, competitive gains, and thus synergy, will not occur.

Engines for the Boeing 777

The ferocious competition among the potential engine suppliers for the Boeing 777—General Electric, Pratt & Whitney, and Rolls-Royce—is an excellent lesson in this concept of contestability even though no acquisition is involved.

In 1994, it was expected that supplying the 777 engines would be highly profitable (as the aircraft engine business has been traditionally) and that Pratt & Whitney and General Electric would hold the number 1 and number 2 positions in the business, respectively. At that time, Pratt had more than half of all orders, and it appeared that Rolls-Royce would be a distant third. But Rolls-Royce came in with rock-bottom pricing—more than 50 percent below list prices—and seized the number 2 spot while threatening Pratt & Whitney by winning a major Singapore Airlines bid.[9]

The ability to contest product markets must be driven by changes in competitiveness in preceding parts of the value chain of the businesses. Just to stay in the game, these aircraft manufacturers have had to slash costs by cutting workforce size, closing manufacturing and office space, subcontracting, and moving subassembly to cheaper locations. Rolls reportedly is attempting to cut costs an additional 40 percent.[10]

Lockheed Martin/Loral Corporation

Vertical integration acquisitions present other interesting competitor reactions. Lockheed Martin paid $9.1 billion for most of the electronics supplier Loral Corporation. The result is that Loral, as a captive supplier of Lockheed, is now perceived and treated as a competitor by its erstwhile customers.

In a move that surprised Loral's chairman, Bernard Schwartz (now a vice chairman of Lockheed Martin), Harry Stonecipher, CEO of McDonnell Douglas (M-D), announced that M-D would switch its business away from Loral to other potential suppliers of electronic systems such as Litton Industries or Raytheon.[11] Clearly McDonnell Douglas has little incentive to support the operations of a major rival for defense contracts when there are alternative suppliers. So before Lockheed Martin can realize any net synergies from the Loral acquisition, it will need to make up for the substantial lost business resulting from M-D's decision to switch suppliers. A similar scenario may play out in the entertainment business, where former suppliers are now owned by competitors. Such relationships may cause serious problems for Viacom, Disney, Time Warner, and others.

Achieving synergy is a brand new competitive problem for executive teams of acquirers, and their competitors will be watching and reacting in anticipation of changes. Acquirers need to ask which of their competitors will stand by silently while the attempt is made to generate synergy at their expense. In hypercompetitive environments, this expectation is simply unrealistic.[12]

Unfortunately for acquirers, these contestability conditions are necessary but not sufficient. For example, customers may not value the new products or may not want to change their buying habits. The acquisition may require substantial additional investments in the business, even beyond the target's price, that negate any additional operating profitability. If the executives of an acquirer do not understand the target's businesses well enough to consider these issues, they will be extremely hard-pressed to develop a credible outlook for potential performance gains.

The Cornerstones of Synergy

How can acquirers know when they are likely to realize little value gain from an acquisition even at a zero acquisition premium? Here, we put the contestability conditions within a managerial framework.

Figure 2.2 illustrates the cornerstones of synergy. The four cornerstones represent the major elements of an acquisition strategy that must be in place for there to be any likelihood of synergy. The diagram is presented in the context of the premium decision (tackled in the next chapter) and competitor reactions. If any of these four cornerstones is missing when the deal is done, synergy will be a trap; the premium is likely to represent a total loss for the shareholders of the acquirer.

As with the contestability conditions, these cornerstones are necessary *but not sufficient* components to ensure performance gains. Achieving significant synergy is fundamentally difficult even when the essential cornerstones are in place—so even at a zero acquisition premium, synergy will be limited.

Acquirers can easily destroy value in the stand-alone businesses by attempting to gain synergies that have little chance of occurring. Executives who are making the costly mistake of throwing additional resources at a failing acquisition strategy can decrease the value of their businesses and make them more vulnerable to competitive attacks.

FIGURE 2.2

The Cornerstones of Synergy

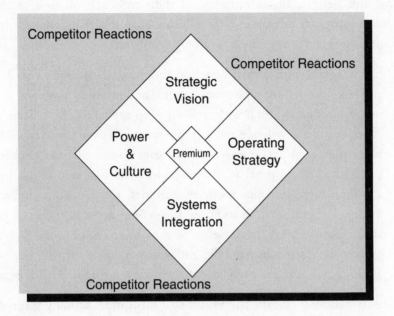

A poor understanding of the fundamentals of synergy can hurt acquirers in three important ways:

1. Post-acquisition planning will be a disappointing waste of managerial resources.
2. The limits to performance improvements will not be understood, so overpayment will be predictable; valuation will consist of hollow and spurious assumptions.
3. Original values of the acquiring and target firms will be severely jeopardized. The premium will be lost, and additional investments to achieve synergy will subtract shareholder value.

Strategic Vision

Strategic vision is where all acquisitions begin. Management's vision of the acquisition is shared with suppliers, customers, lenders, and employees as a framework for planning, discussions, decisions, and reactions to changes. The vision must be clear to large constituent groups and adaptable to many unknown circumstances. Viacom's vision to be the "premier globally branded content provider" is a clear communicable vision, as was AT&T's vision for the NCR acquisition to "link people, organizations and their information in a seamless global computer network."[13] Sears's one-stop shopping concept in financial services was really a wonderful vision:

> Just imagine, with virtual one-stop shopping, a customer could find and buy a house, through Sears; finance and insure it, with Sears; furnish it, decorate it, fill it with well-serviced appliances, from Sears; and contract for a new fence and a home security system, by Sears. Later, he or she could obtain a second mortgage to remodel the kitchen or build an addition, purchase insurance to cover that second mortgage, and then buy the paint, tools, and cabinets for that home improvement—all from Sears. In addition, they could invest in the stock market or buy an IRA, from Sears; or rent a car or subscribe to home movies, at Sears; plus pay bills, order flowers for a relative, deposit a weekly paycheck, and even have their income tax figured, all at Sears.[14]

Unfortunately for Sears, the vision that customers actually wanted to or would buy these different products and services in one place *and* improve the core merchandising business was a mirage.

Investment bankers and executives are usually very good at coming up with a compelling and attractive strategic vision statement. Without the other three cornerstones, however, the vision has little use. The vision must be a continuous guide to the actual operating plans of the acquisition. If the vision does not translate into real actions, it can provoke damaging reactions from competitors.

Visions clue competitors in to the acquirer's actual operating strategies. What better time for a competitor to launch an attack on a major market of an acquirer or the target than on the announcement of a major acquisition? American Airlines took critical share points away from United in its major Chicago hub soon after United's (now divested) acquisitions of Hilton Hotels and Hertz in the mid-1980s. At point of sale it might seem intuitive that an airline, hotel chain, and rental car company could create an integrated travel strategy. In fact, these three businesses have little in common in the preceding parts of their business value chains, and the hotel and rental car businesses diverted valuable management attention away from the core airline business.

The Quaker Oats acquisition of Snapple began with a promising vision and a zero premium. The November 1994 acquisition was, at $1.7 billion, the largest in Quaker's history. William Smithburg, chairman and CEO of Quaker, pronounced that the acquisition "brings together the marketing muscle and growth potential of two of the great brands in an increasingly health-conscious America: Gatorade in sports drinks and Snapple in ice teas and juice drinks."[15]

The stock market didn't get it, though. Quaker paid a zero premium for Snapple yet lost 10 percent of its market value, or nearly $500 million, on announcement of the acquisition. Snapple went on to lose $100 million in 1995 and even decreased its planned marketing budget. Why? Quaker was not the only company to notice the iced tea and fruit juice market. PepsiCo relaunched its Lipton's Brew brand of ready-to-drink iced teas, and Coca-Cola launched its Frutopia brand of fruit drinks with $30 million of advertising and $150 million in increased production capacity for the brand. In July 1996 Quaker announced a plan to *give away* $40 million of Snapple to shore up projected market share losses to the new products of Coca-Cola and PepsiCo.[16] This was in addition to a planned $30 million in advertising. If synergies ever emerge from the Quaker–Snapple acquisition, it is highly unlikely they will come from the product market. Vision is only the beginning.

Operating Strategy

Management's operating strategy must respond to the contestability questions posed earlier: What can be further sustained or improved along the value chains of the businesses that competitors cannot challenge, and how can competitors be attacked and disabled?

The operating strategy cornerstone determines where any contestability gains can occur. Given that most major acquisitions involve little pre-acquisition planning, most acquisitions have no real operating strategy on the day the deal is completed. Instead there is a restatement of the vision with comments about how good the "fit" is between the assets of the acquirer and the target. But actions speak louder than words, and without an operating strategy the vision is just words.

For example, Time Warner's acquisition of Turner Broadcasting System leaves much in doubt concerning the changes in the competitive strength of the companies. Chairman Gerald Levin has claimed that 35 percent of the new company will be owned by people who "understand the media business and the powerful nature of where it's going."[17] Does this mean that the companies will be managed better than before? An operating strategy arising out of the acquisition must address how it will be more difficult for Viacom, Westinghouse, Disney, and News Corp. to attack Time Warner–TBS along the value chains of the businesses in which they all compete.

Shareholders lost over $2.2 billion of market value in just two months following the announcement of this acquisition (over $1 billion on announcement), so the challenge for Levin is to convince the markets, current and potential customers, and competitors that positive change will occur. Simply having a "compelling fit" among the businesses, even where the businesses may have great competitive competencies, will not generate improvements in performance.

The operating strategy must address how the new company will be more competitive along the entire value chain of the businesses. Acquisitions are often an attempt to divert attention away from a failing core business with the hope that the acquisition might provide a miracle for the acquirer. If answers are not forthcoming to the contestability questions, what becomes obvious is a vision with no strategy that will increase competitiveness or generate performance gains. The following examples clearly illustrate this problem.

Sears, Roebuck and American Can. A telling contrast is that of Sears's experiment in an integrated financial services strategy with that of American Can's transformation into Primerica. The major moves of both these companies into financial services, following prolonged weakness in their core business, occurred at about the same time but represented very different strategies.

After years of declining market share and performance in merchandising, Sears considered a number of diversification opportunities. It had a history of success with Allstate as a stand-alone insurance business, and Allstate itself had made several diversifying acquisitions during the 1970s. These included a California savings and loan, a mortgage origination and insurance company, and a significant investment in Coldwell Banker, a commercial and residential real estate firm. In October 1981 Sears acquired Dean Witter Reynolds and Coldwell Banker in the same week. From the one-stop shopping vision described in the last section, Edward Telling, then chairman of Sears, explained the Sears Financial Center strategy:

> The synergy comes in when we develop products in one business that another can sell. The sophisticated investor now expects to be taken through the entire spectrum of financial products, from insurance, credit, real estate, to financial instruments such as equities and commercial paper. . . . I hope that we will quickly start to cross-pollinate the deserving, promotable people through the different businesses, so that all of us have a better understanding of each business.[18]

The problems of the strategy quickly became apparent in different parts of the value chain and in the different businesses. The merchandising group, the core business, performed progressively worse through the 1980s and achieved dismal results by the end of the decade. Net synergies in the Sears Financial Centers never materialized. There were four major reasons.

First, as Sears learned, real estate and mutual funds do not sell well in high-stimuli environments. It seemed reasonable to put a financial counter near high-traffic areas such as automotive and sporting goods, but these are not the type of distractions that real estate or securities brokers would identify as sales enhancers. Second, different types of financial services require different marketing, sales, and distribution channels. Mutual funds are mass marketed and tend to be *sold* to investors. Real estate and mortgages are *purchased* and require a very different customer approach and service. There is little commonality between these businesses even at the product market. Third, for there to be any possibility of synergy, cross-marketing had to occur, and these businesses would have to share information. This turned out to be an unrealistic expectation because these are highly entrepreneurial businesses. Finally, the development of the Sears Financial Centers required more than $250 million of expenditures above the initial purchase price of the acquisitions. Because the freestanding offices of Dean Witter and Coldwell Banker remained intact and were where most of the business was actually done, the Sears Financial Centers were actually expensive prospecting locations.

In September 1992, after intense pressure from institutional investors, Sears announced the spinoff of Dean Witter and Coldwell Banker and decided to focus on its troubled merchandising business.[19] Dean Witter and Coldwell Banker were not bad businesses, but Sears's strategy did not yield synergy. Instead, the company allowed its core merchandising business to deteriorate while it tried to create a synergistic financial supermarket.

Unlike Sears, American Can did not search for synergy with the core canning business but aimed at *replacing* the core business. American Can began to withdraw from canning in the late 1970s when it realized that remaining competitive in the mature can manufacturing business would require major capital investments, low growth, and low returns to capital. Like Sears, the company's strategy led to the financial sector. William Woodside, the chairman of American Can, wanted to reallocate assets from the capital-intensive businesses to focused, specialized businesses that were distribution intensive and required low capital investment.[20]

After AmCan sold its paper business in 1982, it acquired Associated Madison Companies, a life insurance holding company owned and managed by famed investor Gerald Tsai. Following this acquisition, Tsai was put in charge of the investment committee and future acquisitions in financial services. Rather than acquire businesses that would compete with companies such as Sears or Merrill Lynch, Tsai focused on buying companies that filled the needs of clearly defined groups. These companies were operated as independent companies but used low fixed cost delivery systems such as A. L. Williams' 110,000 part-time agents and third-party endorsed sales. By the beginning of 1987, AmCan's stock price increased four times as it divested itself of the packaging business and changed the company name to Primerica. Synergy was not a goal here. But moving capital to higher valued uses where individual businesses could push more product at a lower cost than they could before being acquired yielded success.

AT&T/NCR. The AT&T acquisition of NCR in 1991 is a lesson on the absence of the operating strategy cornerstone. It is a mystery why, after losing an estimated $2 billion in its own computer business between 1985 and 1990, AT&T's directors were willing to approve the payment of a $4.2 billion premium for the NCR acquisition—a 125 percent premium above the pre-bid share price of the company. Charles Exley, chairman and CEO of NCR at the time, accused AT&T of merely trying to bail out its own failed strategy for marketing computers.[21]

He may have been right on target. After paying the extraordinary premium for NCR, AT&T voluntarily left NCR executives in place to conduct business as usual for two years after the acquisition. In fact, they were even put in charge of AT&T's old computer production and marketing business. NCR executives were merely asked by AT&T to "look" for synergy.[22] The vision was that there would be "convergence" between computers and communications, but AT&T's technological advantage was in telecom switches, not in the corporate or consumer computer business.

By 1993, when earnings began to decline, AT&T signaled somewhat belatedly that it had a strategy for NCR after all. It appointed its own executive, Jerre Stead, to run the computer division but synergies did not materialize. In fact, between 1993 and 1995 most of NCR's top managers left the company. Costs increased dramatically as hundreds of new sales teams in over one hundred countries were set up and the company was pushed into new markets and industries where it had little experience. The result was that AT&T shareholders lost the entire premium that was paid to NCR shareholders and racked up losses of $720 million in 1995 alone.

Vision and operating strategy are necessary but not sufficient to ensure performance gains from an acquisition. The other two cornerstones—systems integration, and power and culture—are closely related. Systems integration focuses on the physical integration plans that must be in place to implement the strategy (such as integration of sales forces, distribution systems, information and control systems, and R&D and marketing efforts). Power and culture focuses on the reward and incentive systems and the control of information and decision processes at various levels of the organization. When these cornerstones are missing, the consequences go far beyond a failure to generate synergy.

Systems Integration

The problem of systems integration is a component of the implementation side of acquisitions. Systems integration must be carefully considered before the acquisition and must support a clearly defined operating strategy. Management must decide which operations will be integrated and which will be stand-alone, while maintaining awareness of the preexisting performance targets. It is much like driving a car 100 miles per hour and trying to make adjustments to the engine while moving.

The folklore that mergers that are strategically related should outperform those that are not is rooted in systems integration. If synergies are expected to come from cost savings in large organizations, they must emerge from eliminating duplication. Systems integration planning must lie at the heart of this strategy. This means that future systems integration plans must be planned in advance, and in considerable detail, before the acquirer calculates a bid price for the target. Otherwise the acquirer will not know what it is paying for and, even worse, will not know when the acquisition is simply a resource drain on stand-alone operations.

Acquirers must understand that there can be very distinct postacquisition integration environments. There are several possible scenarios:

1. The company is acquired as a stand-alone.
2. The company is acquired as a stand-alone but with a change in strategy.
3. The target is to become part of the acquirer's operations.
4. The target and acquirer are to be completely integrated.
5. The target takes over the acquirer's existing business and is integrated into the target's operations.

Different degrees of integration can pose different types of problems. If they are poorly considered, they can damage the underlying businesses.

Northwest Airlines/Republic Airlines. In 1986, Northwest Airlines (NWA) completed what was the largest acquisition ever in the airline industry: the $884 million acquisition of Republic Airlines. The acquisi-

tion nearly doubled the size of NWA, making it the fifth largest do-
mestic airline. But within two hours of completion of the acquisition, the airline's Twin Cities operation had ground to a standstill.[23]

NWA and Republic had been prohibited from engaging in detailed pricing and scheduling discussions prior to the acquisition because of federal antitrust regulations. Senior management had little
idea how the two computer systems interfaced, and when they put
the two systems together, neither pilots nor passengers knew what
was going on.

But integration of crew and gate scheduling was only the beginning of a long-term problem. Human resources integration was a disaster. The unions representing NWA employees were different from
those representing Republic, and power struggles ensued. Having
only recently made severe wage concessions, Republic's employees
came to the merger with lower pay schedules than those of NWA. At
the Detroit hub, disgruntled baggage handlers tore off destination
tags, and employees in Memphis mounted an unofficial work slow-
down that destroyed on-time performance. A story even emerged
that former Republic employees in Detroit shut down the sewage
system by simultaneously flushing their "People, Pride, Performance" buttons down the toilets.

Northwest was dubbed "Northworst" by frequent flyers. Less than
a year after the merger, it topped the government's list of passenger
complaints. Complicating these matters, on August 16, 1987, Northwest flight 255 crashed after takeoff from Detroit due to pilot error—
the second worst disaster in American aviation history. In 1989, NWA
was bought out by a group of private investors, and senior management resigned.

Unisys—Burroughs/Sperry. The merger of computer makers Burroughs
Corporation and Sperry Corporation in 1986 to form Unisys, the
largest computer industry merger in history, is an example of how in-
tegrating certain pieces well will have little effect if others are poorly
executed. The chairman of Burroughs, W. Michael Blumenthal, justified the decision to pay a 50 percent premium for Sperry "because
through this merger we will realize economies of scale, procurement
efficiencies, product rationalization, and in the end, further price

competitiveness." The plan was to maintain both companies' computer architectures but integrate all other aspects of the company.

The human side of the merger was orchestrated by well-known organizational psychologists Philip Mirvis and Mitchell Lee Marks. Unisys was touted as an example of a major merger where careful consideration was given to employee attitudes of both companies and the making of credible pledges to employees of partnership and meritocracy. But the integration of the distribution systems, a critical piece of the value chain for any company, particularly for a computer company, was a catastrophe. Because of the pressure to meet the performance numbers that Blumenthal had promised, Unisys rushed the implementation of a new corporate-wide centralized distribution system that combined the very different order-entry and billing procedures of the two companies. A former Unisys executive described the ensuing turmoil in this way:

> We pulled the switch and brought everything to its knees and it is still limping. We put a massive overload on the system. We probably did things we probably should not have. For instance, the amount of money we will save by not developing a new order-entry and billing system for the company we are going to more than blow on our inability to track our product shipments. It is a classic problem of the two systems being too big to run parallel. If I had really thought things through, I would have dug my heels in and said add a year to all your plans and let's do it right.[24]

As a result, equipment orders were notoriously late, and customers were regularly frustrated by missing parts and slow customer service—not the recipe for success in the viciously competitive computer business of the late 1980s. By November 1990, the stock price of Unisys was less than $3 per share—over 90 percent of shareholder value was destroyed.

Sony/Columbia-TriStar. Vertical integration acquisitions carry with them a unique integration problem, as Sony learned with its $3.4 billion acquisition of Columbia Pictures Entertainment from Coca-Cola in 1989.

In vertical integration acquisitions, the integration begins at the link between the two companies. Since this is almost by definition a new business, the acquirer may not have an executive team or an appropriate control system in place to run the acquisition—and costs can veer out of control. Sony's strategy rested on the assumption that having a commanding position in the software business (movies) could influence consumption patterns in the hardware market, such as high-definition television. But first, Sony needed executives to run Columbia.

Sony hired Peter Guber and Jon Peters at a cost of $700 million— $200 million in salary plus $500 million to settle a breach of a long-term production agreement Guber and Peters had with Warner Brothers. Guber and Peters, neither having studio management experience, went out to find executives *with* experience to run Columbia and TriStar (which was acquired along with Columbia). Their spending did not stop there.

As part of the settlement with Warner Brothers, Columbia had to trade its Burbank studios for an old M-G-M production facility, which cost an additional $100 million to upgrade at the lavish standard of Guber and Peters. Additional expenses included a fleet of jets and the purchase of a florist shop so that Columbia's executives could enjoy fresh flowers delivered daily.[25]

Synergies never materialized between hardware and software. The company ranked last in market share among the large Hollywood studios. And in November 1994, only five years later, Sony announced that it was taking a loss of $3.2 billion on the studios.[26]

Power and Culture

For almost thirty years numerous articles, both academic and popular, have discussed the potential troubles of power and culture clashes between merging organizations.[27] Most of these, however, lament that managers are more concerned about the financials than the soft side of acquisition management. The danger of isolated power and culture approaches to acquisitions is that they can often be used as an alibi for anything that goes wrong.

In fact, the issue of culture in acquisitions has not been studied in the context of how it would improve performance. The implicit assumption has been that if only the cultures were managed well, per-

formance gains would occur. Thus culture and power issues have remained soft issues, easily dismissed by many parties involved.

We need to consider the "why" (the economics) of culture to put
this cornerstone in the context of synergy. Cultural tensions *can* un-
dercut mergers and imperil synergies. Consider the following anec-
dote:

> When Warner Bros. CEO Robert Daly walked into the first post-
> merger gathering of senior Time Warner management in the Bahamas
> nearly five years ago, he felt a hand on his shoulder. It was a Time Inc.
> brahmin whom he had never met. The magazine man asked the studio
> exec if he ever considered that General Motors buys $30 million worth
> of advertising in Time Inc. publications before Daly acquired "Roger
> & Me," a scathing cinematic indictment of the automaker.
>
> Daly replied: "No. Did you consider that Warner Bros. spent over $50
> million on 'Batman' before Time ran its lousy review of the movie?"
> The Time exec smiled, patted his new colleague's shoulder and sug-
> gested they both continue their jobs their own way.[28]

Anthropologists and sociologists have over a hundred definitions of
culture, but the classic definition is a "shared set of norms, values, beliefs, and expectations."[29] This shared set of norms, values, beliefs,
and expectations is developed over time and passed down or forward
through the generations of managers. Although a corporate culture
may have developed slowly, it is acquired as a whole, on the spot, in
a merger. And these companies may have very different information
and decision processes and incentive and reward systems. But the issue for acquirers is not whether the cultures are similar or different
but whether the changes necessary to support the strategy will clash
with *either* culture.

Two questions about culture are particularly relevant to mergers
and acquisitions: (1) When will problems of conflict and cooperation
arise? and (2) How will they be solved? Some problems may arise
from what would be considered differences in standard operating
procedures, such as conduct of performance evaluations, chain of
command, methods of communication, and capital allocation ap-
provals.

The larger problems stem from the reshuffling of power and the unwritten expectations of payoffs of cooperating versus competing in the course of doing business in the new company. It is the uncertainty and ambiguity surrounding acquisition events that *will* cause executives and employees in general to defend positions they may have taken years to build. Key executives or knowledge workers who are crucial to the business as a stand-alone may leave in anticipation of these problems and join the competition.

The solution to the problems will lie in the incentive and other reward systems established for the new company. Are there clearly defined incentives that will drive the desired cooperation and coordination between previously independent businesses? In other words, if one side cooperates, will the other side honor its implied commitment or will it cheat when there is an incentive? That people will defect in anticipation of others' defection spells disaster in acquisitions where cooperation may be essential.

In the Time Warner example just given, the players agreed to maintain their individual power rather than work together in a common strategy to generate performance improvements (assuming a strategy existed).

Unless rewards and incentives support a real strategy with real integration plans, management of culture means little with regard to generating performance improvements. As Gerald Levin of Time Warner has said, "My philosophy is to let things happen naturally so that they make sense from the ground up instead of hammering it in from the top down."[30] Cooperation will not magically occur in entrepreneurial-based cultures unless incentives and rewards are created that will induce changes in behavior.

On the other hand, the inappropriate change of incentive systems can cause problems of its own. In 1990, two years after the Commercial Credit acquisition of Primerica, Sandy Weill, chairman and CEO, moved to change the incentive systems of the 110,000-strong part-time sales organization of the A. L. Williams insurance division by establishing specific targets and comparative evaluations by which to measure performance. It backfired immediately, and for two years, the writing of new insurance business was in a free fall. An A. L. Williams manager explained: "Controls don't work here because they imply a downside—they don't just reward good performance, but imply negative consequences for low performance. That doesn't sit well with most of our agents. If they feel that they're going to be subjected to quotas and performance evaluations, they might as well stay home."[31]

Careless changes in decision authority can also result in unexpected changes in profitability, as AT&T learned in its NCR acquisition. In 1993, when AT&T executives took over the NCR division after having been left under the control of former NCR management, Jerre Stead moved to flatten the old NCR hierarchy and "empower" more people. Sales representatives then had more authority to approve contracts that actually represented lower-margin business. Previously these contracts would have been rejected, but sales representatives who were compensated on revenues and not on margin had tremendous incentive to push through the business. The result was more business but lower profits.[32]

Predictable Overpayment

The intensity of the challenge of generating synergies should now be apparent. The central theme of the next chapter and the empirical study presented in Part 2 is that *price does not represent potential value*—and thus it becomes a predictor of acquisition value losses. This conclusion goes well beyond the simple prediction that acquirers overpay because of a winner's curse in a bidding auction.

Let us consider the following five acquisitions with two different synergy scenarios:

Premium	Synergy A	Synergy B
100%	80%	15%
80	60	15
60	40	15
40	20	15
20	0	15

The two scenarios (A and B) represent two categories of post-acquisition performance gains expressed as a percentage of the premium recovered. If price on average represents value, then synergy should occur in the amount dictated by the premium. In other words, a 60 percent premium should be associated, on average, with a 60 percent increase in value through actual performance gains. But suppose that in acquisitions, price is *not* correlated with potential value. In other words, suppose that this potential is in fact limited across acquisitions. Predictions about overpayment up front (ex ante) would then be possible, and integration issues could be considered within more of a performance context.

From an after-the-fact (ex post) perspective, "overpayment" occurs in each of the five cases in both scenarios. However, in synergy scenario A, the level of the premium gives no information about the amount of up-front risk of failure. A loss of 20 percent occurs in each acquisition. In this scenario, synergy is highly correlated with the premium, as would be predicted by the assumption of a competitive markets view. The result is consistent with what is often called the winner's curse: you win the contest but don't like the prize. Acquirers tend to overpay, but there seems to be good reason to make the acquisition if they paid just a little less.

On the other hand, if synergy does not occur or there are limits to the realization of synergy, as in synergy scenario B, then the predictive power of the premium becomes meaningful. That is, the level of the acquisition premium predicts the amount of losses. It is scenario B that represents the likely payoffs of the acquisition game. I will suggest in the next chapter that this 15 percent is actually very generous.

3

Do You Feel Lucky?
The Acquisition Premium

After several months of research and in-depth interviews with 13 experts in merger and acquisition premiums, I have reached two conclusions: (1) everyone is interested in premiums, and (2) no one knows what they mean.

—Thomas Penn, "Premiums: What Do They Really Measure?" (1981)

The market, like the Lord, helps those who help themselves. But, unlike the Lord, the market does not forgive those who know not what they do. . . . A too high purchase price for the stock of an excellent company can undo the effects of a subsequent decade of favorable business developments.

—Warren Buffett, *Berkshire Hathaway 1982 Annual Report*

Imagine there is an apartment you truly want to own on a lovely block of Greenwich Village in New York City. You and all of your friends agree that it is better to live there than where you live now. You'll feel better. What's more, the apartment is a fixer-upper, and you figure you can increase the $100,000 appraised value by at least 25 percent. Unfortunately you are dealing with an unmotivated seller who is asking $150,000 for the apartment—more than you want to spend but you really want this apartment. You have spent so much time searching for the right place, and this one is a perfect fit. (Besides, all of your friends have apartments so much nicer than the one in which you currently reside.) Do you go ahead with the transaction at a price of $150,000? It depends on whether feeling better about your apartment is worth $25,000 to you. Because even if you make the improvements you think are possible and even if they add 25 percent to the appraised value, you will have permanently sacrificed at least $25,000 right at the point of purchase.

Or suppose you just arrived in Las Vegas, a trip you have been planning for a long time. You have never been to Vegas before, but you have read all the books about the various casino games, and you are sure you will make a killing. On the way to the casino, an attractive hotel employee beckons you to a room to play a very special game. You are offered the following payoff distribution: a fair coin will be flipped where heads (H) = $20,000 and tails (T) = $0. It will cost you $9,000 to play the game. Thus,

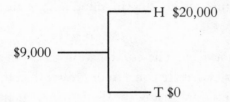

You think for a moment and realize that according to the law of averages, if you could play this particular game one hundred times, you could make a great deal of money—$100,000. That is, you pay to play whether you win or lose, and you expect to win 50 times, for a net gain of $100,000 [(50 × $20,000) − (100 × $9,000)]. On the other hand, you also realize that you could be wiped out after just a couple of plays before the law of averages sets in.[1]

The essential lesson here is that it is important to separate the distribution of payoffs from the price to play the game.

In fact, these examples are a lot like the acquisition game. The acquisition premium is paid up front to play the game, and we know it with certainty. The actual post-acquisition management and integration will yield some uncertain stream or *distribution* of realized payoffs or synergies *sometime in the future*. It will become clear how the timing of these synergies in the future can dramatically affect how much needs to be earned to justify the premium.

Acquirers have two important things to consider: (1) the economics of the acquisition premium, and (2) the probability of achieving synergy in a competitive industry. These are the things that the stock market considers when acquisitions are announced. Stock market reactions to acquisition announcements are market forecasts of the probability and amount of losses or gains, given the price the acquirer will pay to play the game.

The discussion in this chapter centers on the alignment between the required performance improvements embedded in the premium and a likely amount that is achievable. Again, markets will forecast the expected net present value of the decision, where

NPV = Synergy − Premium.

From a planning perspective, it is essential to recognize that premiums are paid up front, but the synergies do not occur until sometime in the future. With this in mind, there are three potential outcomes:

1. *Synergy ≥ Premium*. The combination results in discounted positive synergies that are equal to or greater than the premium paid for the acquisition (that is, the discounted benefits are equal to or greater than the premium required to play the game).
2. *0 ≤ Synergy ≤ Premium*. The combination results in discounted synergies that are positive, but the amount of these synergies is less than the premium paid.
3. *Synergy < 0*. The combination results in diseconomies (i.e., negative synergies) in addition to a total loss of the premium paid.

The Synergy Concept: Expectations versus Realizations

A merger or takeover premium is the amount the acquiring firm pays for an acquisition that is above the pre-acquisition price of the target company. Why would a management team pay more for an existing set of assets than anyone else in the world is willing to pay, and what must this premium represent?

We hear often regarding acquisitions that the financials looked fine on paper, but the acquisition was simply poorly executed. Yet if acquirers understood the fundamentals of the synergy trap, they would have realized that the financials did *not* look fine.

In the tradition of the financial economics literature, the acquisition premium represents the *expectation* of synergy in a corporate combination. According to this explanation, acquirers pay a premium because the expected value of the whole (combination) is greater than the expected value of the sum of the independent parts (value [bidder + target] > value [bidder] + value [target]).[2]

Given the overwhelming evidence of value destruction in acquisitions, we must challenge the belief that expectations reflect realizations. When we consider that the acquisition premium implies certain requirements of performance improvements and calculate the probability of achieving these improvements, we can predict the probable losses to shareholders of acquiring firms. But first we must take the definition of synergy further in terms of operational value drivers. Then, using various techniques, we can show just how hard these drivers need to work.

Recall that *realized* synergies are actual improvements in combined performance above what the two firms were already required to accomplish independently. In simple terms, synergy is realized when cash flows are increased (through higher revenues from increased product sales or higher prices and/or through lower costs) or when the discount rate on projected cash flows falls below what was reflected in the firms' pre-acquisition share prices. Although the discount rate is an easy variable to adjust in a Lotus spreadsheet, it should not be considered a manageable value. The value of an acquisition must depend on achievable cash flows.

Discount Rate

Managers are well advised to consider the discount rate—the cost of capital—as an immutable fact of life. Investors demand a price to finance risky projects. Managers can take this price or leave it. It is generally impossible for managers to lower the cost of capital with an acquisition.

With respect to the cost of debt, most large organizations already have favorable borrowing rates. Moreover, the cost of debt is usually a function of the default risk of the project being financed.

With respect to the cost of equity capital, the issue is the systematic risk, or beta, of the equity. Shareholders can readily diversify or otherwise manage the beta of their securities portfolio in any way they like. *Executives need not concern themselves with the size of their company's beta.* The resulting beta from a combination of two companies will be a mathematical average.[3]

More to the point, different projects and businesses within a company have different costs of capital. An investment in an R&D project will have a different cost of capital than an investment in a T-bill. The overall cost of capital of an acquirer (or any company) is simply the average of the costs of capital of the various businesses and projects in which the parent company is invested. Thus, managers should understand that the discount rate for an acquisition will be a function of the cost of debt and the cost of equity for the acquisition being financed. When a potential acquirer is valuing an acquisition candidate, the appropriate cost of capital is that of the target (including any changes in strategy post-acquisition), not that of the acquirer.

It is seductively and dangerously simple to justify a higher premium by assuming slight changes in the discount rate. The issue executive teams need to be concerned with is the improvement in cash flows above what is already expected.

Cash Flows

The common script about where actual synergies or performance improvements may arise in corporate combinations revolves around economies of scale, economies of scope, more efficient management, the redeployment of assets to more profitable uses, improved production techniques, the exploitation of resulting market power, or the combination of complementary resources.[4] In short, these improvements fall under what I have described as competing better by either further limiting competitors' ability to contest markets or by gaining the ability to contest competitors' markets without their ability to respond.

The prize in this contest is called *free cash flows*—the funds available to suppliers of capital after all required investments in the business are made. These funds can be paid out in the form of interest or dividends, or both. Modern valuation techniques revolve around the estimation and discounting of free cash flows.

From a business planning and analysis perspective, free cash flows are the after-tax operating cash flow minus additional investments in working capital and net fixed assets required to fund the future business plans. Figure 3.1 details the components of free cash flow and the *value drivers* that affect each component. Performance gains from an acquisition strategy must ultimately be the result of managers' control of these value drivers.

Acquisition premiums are additional investments in the business that the stand-alone businesses did not need to make. Unless specific changes in the value drivers can be identified, there is no way to justify a premium.

Management researchers and industrial economists have described the additional costs that can easily arise from the increased bureaucratic complexities and frictions resulting in corporate combinations. These affect the operating profit margin, as do increased expenses, such as advertising or R&D. Additional investments may also be required to generate the desired improvements. These additional required investments will be accounted for in additional working capital and fixed asset requirements. If free cash flows do not increase, no additional value will be created.[5] Moreover, there is the possibility of negative synergies.

Negative synergies occur when a newly combined entity receives lower combined revenues or incurs higher costs. Not only does the acquirer lose the entire premium, but the acquisition makes it easier

FIGURE 3.1

Components and Value Drivers of Free Cash Flow

Free Cash Flow		*Value Drivers*
	Revenues	Sales growth rate
minus	Expenses	
equal	Operating profit	Operating profit margin
minus	Tax on operating profit	Cash tax rate
equal	Net operating profit	
minus	Investment in net fixed assets	Additional fixed asset requirements
minus	Investment in working capital	Additional working capital requirements
equal	Free cash flow	

for competitors to contest their businesses. The growing body of evidence of disastrous performance from some very visible mergers and takeovers (e.g., Novell and WordPerfect, Quaker Oats and Snapple, Eli Lilly and Hybritech, Burroughs and Sperry) is testimony that negative synergies are in fact very common.

Now let us reconsider the three scenarios introduced at the beginning of this section in the context of free cash flows.

1. *Synergy ≥ Premium*. This first scenario would clearly be considered a successful acquisition. The dollar amount of positive synergies (discounted) exceeds the premium paid for the target. In the case of excess positive synergies, value would be created for the shareholders of the acquirer, and this would be reflected in increases in accounting-based performance measures.

2. *0 ≤ Synergy ≤ Premium*. This case is potentially the most important to consider because it is possible for researchers as well as managers to reach different conclusions about the ex-post success of the corporate combination. It is also likely the most frequent outcome in acquisitions. This scenario might not necessarily be considered an unsuccessful combination from a company-level cash flow perspective, because positive synergies do exist. It would be possible to observe improvements above what was already expected (pre-acquisition) in some corporate performance measures. However, returns did not increase enough to compensate shareholders for the premium paid. Thus, from the perspective of the shareholders of the acquirer, the managers paid too much for the acquisition, and these shareholders experienced a reduction in their wealth.

3. *Synergy < 0*. This is clearly a case of pure value destruction. Observed corporate performance measures of the combined firm clearly decrease. The result is a complete loss of the premium paid for the acquisition (i.e., wealth transfer to the shareholders of the target), in addition to further operating losses as a result of the corporate combination. The merger between Burroughs Corporation and Sperry Corporation to form Unisys is an example of a merger creating tremendous negative synergies.

Now we turn to the burden of the premium decision. The premium dictates what must be accomplished with the acquisition strategy.

The Resource Allocation Decision: An Introduction

The mechanics and inherent risks of the resource allocation decision may help explain what is becoming overwhelming evidence of declines in profitability following mergers and takeovers.[6] I will examine this problem from a variety of perspectives. First, let us turn to how paying a premium might affect profitability. We will use the analogy of an investment in a financial instrument.

Consider a ten-year corporate bond with a coupon rate of 10 percent, a face value of $1,000, and a required rate of return (discount rate) of 10 percent. Clearly this bond should trade at par (it has a value of $1,000), and an investor will earn a yield to maturity of 10 percent. Now imagine that someone offers $1,700 for this bond that has been selling for $1,000. What will change? The return (the profitability) of this bond declines dramatically. How dramatically? This $700 premium drives the yield to maturity on this bond down from 10 percent to 2.15 percent.

This problem is precisely what top managers face when committing resources for corporate acquisition strategies. By allocating resources in the form of paying large premiums for already existing assets and technologies, managers drive the profitability measures of the acquired firm (and ultimately the new entity) downward immediately. This is the so-called dilution effect. It is real.

Consider the effect on the return on assets (net income/total assets). Paying a premium raises the asset base of the acquired firm and causes an immediate drop in profitability measures.[7] Just to break even, the net income needs to increase to an amount that brings the return on assets ratio back to pre-merger levels. Required synergy is the additional free cash flows that managers must bring in to accomplish this break-even target. In many high-premium acquisitions, synergies may need to be more than twice the pre-merger net income of the acquired firm, and herein lies the synergy trap. Later we will consider what "high" premiums are in the context of realistic improvement scenarios in a competitive environment.

Given that so much management and industrial-organization economics research judges performance based on profitability measures and searches for explanations of the variance in these measures, the premium variable can provide significant explanatory power.

Consider the conclusions of a recent paper by Ravenscraft and Scherer on divisional sell-offs: "By far the leading force in explaining a corporation's sell-off decision is profitability [measured as operating income/assets] at the line-of-business level. Company managers apparently view low accounting profits as a powerful signal of unsatisfactory performance. Acquisitions, and particularly conglomerate acquisitions, are significantly less likely to stand the test of time than original or de novo entry lines."[8]

This is an extremely important concept for practicing managers to understand because premiums translate into specific required performance improvements for the new firm to meet. This may appear obvious, yet acquisitions researchers routinely dismiss this concept when considering the performance of acquiring firms. The prevailing argument is that value creation is a long-term problem that occurs after the acquisition, and only where the acquisition is implemented appropriately will the value potential be realized.[9]

That is too long to wait. Premiums averaged 50 percent in the later 1980s; many were 100 percent or more. It is imperative to understand the predictable effects of the premium decision. If the free cash flow on a discounted basis does not improve sufficiently, managers have simply driven down corporate performance.

The rest of this section will consider the implicit meaning of the premium in the context of such commonly recognized valuation tools as the price/earnings and equity market value/book value ratios. By analyzing the implicit changes in the factors that influence these classical valuation models, we can gain some understanding of what executives are implicitly claiming they can accomplish (whether or not they know it). Then we use numerical simulations to simulate the dynamics of this problem from a free cash flow planning basis.

Price/Earnings Ratio

The P/E ratio carries with it information about implied anticipated growth opportunities for a firm. Given a required rate of return (r) and an average earnings per share (EPS), we can think of the price of a share (P_0) as the present value of an earnings stream with no growth plus the present value of future growth opportunities (PVGO). Thus, it can be easily shown that:

$$P_0/EPS_1 = 1/r + PVGO/EPS_1$$

A premium paid for a target firm drives up the P/E multiple and, implicitly, the implied profitable growth in earnings needed to justify the increased multiple. Recall that synergy has to be increases in future growth or profitability over what is already anticipated for the future. For example, more than 85 percent of the current stock market value of companies such as Ralston or General Mills is based on cash flow expected beyond a five-year horizon. Thus, driving up the P/E multiple means increasing these future expectations even more.

Equity Market Value/Book Value Ratio

Recent literature in strategy has discussed the importance of the equity market value/book value ratio (MV/BV) in value-based planning models.[10] These authors find that the MV/BV is a function of the spread between return on equity (ROE) and the cost of equity capital (k_e) and the number of years this spread can be maintained. Figure 3.2 shows the functional relationship between the MV/BV and the ROE–k_e spread. Using Value Line data for three- to five-year estimates of the ROE–k_e spread and the current MV/BV for the Dow Jones 30 Industrials, the functional relationship is clear.[11]

The payment of an acquisition premium drives the MV/BV upward and potentially destroys the functional relationship between MV/BV and the ROE–k_e spread. Clearly the ROE–k_e spread will have to widen to make an acquisition premium justifiable. This will be especially problematic if an acquisition results in declines in ROE.[12]

To illustrate the problem using this approach, I adapt what is essentially a classical valuation model used by the CS First Boston equity research group.[13] Instead of looking at the implied ROE given a current share price, I adapt the model to compute the ROE given the current share price of the target plus the acquisition premium. In this model, the assumption is that a firm's current equity market value must be directly related to the firm's expected future book value, where this book value is a function of the future returns on the firm's equity. The model has several embedded assumptions, but it is simple and provides a useful introduction to the concept of increases in economic rents that a firm must earn on its invested capital for a given percentage acquisition premium.

FIGURE 3.2

Market to Book Ratios versus ROE $- k_e$

Dow Jones Industrials, 1992

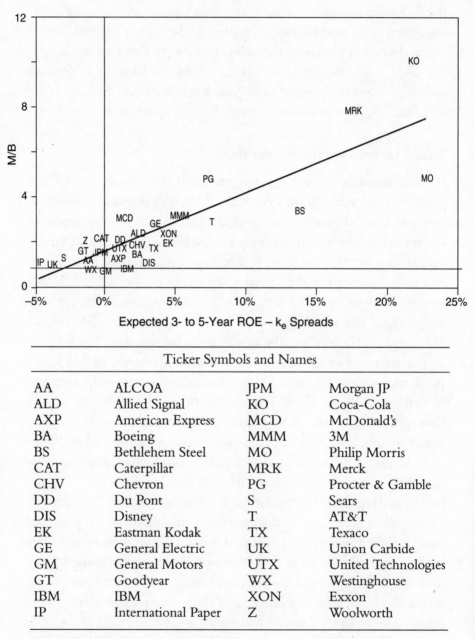

Expected 3- to 5-Year ROE $- k_e$ Spreads

Ticker Symbols and Names			
AA	ALCOA	JPM	Morgan JP
ALD	Allied Signal	KO	Coca-Cola
AXP	American Express	MCD	McDonald's
BA	Boeing	MMM	3M
BS	Bethlehem Steel	MO	Philip Morris
CAT	Caterpillar	MRK	Merck
CHV	Chevron	PG	Procter & Gamble
DD	Du Pont	S	Sears
DIS	Disney	T	AT&T
EK	Eastman Kodak	TX	Texaco
GE	General Electric	UK	Union Carbide
GM	General Motors	UTX	United Technologies
GT	Goodyear	WX	Westinghouse
IBM	IBM	XON	Exxon
IP	International Paper	Z	Woolworth

Source: Value Line, 1992.

Let MV be the pre-acquisition market price of the target plus the premium, PV be the present value of the future book value, and BV be the current book value. In an efficient market, the market price will reflect the present value of the expected future book value so MV = PV. We have:

$$PV = BV(1 + ROE)^n/(1 + k_e)^n$$

where ROE is the return on equity, k_e is the cost of equity (required rate of return on equity), and n is the number of periods expected for the acquisition to recoup the premium. Obviously, where ROE = k_e, PV = BV.

Substituting MV for PV and rearranging terms (just some simple algebra), we have:

$$ROE = (1 + k_e)\ (MV/BV)^{1/n} - 1$$

Now if we let BV be the pre-acquisition market price, the MV/BV ratio represents the premium. For example, a ratio of 1.0 is equivalent to paying a zero premium, a ratio of 1.5 is equivalent to paying a 50 percent premium, and so on. The result is a convenient way to show how much acquirers must increase the economic rents earned by the target company. Economic rents can be measured by the spread between the return on capital and the cost of capital. At a zero premium, the additional required spread in returns is also zero. And as the premium increases, so does the required spread. By definition, these economic rents must be gains in competitive advantage.[14]

Figure 3.3 illustrates the application of this model for different time periods and premiums. For example, for a 100 percent premium with a current ROE of 15 percent, ROE must *increase* by 11.97 percent (26.97 − 15.00) for seven years beginning immediately just to break even. This simple model has some assumptions that limit its usefulness as a tool for planning, but it does show how, in a commonly used valuation technique, premiums have implicit, measurable meaning.[15]

We now get down to brass tacks. The following approach illustrates exactly what these acquirer executives (or their investment bankers) should have explicitly been valuing in their pre-acquisition strategic and organizational analyses. The contestability conditions described in Chapter 2 must ultimately be satisfied in these terms to justify any premium.

FIGURE 3.3

Implied ROE for Different MV/BV Ratios and Investment Horizons

MV/BV	1 Year	2 Years	3 Years	4 Years	5 Years	6 Years	7 Years	8 Years	9 Years	10 Years
1.0	15.00%	15.00%	15.00%	15.00%	15.00%	15.00%	15.00%	15.00%	15.00%	15.00%
1.25	43.75%	28.57%	23.88%	21.60%	20.25%	19.36%	18.72%	18.25%	17.89%	17.59%
1.50	72.50%	40.85%	31.64%	27.27%	24.71%	23.04%	21.86%	20.98%	20.30%	19.76%
1.75	101.25%	52.13%	38.58%	32.27%	28.62%	26.24%	24.57%	23.33%	22.38%	21.62%
2.0	130.00%	62.63%	44.89%	36.76%	32.10%	29.08%	26.97%	25.41%	24.21%	23.25%

$$\text{ROE} = (1 + k_e)(\text{MV/BV})^{1/n} - 1$$

k_e = cost of capital

n = investment horizon (number of years required to sustain a given ROE – k_e spread)

MV/BV = premium ratio

Required Performance Improvements: A Simulation Approach

The resource allocation in the acquisition process occurs at time zero and thus is known with certainty. Required synergy, or what I will call *required performance improvements* (RPIs), occur in the future and are uncertain. The analysis will show that RPIs are dynamic and may turn out to be far greater than top management teams ever imagined. We will also consider a realistic probability distribution for these improvements in a competitive business.

I follow a very conservative approach in simulating RPIs given the payment of an acquisition premium. Specifically, I assume that the performance of the acquired firm never falls below pre-merger levels and the firm sustains the required rate of return on pre-merger operations; there are no decreases in demand and no negative synergies. I also assume that there are no additional investments or administrative costs required to generate synergies. The focus is on exactly how much operations must *improve* (on a free cash flow basis) to justify the resources committed by management and the likelihood of achieving these improvements. This analysis will provide a theoretical and practical foundation for understanding the dynamics of post-acquisition performance and the up-front risk embedded in the premium.

Let us first consider the payment of a $10 million acquisition premium. Figure 3.4 shows the annual required synergy that must be realized assuming a 15 percent required rate of return and using a simple amortization method (i.e., equal annual improvements). The required rate of return is the appropriate cost of capital that reflects the risk class of the expected cash flows. The figure is derived by assuming that there are zero improvements until the ith year, an assumption that can be easily relaxed. For example, where i = 1, performance gains begin immediately; where i = 3, they do not begin until year 3. Thus, in the figure, year 1 shows what management must achieve on an equal annual basis over a ten-year period ($1.99 million per year) to make this corporate acquisition strategy successful. Similarly, the plot of year 3 shows how much the annual synergy must increase if synergies are not realized in year 1 and year 2 and

FIGURE 3.4
Annual Required Performance Improvements for a $10 Million Premium

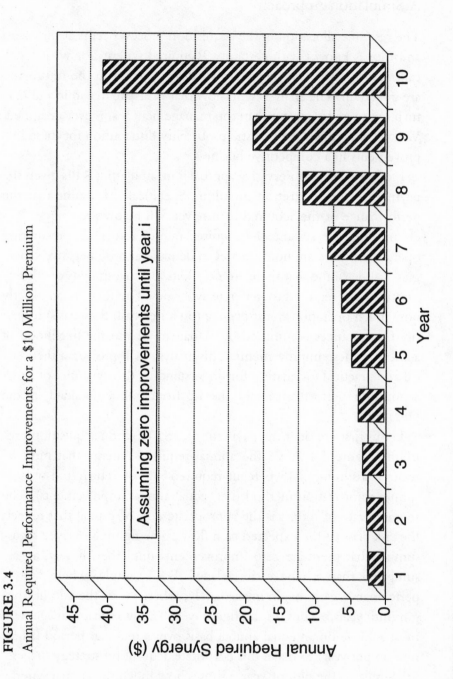

FIGURE 3.4 (continued)

$ Premium	Year i									
	1	2	3	4	5	6	7	8	9	10
$10M	$1.99M	$2.41M	$2.95M	$3.66M	$4.62M	$6.00M	$8.10M	$11.65M	$18.82M	$40.46M

$$RPI = \frac{\$ \text{ PREMIUM}}{\sum\limits_{t=i}^{N} \left(\dfrac{1}{(1+r)^t} \right)}$$

RPI = Required Performance Improvements
r = cost of capital
N = number of years in planning period
i = year in which performance improvements begin

begin only in year 3 ($2.95 million for years 3 through 10). RPIs are dynamic and must discount back to the up-front acquisition premium.

IBM's $3.3 billion acquisition of Lotus represented a premium of over $1.65 billion. Industry experts expect that it will take several years for the Lotus acquisition to yield improvements.[16] Moreover, these improvements must be above those already expected (see Figure 2.1). Figure 3.4 serves to demonstrate the extraordinary challenge embedded in their acquisition strategy if the industry experts are correct.

As in all simulations, the preceding analysis deserves some comments on its realism, particularly from a day-to-day management perspective. Recall that management teams have paid over $20 billion in fees for advice on the value of doing acquisitions. Thus, these premium payments did not just come out of thin air. Managers of acquiring firms made resource allocation decisions supported by projections of performance improvements done either internally or by their outside advisers. The reporting and planning teams of the acquiring firms must work with these projections on a day-to-day basis following the acquisition.

Figure 3.5 extends the process in Figure 3.4 for different percentage premiums. This allows us to compare the required managerial performance environments across acquisitions with different percentage premiums. We examine the required percentage increases (on an equal annual basis relative to the pre-acquisition share price of the acquired firm) for a 25 percent, 50 percent, 75 percent, and 100 percent premium. This simulation shows the required increases in ROE (in terms of increases in free cash flow) and, if the target has no debt, return on assets (ROA).[17] *The results are dramatic.*

For example, assuming synergies begin occurring *immediately,* ROE (ROA) must be 10 percent higher every year for the 75 percent premium than for the 25 percent premium. If there is any delay, the required returns increase dramatically. For a 75 percent premium, if performance gains do not begin until the third year, an acquirer would have to generate an increase in returns for the target of over 22 percentage points in the third year and maintain it for the next seven years. And these increases are required just to break even. This analysis includes no value creation, only value preservation for the acquiring firm.

Management scholars and practitioners have often given integration advice that would explicitly lead to required managerial performance moving to the right in Figure 3.5. For example, Jemison and Sitkin suggest that managers should reach agreement only in principle on integration issues before doing an acquisition and leave the details of integration until after the acquisition. They believe that long-term integration planning is not very realistic. Nelson and Lagges, principals with A. T. Kearney, advise, "During the first year, it is important to combine two cultures and organizations, but it is fatal to get bogged down in heavy operations integration. Start out by picking the low-hanging fruit." These practitioners note that the integration of manufacturing and distribution normally requires several years.[18]

It is not that these scholars and consultants are giving bad advice, but for an average acquisition premium of over 40 percent, it is crucial to understand exactly what required performance environment acquirers are creating for themselves if significant performance gains are not expected to begin immediately. The evidence is that most acquiring firm managers do not have detailed integration plans in the beginning and move incrementally after the acquisition.[19] The preceding analysis (Figures 3.4 and 3.5) squarely challenges how most premiums could ever be approved under these circumstances. It is the basis for understanding how the acquisition premium can be used to predict losses.

Let us now consider a realistic competitive scenario and consider the *probability* of achieving the required improvement in returns in each year for the four percentage premium cases. Formally, let X be a continuous random variable that takes values from zero to infinity because of our assumption of no diseconomies. Thus we need a probability distribution, $f(x)$, for $0 \leq x < \infty$, where $\int_0^\infty f(x)\, dx = 1$.

Because we want low-return events to have a higher probability than high-return events and with no jumps in the distribution, we desire $f(x)$ to be continuous (that is, smooth) and monotonically non-increasing in x. Given the evidence of the difficulty of generating

FIGURE 3.5

Required Increases in Returns (ROE/ROA) for Different Percentage Premiums

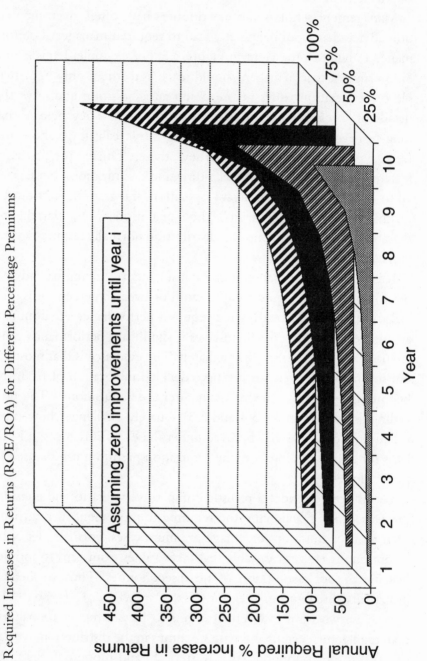

FIGURE 3.5 (continued)

% Premium	Year i									
	1	2	3	4	5	6	7	8	9	10
25%	4.98%	6.03%	7.37%	9.14%	11.55%	15.00%	20.25%	29.13%	47.04%	101.14%
50%	9.96%	12.05%	14.74%	18.28%	23.11%	30.00%	40.51%	58.25%	94.08%	202.28%
75%	14.94%	18.08%	22.10%	27.42%	34.66%	45.00%	60.76%	87.38%	141.12%	303.42%
100%	19.93%	24.10%	29.47%	36.56%	46.22%	60.00%	81.02%	116.50%	188.17%	404.56%

$$\left(\frac{RPI}{P_0} \right) = \frac{\dfrac{\$ \ PREMIUM}{P_0}}{\displaystyle\sum_{t=i}^{N} \left(\frac{1}{(1+r)^t} \right)}$$

RPI = Required Performance Improvements
P_0 = pre-acquisition price of target company
r = cost of capital
N = number of years in planning period
i = year in which performance improvements begin

performance improvements, we want to allow a positive probability of earning no synergy and want the probability of extraordinarily high improvements to be negligible. Thus we desire $f(x)$ to have the following properties:

1. $f(x)$ is continuous.
2. $\int_0^\infty f(x)\,dx = 1$.
3. $\lim_{x \to \infty} f(x) = 0$.
4. $f(0) > 0$.
5. $f(x)$ is nonincreasing in x.

A probability distribution that satisfies the above conditions is the exponential distribution and hence our choice. Again, consistent with the assumptions in the first RPI analysis, we do not allow for negative synergy. In technical terms, we truncate the distribution at zero. We are assuming that acquirers can avoid the part of the synergy trap where they destroy the value of the stand-alone businesses beyond losing the premium. This simply makes the analysis more conservative and gives the acquirer the advantage.

An exponential distribution is used because it is likely that the probability of realizing synergy is both decreasing in the size of the required synergy and decreasing at an increasing rate. Figure 3.6 incorporates an exponential distribution with a mean annual return of 15 percent to estimate the probabilities of achieving the returns that are required under the scenarios simulated in Figure 3.5.

An expected improvement in performance of 15 percentage points above normal operations is a reasonably generous assumption in a competitive business. Again, this assumption can be altered for practical analysis, but there needs to be a good reason. Figure 3.6 shows how unlikely it may be for managers to earn the required returns from some acquisitions even if synergies begin occurring immediately.[20] These are the probabilities of earning the RPI percentage or higher.

The probabilities drop dramatically as we delay achieving synergy and as we move to higher premium levels. Note that different performance numbers can be used in the analysis, but the picture will be the same. These are the underlying fundamentals of the acquisition game: *an up-front premium paid with embedded RPIs for some distribution of uncertain future performance above what is already expected.*

Figure 3.7 simulates the expected gain/(loss) for our $10 million acquisition premium under the four percentage premium scenarios. Given an expected marginal performance improvement of 15 percent, it is clear that if managers believe in "long-term" payoffs for their resource allocation decision, they may be locking in losses from the start of the acquisition process. It is the dynamic nature of RPIs that punishes poor acquisition planning. Even if synergy begins immediately, when the premium crosses 25 percent the likelihood and amount of losses increase dramatically. Some authors have argued that poor initial stock market performance for an acquiring firm may be misleading because the real payoffs from an acquisition often take many years to unfold.[21] My analysis suggests that this belief may be problematic and executives must beware of this "wisdom" when seated at the negotiating table with the corporate checkbook. Recall that I used generous assumptions in these simulations—adding 15 percentage points to current returns is an intense challenge for any business. It would not be unusual for actual results to be even worse.

The central theme here is that resources allocated up front for an acquisition have an opportunity cost that, if not met, will result in negative net present values for the acquisition and value destruction for the acquirer. Obviously, the size of the acquired firm relative to the size of the acquiring firm will have a great impact on the subsequent performance of the combined firm. The larger the acquisition size and the less value recovered through synergy, the greater will be the value destruction for the shareholders of the acquiring firm.[22]

The elements of time and probability considerations have been absent in analyses of acquisitions to date, yet this is where the strategy and finance meet head-on. The element of time is absolutely crucial in acquisitions, for two reasons. First, from a planning perspective, if acquirers do not begin to realize RPIs immediately, they grow quickly with time to an amount that is unachievable. Second, and even more important, time kills the acquirer, because the acquirer has sent notice to its competitors that it expects to be a better competitor. The longer that synergies do not materialize, the more likely it is that competitors will respond before the company realizes *any* gains—one more way to fall into the synergy trap.

FIGURE 3.6

Probability of Achieving Annual Required Performance Improvement or Higher

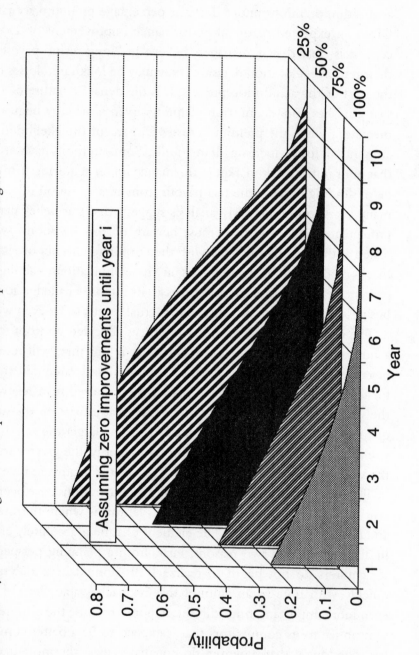

FIGURE 3.6 (continued)

% Premium	Year i									
	1	2	3	4	5	6	7	8	9	10
25%	0.7174	0.6692	0.6119	0.5438	0.4629	0.3679	0.2592	0.1435	0.0435	0.0012
50%	0.5147	0.4478	0.3744	0.2957	0.2143	0.1353	0.0672	0.0206	0.0019	0.0000
75%	0.3693	0.2997	0.2291	0.1608	0.0992	0.0498	0.0174	0.0030	0.0001	0.0000
100%	0.2649	0.2005	0.1402	0.0874	0.0459	0.0183	0.0045	0.0004	0.0000	0.0000

$$P\left(X > \frac{RPI}{P_0}\right) = \int_x^\infty \lambda e^{-\lambda x} dx$$

RPI = Required Performance Improvements

P_0 = pre-acquisition price of target company

X = improvement in returns

λ = 1/ mean achievable performance improvement in any year

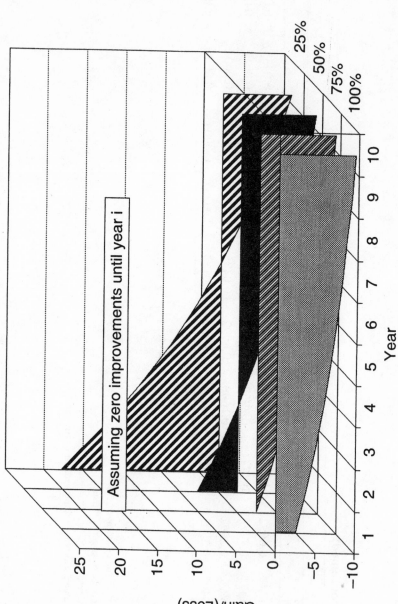

FIGURE 3.7

Expected Gain/(Loss) for a $10 Million Premium at Different Percentage Premiums

FIGURE 3.7 (continued)

% Premium	Year i									
	1	2	3	4	5	6	7	8	9	10
25%	$20.11	$14.90	$10.36	$6.41	$2.98	($0.00)	($2.59)	($4.85)	($6.81)	($8.52)
50%	$5.06	$2.45	$0.18	($1.79)	($3.51)	($5.00)	($6.30)	($7.42)	($8.41)	($9.26)
75%	$0.04	($1.70)	($3.21)	($4.53)	($5.67)	($6.67)	($7.53)	($8.28)	($8.94)	($9.51)
100%	($2.47)	($3.78)	($4.91)	($5.90)	($6.75)	($7.50)	($8.15)	($8.71)	($9.20)	($9.63)

$$\text{Gain/(Loss)} = P_0(.15) \sum_{t=i}^{N} \left(\frac{1}{(1+r)^t} \right) - 10$$

P_0 = pre-acquisition price of target company

r = cost of capital

N = number of years in planning period

i = year in which performance improvements (15%) begin

The Seductiveness of Financial Valuation Models

At the beginning of the book I suggested a paradox concerning the evidence of such disappointing acquisition performance. In addition to paying premiums, acquirers allocated over $20 billion during the past fifteen years for advice about the fair value of the companies they were acquiring. We have not gotten to the actual empirical study yet, but based on the description of the synergy trap and the implicit RPIs of premiums, it should be becoming clear how the acquisition premium can be an up-front predictor of value destruction for acquirers.

So where do these numbers come from? As a former director of Coopers & Lybrand once told me, "Lotus is the culprit in failed acquisitions. It is too easy to assume anything you want in perpetuity without any understanding of the economics of an industry, and package it in a beautiful report."[23]

But the legal system also encourages acquirers to overpay. Shareholders of acquirers traditionally have had little legal recourse against managers who waste capital in predictably bad acquisition decisions. On the other hand, the shareholders of the target firm have a great deal of power and recourse. Virtually all of the merger law from the 1980s was for the protection of the poor shareholders of the target firm—the shareholders on the receiving end of the value transfer. And after the landmark case of *Smith* v. *Van Gorkom* in 1985, the officers and directors of the target firm could be held personally liable for not making an informed decision about the appropriate selling price of the company (e.g., not searching for higher prices from other potential bidders).[24]

Acquisition prices have to gravitate around comparables, often called *compaqs* (comparable acquisitions), at a given point in time. Essentially, the price an acquirer will be required to pay for a given acquisition will be based on the going multiple of cash flow or EBITDA (earnings before interest, taxes, depreciation, and amortization) at the time at which comparable acquisitions have been priced. An officer or director of a target firm who approves the sale of the company for less will probably get sued. Thus, acquisition prices are usually exogenously determined by the market and have little to do with any potential value that can be created by the acquirer.

How are these numbers justified? Valuation models are sensitive to what appear to be only slight changes in assumptions about growth rates, cost of capital, and terminal value. In fact, most valuations turn on three leverage points: (1) Free cash flow forecasts for five to ten years, (2) a terminal or residual value assumption at the end of the forecast period, and (3) a discount rate or required rate of return. The value of a company is determined by discounting the intermediate cash flow and the terminal value (sometimes called residual value) as follows:

$$\text{Value} = \sum_{t=1}^{N} \frac{FCF_t}{(1+r)^t} + \frac{TV_N}{(1+r)^N}$$

where r is the appropriate cost of capital, FCF is free cash flow, and N is the number of years in the forecast period. Terminal value (TV) at the end of the forecast period is commonly expressed as a perpetuity with growth (the sum of an infinite geometric series),

$$TV_N = \frac{FCF_{N+1}}{(r-g)}$$

where g is the growth rate of free cash flow in perpetuity.

The following brief analysis demonstrates just how easy it is to generate almost any value needed by changing certain assumptions only slightly. Figure 3.8 presents a concise sensitivity analysis of the value of an acquisition target using the above valuation model and two different series of free cash flow. The actual numbers for 1995 are given, and the numbers for 1996 through 2005 are the ten-year forecasts (2006 is used for the terminal value calculation). Series 1 is a stable growth scenario. Series 2 is a common emerging technology scenario where current cash flows are negative but are expected to improve greatly over the next ten years. The sensitivity analysis for each series is given by allowing the cost of capital (r) and the r − g spread to vary. For example, the value of company in series 1 with a cost of capital of 14 percent and an r − g spread of 8 percent (implying a growth rate of 6 percent) will give a market value of $1.23 billion. (Where there is no debt, the market value will represent the equity value.)

FIGURE 3.8

Seductiveness of Valuation Models

Series 1: Total Free Cash Flow to Firm (in $ millions)

1995A	1996	1997	1998	1999	2000	2001	2002	2003	2004	2005	2006
$100.00	$105.00	$110.25	$115.76	$121.55	$127.63	$134.01	$140.71	$147.75	$155.13	$162.89	$171.03

Series 1: Valuation Sensitivity Analysis

	r – g Spread Terminal Value	Value of the Target				
		0.04	0.06	0.08	0.10	0.12
		$4,276	$2,851	$2,138	$1,710	$1,425
Cost	18%	$1,373.3	$1,101.0	$964.8	$883.1	**$828.6**
of	17%	1,468.0	1,171.5	1,023.3	934.3	875.0
Capital	16%	1,571.4	1,248.3	1,086.7	989.8	925.2
	15%	1,684.2	1,331.8	1,155.7	1,050.0	979.5
	14%	1,807.4	1,423.0	1,230.7	1,115.4	1,038.5
	13%	1,942.3	1,522.4	1,312.5	1,186.5	1,102.6
	12%	2,090.0	1,631.1	1,401.7	1,264.0	1,172.2
	11%	**2,252.0**	1,750.0	1,499.0	1,348.4	1,248.0

Series 2: Total Free Cash Flow to Firm (in $ millions)

1995A	1996	1997	1998	1999	2000	2001	2002	2003	2004	2005	2006
($20.00)	($16.00)	($12.00)	($8.00)	($4.00)	—	$50.00	$60.00	$72.00	$86.40	$103.68	$114.05

Series 2: Valuation Sensitivity Analysis

		Value of the Target			
r – g Spread	0.04	0.06	0.08	0.10	0.12
Terminal Value	$2,851	$1,901	$1,426	$1,140	$950
Cost 18%	$611.5	$429.9	$339.1	$284.6	**$248.3**
of 17%	666.2	468.5	369.6	310.3	270.7
Capital 16%	726.2	510.8	403.1	338.4	295.3
15%	792.1	557.2	439.8	369.3	322.3
14%	864.6	608.2	480.0	403.1	351.9
13%	944.3	664.3	524.3	440.3	384.3
12%	1,032.0	726.0	573.0	481.2	420.0
11%	**1,128.7**	794.0	626.6	526.2	459.2

r = cost of capital; g = growth rate of free cash flows beyond the forecast period; boldface numbers = range of attainable values

Now suppose that *compaqs* in a given industry in early 1996 are commanding multiples that would imply a 30 percent acquisition premium. No problem. By decreasing the discount rate by 2 percent (to 12 percent) and allowing the growth rate to remain the same 6 percent in perpetuity gives a value of $1.63 billion—a 32 percent premium! And for series 2, the same change will result in a premium of 51 percent. A close look at the figure shows how making what would appear to be slight changes (in free cash flow growth rates or the cost of capital) can drive an incredible range of values.

The culprit is the terminal value calculation, especially for series 2, where cash flows are negative in the beginning and thus most of the value is driven by the terminal value. When perpetuity with growth models are used (as is very common), the assumption is that profitable growth will go on forever. With this approach, just a few small assumptions can make a company seem undervalued or worth almost any premium.

At this point it should be clear how dangerous these models are in acquisitions. It is absolutely essential to focus on improvements that can be reasonably expected. Remember that these improvements are competitive gains beyond what is already built into pre-acquisition prices. If the premium is being driven by terminal value assumptions of new profitable growth that will go on forever and will not begin until five or ten years from now, it is unlikely this performance will ever occur.

Do *you* feel lucky?

4

Tools and Lessons
for the Acquisition Game

Acquisitions require tremendous discipline. That is, the courage to
walk away from an acquisition opportunity that is attractive in every
way except price. Over the years we have made that walk many times.

—Robert Cizik, Chairman and CEO, Cooper Industries (1995)

Officers and directors owe a duty of care and a duty of loyalty to their corporations and their shareholders. The business judgment rule protects those officers and directors
where their decisions are *informed* decisions.[1] The long-overdue integration of strategy and finance that this book represents introduces a
standard by which to evaluate what constitutes an informed acquisition decision.

Most companies make few, if any, major acquisitions. Because
these are exciting but rare events, they easily fall into a category
called, "Wow! Grab it!" type of decisions. The elation and "raring-to-
go" feeling associated with a decision that will dramatically change
the size and shape of a company overnight are undeniable. In *Crucial
Decisions,* Irving Janis describes the "Wow! Grab it!" decision rule as:
"This is better than you could hope for, so grab it; don't take any
chance of losing the wonderful opportunity by wasting time looking
into it any further."[2]

Major acquisitions require deeper analysis than that. In Part 1 of
this book, I have shown managers why they need to look before they

leap. In the next part, I present a comprehensive empirical study of acquiring firm performance that quantifies the risks of these decisions. The evidence surrounding the losses to acquirers cannot be ignored. Other corporate decisions causing only a fraction of these losses bring public outcry. Losing millions, even billions, of dollars of market value on the announcement of a major resource allocation decision means something is wrong. Markets have seen the acquisition game played too many times before. Most companies contemplating a major acquisition have not.

I have presented acquisitions as a unique business gamble. With the fundamentals developed here, we can predict the fate of most acquisitions, no matter how "strategic" they appear to be. We can make reasonable predictions of *how much* value will be merely transferred from the shareholders of the acquirer to the shareholders of the company being acquired. In Part 2 of this book, such predictions are tested across twenty-eight measures of shareholder performance spanning different periods of time. I found that losses can be predicted, and the higher the premium, the larger the losses.

Once again, the value to the shareholders of an acquirer is the net present value of the decision:

NPV = Synergy − Premium.

This assertion might be evident, but it is the necessary starting point. It yields what I have called the acquisition game: an up-front premium is paid for some uncertain stream of benefits or payoffs sometime in the future. Managers need to consider the likelihood of different scenarios of these payoffs (synergy), or they will actually know more about the payoffs in blackjack than for an acquisition.

Before a likely amount of synergy can be determined, we have to consider carefully what exactly synergy is and what competitive conditions must be met before anything good is likely to occur. The premium is the amount that acquirer shareholders would not have to pay to buy the shares of the target company on their own, so synergy must be increases in performance above some base case.

Existing stock market prices are formed on the expectations of the future. It is these preexisting performance expectations that create the base case. Synergy, then, must be performance gains above those that are already expected. This forms the competitive challenge. Synergy must imply gains in competitive advantage—that is, competing better than was previously expected. *Unless synergy is considered in this context, the trap begins to open, and planning and valuation have little meaning.*

Just putting two companies together that appear to be similar or complementary in some way will yield nothing unless the marriage can pass at least one of the contestability conditions:

1. Acquirers must be able to further limit competitors' ability to contest their or the target's current input markets, processes, or output markets above what is already expected, and/or
2. Acquirers must be able to open new markets and/or encroach on their competitors' markets where these competitors cannot respond.

Four organizational cornerstones must be in place for synergy to be anything but a trap: (1) strategic vision, (2) operating strategy, (3) systems integration, and (4) power and culture. These cornerstones must be set from the beginning. Post-acquisition is the wrong time to begin working out "the details" because competitors will not sit still while the acquirer attempts to generate synergies at their expense. Moreover, without the details, how could an acquirer ever conduct a valuation of improvements or negotiate on price?

Even when the cornerstones are in place, the acquisition premium dictates massive required performance improvements (RPIs) that in most cases quickly dwarf the amount of performance that could reasonably be achieved. Making matters even worse from a planning basis, the RPIs are dynamic. If delays in synergy are expected, the RPIs get bigger—much bigger—and markets and competitors know this.

In most acquisitions, the premium does not represent potential value. I illustrated this concept with the acquisition synergy scenarios at the end of Chapter 2. These elements of the acquisition game show how synergy can be measured, how difficult the management problem truly is, and, finally, why the amount of overpayment is predictable.

So the acquisition game *is* akin to running on a treadmill. Recall the illustration from Chapter 1: *Suppose you are running at 3 mph, but are required to run at 4 mph next year and 5 mph the year after. Synergy would mean running even harder than this expectation while competitors supply a head wind. Paying a premium for synergy—that is, for the right to run harder—is like putting on a heavy pack. Meanwhile, the more you delay running harder, the higher the incline is set.*

Utilizing the preceding principles, we can identify three main sources of tension that arise in the management of an acquisition strategy: (1) prior expectations and additional resource requirements, (2) competitors, and (3) time, value, and the premium. These issues create difficult and even paradoxical problems for managers.

Prior Expectations and Additional Resource Requirements

The stock market price of the target company before the acquisition will in most cases have substantial expected improvements already built in. What might appear to be post-acquisition performance gains may have nothing to do with synergy. Additional costs or investments such as increased R&D, new executives, golden parachutes, new plants, or increased advertising can negate any additional benefits in addition to damaging prior expectations. Finally, acquisitions can divert important managerial resources away from the acquirer's other businesses.

The lesson: Pay close attention to what is required to maintain value in the stand-alone businesses. This is the base case. When acquirers make organizational or strategic changes to gain the value they paid for in the premium, they run the risk of destroying the growth or value that was already priced by the markets. Additional investments in the businesses are like additions to the premium and must be considered as such if maintaining value is the objective.

Competitors

If proposed changes in strategy or cost-cutting measures are easily contestable by competitors, there will be no synergies. The result is that acquirers will likely need to make major additional commitments if the changes have a chance of improving competitive advantage.[3] On the other hand, acquirers must question whether integration moves will cause inflexibility, such that the moves of their competitors become difficult to contest. For example, workforce cuts might help efficiency but slow competitive response in the next round of competition. Finally, the longer the acquirer delays in implementing a post-acquisition strategy, the more time competitors have to learn what an acquirer is attempting to do. They *will* find ways to challenge the acquirer's anticipated moves before "improvements" even begin.

The lesson: Synergies will be the result of competitive gains and must be viewed in this context. An acquisition strategy will not create synergy with only a vision of why it might be a good thing to do. Unless acquirers carefully consider the other three cornerstones of synergy, the additional resources that will be needed to put them in place, and where these changes will improve performance along the value chain, synergy is a trap. The transition to the post-acquisition integration phase must be done quickly and decisively. Otherwise transition management becomes a resource drain and can make the acquirer even more vulnerable to competitors.

Time, Value, and the Premium

The premium translates into required performance improvements that only grow with time, so improvements need to begin immediately. But many improvements can come only from changes that take significant time to plan and implement (distribution, product development, new plant locations, executive succession), and rushing them may prove to be a disaster.

The lesson: Do not value the proposed acquisition in one shot. The market has already valued expected future performance of the target company as a stand-alone. The premium must represent improvements above this. Thus, acquirers need to value the improvements— *when* they are reasonably expected to occur. There is no credible way to enter negotiations on price if these issues are not clearly considered. It is difficult to do, but without doing it, the premium is a predictor of how much value will be destroyed. Losses can be "locked in" right up front even where substantial improvements are made down the road. Finally, missing performance targets that were probably unachievable in the first place is no signal to raise the stakes. Firing key executives, cutting back R&D, or doubling advertising or sales bonuses often means just getting deeper into the synergy trap.

The objective of the first part of this book and the comprehensive empirical study that follows is to improve our understanding of acquisition fundamentals and the history of acquisition performance. Gambling billions on one of the biggest decisions a company makes without the fundamentals has been vividly described by Robert Lutz, former president of Chrysler Corporation:

> Suppose you're in a road race on a public road, and you have a chance to pass the car ahead of you—only to do so would require crossing the double-yellow line and passing on a blind curve. Would this high-risk strategy bring you "high reward" if the road ahead were completely clear? Of course, it would.
>
> But what would happen if, say, there was a cement truck around that blind corner? What happens to your reward then?
>
> We know that no matter what business you're in, you don't try to find competitive advantage by passing on blind curves. Sure, that's something you might do . . . but, at the end of the day, that's a "strategy" which leads absolutely to nowhere![4]

Even well-planned acquisitions at modest premiums can fail—all the more reason that acquirers must not walk into major acquisitions with their eyes closed. The risks are too high.

Before senior executives can justify paying *any* acquisition premium they must be able to answer the following questions:

- What are the stand-alone expectations of acquirer and target?
- Where will performance gains emerge as a result of the merger?
- Which competitors are likely to be affected?
- How will those competitors likely respond?
- What are the milestones in a 24-month implementation plan?
- What additional investments will be required?
- Who are the key managers responsible for implementation?
- Why is this deal better than alternative investments?

Without credible answers to these basic questions, acquirers will be well on their way to losing the acquisition game from the beginning and their shareholders will pay the price.

Saving a company and its shareholders significant wealth by walking away is a very good decision. After all, acquisitions are strategic *alternatives.* If destroying shareholder value is a manager's best alternative, something is wrong. *Strategy is about creating value.*

Part 2 is a comprehensive study examining the determinants of acquiring firm performance. The average size of the acquiring firms in the study is $2.31 billion, with a range from $27 million to $34 billion. The average size of the targets is $753 million, with a range of $17 million to $8.3 billion. The average relative size of the acquisitions in the study is nearly 50 percent. These are major acquisitions. The vast majority (over 72 percent) are single-bidder auctions. The premium ranges from −6.9 percent to 107 percent, with an average of approximately 30 percent. The major empirical results are summarized as follows:

1. Acquisition strategies, on average, destroy value for the acquirer.
2. The stock market losses—or gains—on announcement of acquisitions are indicative of long-term performance.
3. The *level* of the acquisition premium has a strong negative effect on performance across all twenty-eight measures of shareholder performance; the higher the premium, the larger the losses.
4. The presence of multiple bidders has a negative impact on performance, but this effect is independent of the negative effect of the premium. In other words, acquirers do not need to participate in multiple-bidder contests to predictably overpay.
5. Strategic relatedness moderates the value-destructive effect of the premium but has no independent effect on the performance of acquirers. In fact, by conditioning on the premium, I show how unrelated acquisitions can outperform strategically related acquisitions.
6. The use of cash for acquisitions results in better performance than the use of equity (stock).

7. Contested acquisitions result in the payment of higher premiums than uncontested acquisitions.
8. Executing an acquisition through a tender offer versus a "friendly" merger has no independent effect on performance, nor is there a difference in the premium paid.
9. There is no consistent effect of the relative size of the acquisition on performance.

PART 2

AN ANALYSIS OF CORPORATE ACQUISITION STRATEGIES

5

Acquirer Performance and Risk Taking

The empirical study in Part 2 sets forth to answer four major questions:

1. Do corporate acquisition strategies create shareholder value?
2. Can the acquisition premium be used to predict the performance outcomes of an acquisition?
3. How do other factors (such as strategic relatedness, relative size, method of payment, and mergers versus tender offers) affect performance in the context of the acquisition premium?
4. Will future risk taking by managers in acquiring firms be affected by the size of the acquisition premium decision?

Question 4 is posed to probe what may happen to acquirers after predictably falling into the synergy trap. Do managers escalate their commitment to a failing strategy by taking greater risks after they miss the target RPIs? Once they are caught in the trap, do they make matters worse by exhibiting gambling behavior?

A large body of research in the management literature examines the performance of acquiring firms, but this work has been exploratory in nature and has yielded a stream of conflicting evidence (reviewed in Appendix A). The conflicting empirical evidence has led some strategy scholars to conclude that traditional large-sample empirical research does not contribute to an understanding of acquisition performance.[1] In fact, past studies generally explain less than 10

85

percent of cross-sectional variance in performance. Given that mergers and acquisitions are perhaps the most important discretionary method of implementing strategic change in organizations, managers require more than what has been offered.

Figure 5.1 represents the major decision variables underlying the management literature on acquirer performance.[2] It shows that prior research has examined only linear independent effects of these managerial choices on performance. Most of the literature has actually been only tests of the difference in performance between related and unrelated acquisitions.

This study seeks to show the importance of a resource allocation decision of executive teams—specifically, the acquisition premium—to develop a better understanding of acquiring firm performance as well as offer a reconciliation of the conflicting evidence in the literature.

By treating an acquisition as a resource allocation decision, we can

FIGURE 5.1

Prior Approaches to Examining Acquirer Performance

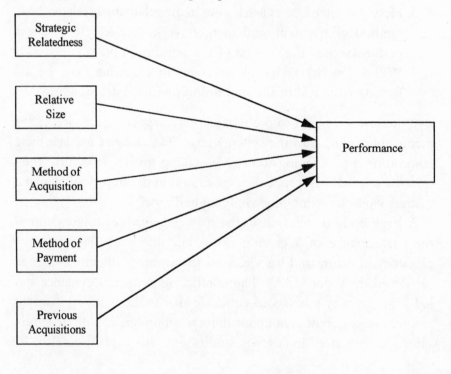

also introduce behavioral theories that may have important implications for understanding differences in the risk-taking behavior of acquiring firm managers post-acquisition. Figure 5.2 shows the conceptual model of this research. Note that the strategic factors that have been discussed in prior approaches are still included in this framework, but now they are placed in the context of the economics of the acquisition premium paid by executive teams in executing a corporate acquisition strategy.

In general, the economic justification for acquisitions in the literature has been the expectation of synergy. Little attention, however, has been given to how paying merger or takeover premiums for these synergistic expectations can or has affected corporate performance or the risk-taking behavior of managers. The central theme of this research is that the payment of an acquisition premium is a strategic resource commitment with embedded required performance im-

FIGURE 5.2

Model of Acquirer Performance and Risk Taking

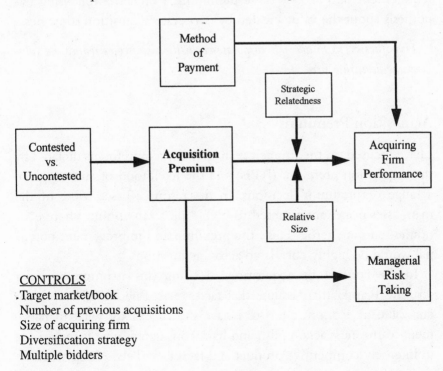

CONTROLS
.Target market/book
Number of previous acquisitions
Size of acquiring firm
Diversification strategy
Multiple bidders

provements that must be examined to understand the dynamics of acquirer performance.

The traditional approach to acquisition performance has subsumed the resource-based view of the firm where factor prices get bid up to their "fair" value in a competitive market. My claim is that many of these premium payments have created required performance improvements that are virtually impossible to realize, even by the best executives in the best of industry conditions. With respect to acquisitions, secondary market participants around the world have already bid on the pre-acquisition value of target firms, so the required synergies implied by the premium must be performance gains above what is already expected for these firms to achieve.

Corporate Acquisitions as a Strategy for Value Creation

Acquisition activity over the past fifteen years has involved many large acquisitions implemented with significant acquisition premiums. Given an average premium of over 40 percent and the performance requirements implied by these premiums, I offer the following hypothesis about the value created by corporate acquisition strategies:

Hypothesis 1: On average, corporate acquisition strategies reduce the value of the acquiring firm.

Acquisition Premiums

I have focused on the implicit management requirements dictated by the acquisition premium (RPIs) and the likelihood of success given a range of premium decisions. In the resource-based view of the firm, asset prices are assumed to be bid up to the point where economic rents are zero.[3] Thus, the premium and improvement potential would be highly correlated across acquisitions.

In the context of acquisitions, I bring this assumption under scrutiny. Rather than assume that factor prices necessarily represent fair value in economic terms, I have shown exactly what management teams must accomplish and have considered what is reasonable in intensely competitive product and factor markets. Along with the required cornerstones of synergy, the analysis provides support for the position that there are severe limits to the improvements that acquiring firm management can generally make with acquisitions. I refer to this as the *synergy limitation view* of acquirer performance.

Markets attempt to forecast the net present value of acquisition decisions. Recall the net present value model of acquisition performance:

NPV = Synergy − Premium.

In the synergy limitation view, we predict a low correlation between the size of the premium and improvement potential such that the level of the premium provides an indication of the degree of up-front (ex-ante) risk of acquisition failure. In Chapter 2, two scenarios of synergy were described for different acquisition premiums:

Premium	Synergy A	Synergy B
100%	80%	15%
80	60	15
60	40	15
40	20	15
20	0	15

The hypothesis of the synergy limitation view is represented by synergy scenario B and yields the major hypothesis of this study:

Hypothesis 2: The larger the premium paid for an acquisition, the worse the subsequent returns for the acquiring firm.

Although the negative premium–return relationship is obvious for any single acquisition, if the premiums paid across acquisitions, on average, represented their value, there should be no relationship between the amount of the premium and performance—the premium would represent the value, and the NPV should be zero. So as long as the expectations of required performance improvements embedded in the premium reflect realizations, on average, the preceding hypothesis would be rejected (i.e., price represents value). This would also hold for synergy scenario A, where overpayment occurs, but the premium gives no prediction of the amount of losses—synergy is still highly correlated with the premium. A high correlation between price and value is precisely what would be predicted by a competitive markets view of the firm but not the synergy limitation view represented by scenario B and Hypothesis 2.

Strategic Relatedness of Acquisitions

The literature regarding the effect of acquisition relatedness has relied on the basic intuition that related acquisitions should generate more synergy than unrelated acquisitions and related acquirers should thus outperform unrelated acquirers.[4] The literature, however, is inconclusive. On balance, no significant difference has been found in returns to the shareholders of acquirers for strategically related versus unrelated acquisitions.[5] In a comprehensive study, Lubatkin concludes that his findings do *not* support the popular belief that "all things being equal, some product and market relatedness is better than none."[6] On the other hand, some research has actually found that acquirers making unrelated acquisitions significantly outperform those making related acquisitions.[7]

The following discussion will offer some insight on the nature of this problem and suggest conditions under which the relatedness of an acquisition will have an effect on performance. More important, I offer an alternative theoretical approach to understanding the importance of relatedness in acquisitions that will help to reconcile the current literature.

There are two major problems in the literature on the effect of acquisition relatedness that may explain insignificant or conflicting findings about the effect of this choice variable. First, there has been little consideration of the degree of relatedness of the acquisition; that is, acquisition relatedness has been measured as a dichotomous (0,1) variable. Second, there has been little consideration of other choice variables that may be driving performance such that acquisition relatedness does not have a direct effect on performance. The models of performance have been incomplete. The first problem I consider in the next chapter on methodology; the second problem I consider here.

There are two distinct dimensions to the acquisition performance problem: (1) the payment of the acquisition premium, and (2) post-acquisition realization of synergy. Consistent with the resource-based view, empirical tests of the relatedness hypothesis in acquisitions implicitly assume the rational economic position that the premium reflects value potential. Consideration has not been given to the required performance improvements that are embedded in the acquisition premium, and relatedness has not been considered in this context.

There is no reason to believe that joining two firms that are related in every way will create synergy. Unless the acquisition can pass one or both of the contestability conditions and has a firm command of the cornerstones of synergy, synergies will be unlikely. In short, the knowledge of whether an acquisition is strategically related or unrelated will say little if anything about synergy potential.[8] This gives the following null hypothesis:

> *Hypothesis 3a: Acquisition relatedness will not have a main effect on acquiring firm performance.*

The objective here is not to discard the relatedness concept but to approach the meaning of relatedness with different reasoning and in the managerial context created by the resources that are committed to make the acquisition, particularly the acquisition premium. Rather than focus on potential synergies, the focus should be on *why* a firm would pursue a related versus unrelated acquisition strategy.

An unrelated acquisition strategy might be a signal that there may not be valuable or sufficient reinvestment opportunities in the current lines of business of the firm. Profitable growth opportunities might be exhausted. Thus, if a top management team is acquiring an unrelated company, it may be sending a strong signal about its confidence in the current business(es).[9]

But is simply knowing whether the acquisition is related or unrelated enough to give an indication of strategic intent or a signal of future performance? It is within the context of the acquisition premium that this approach becomes particularly meaningful. Premiums translate into specific required performance improvements that management teams must accomplish with the acquisition.

At low levels of the acquisition premium, the difference between a related and an unrelated acquisition is, at worst, management's forecast of the profitability of the current lines of business. At higher levels of the acquisition premium, both related and unrelated acquisitions are likely to be failures. For unrelated acquisitions, however, management teams are diverting even more available resources away from the current businesses, perhaps in desperation, in addition to establishing what are unachievable performance objectives in a new business. Further, given that management is *diverting* resources, there will clearly be a low probability of the organizational integration so essential to achieving any of the performance improvements that may be available from an acquisition. Thus, relatedness will moderate the strength of the negative relationship between the premium and acquiring firm performance.

Hypothesis 3b: Acquisition relatedness will have a positive moderating effect between the acquisition premium and acquirer performance. That is, the negative effect of the acquisition premium will be less for related acquisitions than for unrelated acquisitions.

We are also in a position to explore some important questions concerning the relationship between strategic relatedness and the acquisition premium. The following propositions are not formally motivated and so are presented as conjectures:

Conjecture 1: Strategic relatedness will have various effects on performance when conditioning on the acquisition premium.

Because the acquisition premium will dominate the effect of strategic relatedness on acquirer performance, we can replicate conflicting evidence about relatedness simply by conditioning on the proposed effects of other strategic factors—in particular, the acquisition premium. This conjecture is posed specifically to replicate and explore conflicting past results on relatedness and attempt to reconcile the empirical literature.

Conjecture 2: Acquisition premiums are no higher for related versus unrelated acquisitions.

The market for corporate control drives the acquisition premium. Acquisitions are normally priced based on the price paid for comparable acquisitions (*compaqs*). The key job of an investment banker is to inform an acquirer what it must pay for an acquisition. This is consistent with Hypothesis 2 that acquisition premium decisions do not necessarily represent realizable synergies in a competitive industry. If the premium is driven exogenously, there is little reason to believe that related acquisitions will command higher premiums than unrelated acquisitions, on average. Thus, the conjecture is that there will be no relationship between the relatedness of the acquisition and the acquisition premium.

Method of Payment

There is conflicting evidence in the acquisition literature of the management field regarding the effect of the method of payment: the use of cash versus stock as payment in acquisitions.[10]

An argument for the expectation that cash acquisitions will outperform stock acquisitions has been given by Myers and Majluf.[11] Essentially, financing an acquisition with stock (equity) is equivalent to issuing stock. Thus, there is an adverse selection problem because an acquirer would issue equity only when the firm is overvalued; the acquirer must know that the market knows this so an equity issue must be a last resort.

This adverse selection problem can be illustrated as follows: Suppose I tell you that I have between $50 and $200 of cash in my wallet, and I give you and your friends the chance to bid for my wallet, with the highest bidder winning. But just before you hand over your bid, I tell you that I have the right, after examining the bids, to decide whether to accept them. Immediately you will protest, "Hey, that's not fair!" Why? Because you know that I will accept your bid only when I know it is for an amount greater than the amount of cash I actually have in my wallet.

I have just introduced a dangerous (for you) asymmetric information problem into the auctioning of my wallet. I know more about the value of the wallet than you do, and I will accept your bid only when it is beneficial for me. Issuing equity is very similar to this example, regardless of what the funds will be used for. Although sometimes equity issues are appropriate (not the last resort), markets cannot tell the good guys from the bad guys, and equity issues will be met unfavorably by the market.

Cash acquisitions, in contrast, are normally financed with debt. Free cash flow theory suggests that increasing debt levels will establish cash flow requirements that will limit the amount of cash that can be invested at below the cost of capital or wasted through organizational inefficiencies.[12] From a managerial perspective, increasing debt levels should force the immediacy of post-merger synergy realization to prevent defaulting on the debt. Because the cost of equity does not appear as an expense on the income statement (although interest from debt does), managers frequently view equity issues as free money.

Further, since interest on debt is tax deductible, corporate financial officers (CFOs) should utilize debt where possible—but not beyond the point where the level of debt might interfere with ongoing operations if the company fell into financial distress. So presumably managers would choose to issue equity when they know operations are not sufficiently strong to carry the increased debt.[13]

Each of these views yield the following hypothesis:

Hypothesis 4: The payment of cash for acquisitions will result in better performance for acquiring firms than the payment of stock (issuing equity).

The Performance Effects of Mergers versus Tender Offers

There has been a continuing stream of conflicting evidence on the performance effects of mergers versus tender offers in the management literature.[14] Prior analysis, however, has not addressed the nature of the performance effects of a merger as opposed to a tender offer. We need to understand what it is about mergers or tender offers that can affect performance.

Mergers and tender offers are similar in that both command a significant acquisition premium.[15] This is likely the nature of the performance relationship. The execution of an acquisition through a "friendly" merger instead of a tender offer for the shares of the target company should not have an independent effect on performance. If there is an effect, the merger versus tender offer distinction is meaningful in relation to the acquisition premium.

Several authors have distinguished between contested and uncontested (unfriendly versus friendly) tender offers.[16] In a contested acquisition, the management of the target firm resists the acquisition offer. The evidence is that contested takeovers perform worse than uncontested takeovers.[17] Further, contested takeovers bring "white knights" along with very high acquisition premiums. White knights experience significant losses in value.[18] For example, when Kodak acquired Sterling Drug, its market value fell by $2 billion, the full amount of the premium.[19] Thus, the underlying nature of the problem is the contestedness of the process and not simply the arbitrary distinction of merger versus tender offer.[20]

The argument here is that a consideration of the method of the acquisition—mergers versus tender offers—is important only to the extent that these options drive the acquisition premium. Further, given that many tender offers are mutually agreed on, it is more meaningful to consider whether an acquisition is contested rather than whether a form 14-D (for a tender offer) has been filed. This approach challenges the importance of the merger versus tender offer construct and proposes the meaningfulness of contestedness with regard to performance of the acquiring firm. This discussion is empirically testable and yields the following hypothesis:

Hypothesis 5a: The implementation of an acquisition through a contested process will result in the payment of a higher premium than through an uncontested process.

In addition, from the preceding discussion I propose the following null hypotheses:

Hypothesis 5b: The implementation of an acquisition through a tender offer will not result in the payment of a higher premium than through a merger.

Hypothesis 5c: The implementation of an acquisition through a tender offer versus a merger will not have an independent effect on performance.

Relative Size of the Acquisition

The relative size question has yielded mixed results in the acquisition literature in both the finance and strategy fields.[21] As in the merger versus takeover question, the problem may be a lack of consideration of the nature of the relative size of the acquisition. Why should the relative size of any acquisition have an independent effect on performance?

Scholars in the acquisition literature have typically cited the work of Biggadike as the motivation for proposing that the relative size of an acquisition should have a positive effect on the performance of the acquiring firm.[22] However, Biggadike's argument and evidence focused on the nature of the resource commitment to a particular venture—that new ventures required major up-front commitments to improve their chances of success—not the relative size of the venture to the size of the whole organization. Further, Biggadike considered de novo–type ventures, not acquisition strategies.

It is necessary to describe here the relative size considerations for this study. A McKinsey & Company study found that the failure rate of acquisitions fell from 61 percent overall to 54 percent when the acquisitions were less than 10 percent the size of the acquirer.[23] An argument can be made that smaller relative size acquisitions—those less than 10 percent—have a higher chance of success because there will be a more detailed understanding of the businesses and quicker integration potential.

My study examines large acquisitions—those over $100 million—that represent a relative size of at least 10 percent the size of the acquirer. Thus the focus is on acquisitions that represent truly major corporate decisions and represent the majority of the dollar value of acquisitions completed across the economy. In this context, the relative size on its own gives little information about the acquisition other than to be able to say the acquisition is larger or smaller. Relative size should have an effect only to the extent that it allows performance drivers of acquisitions to have effects on the acquiring firm and thus will not have an independent effect. This yields the following hypothesis:

Hypothesis 6: The relative size of an acquisition negatively moderates the relationship between the level of the acquisition premium and acquiring firm performance. That is, the greater the relative size, the more damaging the effect of the premium on acquirer performance.

Managerial Risk Taking Following Acquisition

The simulations in Chapter 3 illustrated the required performance improvements (RPIs) facing managers following an acquisition for different levels of the premium. We can think of the required performance improvements as a target reference point for managers with respect to preserving the value of the firm. The simulations also clearly illustrated that as the premium increases beyond certain levels, the likelihood of realizing the required improvements declines dramatically. It is the knowledge of the synergy trap and the results of the simulation analysis that allows up-front predictions about when managers are likely to miss their performance requirements and by how much.

This chapter has largely focused on generating predictions about the returns to acquirers based on the value consequences of paying an acquisition premium and the interaction of these consequences with other managerial choice variables that have been considered in prior research. In Chapter 2, I detailed the cornerstones of synergy and how future resource commitments will be pure resource drains if these are not considered carefully. It is the likelihood and characteristics of these resource commitments following the acquisition that we can now consider.

Can the size of the premium be used to predict changes in the nature of future resource commitments? If this were possible, predictable value–destroying behavior following the acquisition might be avoided.

These future changes in the nature of resource commitments might take the form of changes in risk taking. In the post-acquisition phase, the changes in managerial risk taking could take two forms: (1) increasing the size of the bet on the current competitive game (such as a major advertising campaign), or (2) committing resources to new, higher-risk competitive games (such as a major distribution system change or R&D venture), or both.

Why would the level of risk taking increase following an acquisition? Initially managers may have built increased risk into post-merger integration plans to obtain a greater chance of positive returns from their resource allocation decision. But given the likelihood that as the acquisition premium increases managers will predictably miss their performance targets, the issue is whether the level of risk taking will change over time.

A manager acting in an economically rational manner should, at any given point in time, evaluate the net present value of future decisions and not be affected by past decisions, which are sunk costs. This includes the extreme of facing the abandonment decision. Simply put, is it better to divest or to continue ownership?

A substantial amount of evidence has shown that the assumption of economic rationality is routinely violated by managers.[24] It is also well documented that managers may exhibit an escalation of commitment to a failing course of action.[25] There are at least two approaches to risk taking that would motivate predictions within this context.

One approach to the escalation of commitment phenomenon has been the self-justification hypothesis. Brockner has written that escalation is determined, at least in part, "by decision makers' unwillingness to admit that their prior allocation of resources to the chosen course of action was in vain (the self-justification hypothesis)."[26] Often managers do not want to admit defeat and will go to great lengths to show their decisions were ultimately justified. This explanation is comparable to the finance literature's managerial hubris concept, which says managers really believe they can achieve the required gains from the acquisition.[27] Some research has even suggested that managers may escalate their commitment to a failing acquisition such that the divestment decision is severely delayed.[28]

The concept of escalating commitment has also been approached from the prospect theory perspective.[29] Prospect theory predicts that individuals will generally be risk seeking when they are losing but risk averse when they are winning—classic gambling behavior. Winning or losing is in relation to an arbitrary reference point. The acquisition premium provides a clear target reference point for managers to meet.

Thus, as managers miss what may actually be unachievable performance targets and fall below their target reference point into the domain of losses, they may increase their level of risk taking to attempt to meet these targets in the future. The analogy to this is a gambler sitting at a blackjack table who increases his bets as he loses. These higher-risk strategies may simply be perceived as necessary by managers given the distance they must cover to preserve value. For example, recall that when synergies failed to materialize in AT&T's acquisition of NCR, and losses began to mount, AT&T spent millions on new sales teams in new markets and industries where it had little experience.

Since higher levels of the acquisition premium will be associated with a greater likelihood of not achieving performance targets, it follows that high levels of the premium will also be associated with increases in risk taking.[30] This analysis suggests the following hypothesis:

Hypothesis 7: Higher acquisition premiums will be associated with increases in managerial risk taking following the acquisition.

The next chapter describes the details of the sample of acquisitions and the methodology used to test the preceding hypotheses of the study.

6

Methodology

Sample

The data sources used to develop the acquisition sample were the *Mergers and Acquisitions* database (IDD Enterprises), the Securities Data Corporation database, the CRSP (Center for Research in Security Prices) tapes, and the *Wall Street Journal Index*. The preliminary sample included all acquisitions of New York (NYSE) or American (AMEX) Stock Exchange targets that were made by NYSE or AMEX acquirers during the period 1979 through 1990.

The objective was to consider acquisitions that represented a significant change or addition to the corporate strategy of the acquirer. Accordingly, target firms were required to be at least 10 percent the size of the bidder in terms of assets or the market value of the equity. In contrast, most other acquisition studies have looked at deals where the average relative size of the acquisition is less than 10 percent; in fact, these studies include a majority of deals that are less than 5 percent the size of the acquirer. From a statistical perspective, the advantages are that I increase the power of the cross-sectional tests and avoid the statistical problems that arise with the inclusion of small acquisitions that are insignificant to the market value of the acquirer.[1]

In addition, bidding firms could not have previously owned more than 5 percent of the target, and the acquisition must have been accomplished in one transaction where the result was ownership of 100 percent of the target. Again, the objective was to examine the results of major discretionary management decisions involving acquisitions that represented discrete changes or additions to current corporate strategy. Acquisitions involving regulated firms (banks, railroads, and utilities) were identified and excluded, as were those involving trusts and limited partnerships. The final sample contained 168 acquisitions. Appendix C lists the complete sample of targets and acquirers and a business description of each.

Acquiring Firm Performance

Consistent with contemporary strategy and financial economics literature on acquiring firm performance, I focus on stock-return measures.[2] Because we are studying the effects of executive decisions, stock-return measures are appropriate; they measure revisions of expectations of future performance and, more important, the effects on shareholder value. Given that shareholders are residual claimants, it is likely that stock-return measures also reflect the welfare of other stakeholders of the organization.[3] The CRSP database is the source of stock price data for determining acquirer performance.

For this research, stock returns are superior to traditional accounting-based measures such as ROA or ROE for two major reasons. First, the decisions we are examining are discrete in nature, and the theory has yielded expectations-based hypotheses. There is substantial evidence that the market evaluates management decisions based on expected long-term cash flow, not on short-term accounting treatments.[4] Second, accounting returns (particularly in acquisitions) can be manipulated and have been criticized as being noisy and unreliable.[5] This might explain why the strategy literature has not relied on accounting measures in studying acquiring firm performance.

Acquiring firm performance (the dependent variable) is measured using seven different windows of stock market returns following the acquisition:

1. Announcement effect measured from day −1 through day +1.
2. Announcement effect measured from day −5 through day +5.
3. Announcement effect measured from day −5 through day T, where T is defined as the day the target firm actually ceases trading. This measure captures news about the acquisition that may occur between the first announcement and the close of negotiations.

4. Month 0 through month 12 (one year).
5. Month 0 through month 24 (two years).
6. Month 0 through month 36 (three years).
7. Month 0 through month 48 (four years).

Although these windows are not independent, they do allow us to test the propositions across the various time periods that have been considered in previous studies of acquirer performance. Moreover, Porter argues that short-window market reactions may not represent actual long-term significance, so this multiperiod approach comprehensively addresses this common concern.[6]

Strategy researchers have expressed reservations about using market-model-based shareholder returns (which adjust raw returns for both trends in past performance and market-wide volatility) to draw meaningful conclusions about the effects of corporate strategies.[7] The major reservation is the potential instability of the parameter estimates of the market model giving unreliable measures of abnormal performance. Thus, to promote generality of results (and test the above assertion) I generate the returns for these seven windows using four different models: (1) market-adjusted returns, (2) market-model returns, (3) mean-adjusted returns, and (4) raw returns or unadjusted total shareholder returns (commonly known as TSRs). The result is twenty-eight measures of the performance dependent variable.

Briefly, market-adjusted returns adjust raw shareholder returns over a given period for the overall market returns (Standard & Poors 500) for the same period. Market-model returns adjust raw returns for the normal returns that would be expected for a given equity security given its past performance and sensitivity to market changes. Finally, mean-adjusted returns adjust raw returns for the mean of past performance of the security over some time period.

For each of the four return generation methods, returns for the short-term event windows 1, 2, and 3 are calculated using daily data, and returns for the longer-term event windows 4, 5, 6, and 7 are calculated using monthly data as follows:

1. *Market-model returns.* An ordinary least squares (OLS) market model is estimated for each security in the sample, using 200 daily re-

turn observations from day −240 to day −40 and using 46 monthly observations from month −48 to month −2 for the short-term and long-term performance periods, respectively. Using the parameter estimates of the market model, excess or abnormal returns $(A_{i,t})$ are estimated for every security for each of the seven time periods (the event periods) as follows:

$$A_{i,t} = R_{i,t} - \alpha_i - \hat{\beta}_i R_{m,t}$$

where α_i and β_i are OLS values from the estimation period, $R_{m,t}$ is the return on the CRSP equally weighted market index for day (month) t, and $R_{i,t}$ is the actual return for security i on day (month) t. The test statistic for significance of the abnormal return estimates is according to Brown and Warner.[8]

2. *Market-adjusted returns.* Returns are calculated for every security for each of the seven time periods (the event periods) as follows:

$$A_{i,t} = R_{i,t} - R_{m,t}$$

The market-adjusted model is essentially the same as the market model where $\alpha_i = 0$ and $\beta_i = 1$ for all securities. Market-adjusted returns are simply the daily or monthly post-acquisition return (see *market-model returns*) adjusted for the return on the market during the same time period. Thus, this measure is free from the so-called parameter biases from the estimation period in the market model of which strategy researchers have expressed concern.

3. *Mean-adjusted returns.* Returns are calculated for every company for each of the seven time periods as follows:

$$A_{i,t} = R_{i,t} - \bar{R}_{i;T1,T2}$$

where $\bar{R}_{i;T1,T2}$ is the average of past performance for each security in the sample, using 200 daily return observations from day −240 to day −40 (that is, mean daily performance one year before the acquisition), and using 46 monthly observations from month −48 to month −2 (mean monthly performance four years before the acquisition) for the short-term and long-term performance periods, respectively. $R_{i,t}$ is as above.

4. *Raw returns* (total shareholder returns). Returns are calculated for every company for each of the seven time periods as follows:

$$A_{i,t} = R_{i,t}.$$

Raw returns are simply the daily (monthly) unadjusted post-acquisition return—capital appreciation or depreciation—plus dividends for each time period.

For each of the preceding methods, day 0 is defined as the day the market could respond to the news of an acquisition proposal by the acquiring firm.[9]

Given the daily (monthly) stock returns that were generated by the four methods, I calculated the dependent-variable measure of acquiring firm performance for each of the seven time periods as follows:

$$CAR_{i;T1,T2} = \sum_{t=T1}^{T2} A_{i,t}$$

where T1,T2 is the interval for each of the seven performance periods described at the beginning of this section.

For calculating the aggregate statistics we need for testing the first hypothesis, I cumulate the returns as follows:

$$CAR_{T1,T2} = \sum_{t=T1}^{T2} AR_t$$

where

$$AR_t = \frac{1}{N_t} \sum_{i=1}^{N_t} A_{i,t}$$

and N_t is the number of firms whose returns are available on day (month) t.

The following section details how the independent variables are measured. The word in parentheses following the independent-variable name is used in the regression tables in Appendix B.

Independent Variables

Acquisition Premium (Premium)

The CRSP database is the source of stock price data for measuring acquisition premiums. The *Wall Street Journal Index* was used to identify the announcement date of a proposed takeover. The measure of the acquisition premium follows directly from the simulations discussed in Chapter 3. The premium is measured as the percentage change in the price of the target firm from five days prior to takeover news to five days after the news, adjusted for the movement in the S&P 500 Index during that time.[10] This measure is also used by Merrill Lynch, Inc. and the *Mergerstat* database. Other time periods were also examined, and they yielded results consistent with those reported here. This measure represents the absolute task of generating required synergies from the acquisition that faces management. It has the advantage of being a ratio-scaled measure and is readily interpretable.

Another potentially independent dimension of the acquisition premium, for which I control, is the implied market value of equity/book value of equity of the target given by the premium. The concept of price paid was operationalized by Kusewitt as the MV/BV ratio of the target at the effective date of the acquisition (Tmvbvt).[11] Although he provided no theory behind the measure and found insignificant results in a cross-sectional analysis of performance, it may be meaningful. Consider the following scenario:

Suppose that two firms are being considered as potential targets by a firm that is implementing an acquisition program. Firm A has had sales and earnings growth of 20 percent over the past three years, with high expectations for the future. Firm B has recently lost market share in a profitable industry and has had an earnings decline of 5 percent over the past two years. Both firms have the same number of shares outstanding and currently sell for $50 per share. How do we consider the managerial relevance of an acquisition premium for these two firms?

In the simulation section I did not differentiate between these two types of firms. In other words, I was concerned about the likelihood of earning synergies—above already existing required rates of return—for any firm in a competitive economy. I did not condition the expectations for synergy realization on the amount of performance expectations already built into the price of the target firm.

In the scenario here, it may be very difficult to significantly improve the operating performance of firm A relative to the improvement potential for firm B. Further, it is likely that high expectations are already built into the price of firm A such that the total required performance needed to maintain value given by some percentage acquisition premium may be much more severe for firm A than for firm B. Thus, an argument might be made that this method of measuring the premium adjusts for the fact that for some companies selling at a low market/book multiple, a high premium may be a better investment than the same premium for a company already selling for a high market/book multiple.

This argument, however, makes a big assumption: that the market is not properly pricing firms with high (low) market/book values. If, in fact, high (low) market/book values are a good forecast of the future performance of the firm, then paying a given premium for a high versus low MV/BV company has the same managerial significance.

Thus, controlling for this variable (Tmvbvt) is, in a sense, a test of two alternative hypotheses: (1) overpayment is more likely for high MV/BV companies than for low MV/BV companies, or (2) high (low) MV/BV companies sell at these multiples for good reason (i.e., appropriate expectations) and thus, the MV/BV multiple does not affect the managerial significance of the premium on acquiring firm performance. The latter hypothesis is obviously the null, and if the expectations reflected in pre-acquisition market pricing are not accurate (on average), then we would reject the null.

Acquisition Relatedness (Relindx)

Relatedness of the acquisition is measured based on SIC (Standard Industrial Classification) commonality. Although this approach has limitations, it is consistent with the approach taken in past cross-sectional work and has received considerable empirical support.[12] The data on SIC codes were checked against four sources: the *Mergers and Acquisitions* database, COMPUSTAT SIC files, Securities Data Corporation database, and Dun & Bradstreet's *Million Dollar Directory.*

I use two methods for operationalizing relatedness. First, for testing the conjectures on relatedness and replicating past evidence I use the traditional dichotomous method—that is, if there is a match between the two firms in any of their principal businesses at the four-digit SIC code level, then the acquisition is related; otherwise, it is considered unrelated. Second, rather than consider relatedness as dichotomous for use in the cross-sectional regression analysis, we achieve a better measure of the degree of relatedness between two firms by calculating the following index: the number of SIC codes in common at the four-digit level divided by the number of distinct SIC codes at the four-digit level. The result is an index with values from 0 to 1 inclusive. For example, suppose firm A has seven four-digit SIC codes and firm B has four four-digit SIC codes, and three of the SIC codes are in common. Then the index value would be 3/8. Results with a dichotomous variable are similar.

Cash versus Stock (Cash)

This is measured as a dichotomous variable (coded 0,1). A zero code includes stock and combination cash and stock payment methods.[13]

Contested versus Uncontested Acquisitions (Contest)

This is measured as a dichotomous variable (coded 0,1). Acquisitions involving hostile takeover bids (the target rejects advances of the bidder, including white knight acquirers) are coded as contested (1 = contested).

Tender versus Merger (Tender)

This is measured as a dichotomous variable (coded 0,1). An acquisition is coded as a 1 for a tender offer if a form 14-D was filed with the Securities and Exchange Commission at the announcement of the proposed takeover.

Relative Size of the Acquisition (Relsize)

Relative size of the acquired firm is measured as the market value of the acquired firm relative to the market value of the acquiring firm one month prior to the announcement date of the acquisition.

Control Variables

Size of the Acquiring Firm (Bmv1). Researchers in the finance and management literatures have demonstrated that firm size can affect performance, and so I include this as a control variable measured as the market value of the acquiring firm at one month before the announcement date of the acquisition.[14]

Number of Previous Acquisitions (Prev). Previous acquisitions may or may not yield a learning effect. This control variable represents the number of other acquisitions previously made by the acquiring firm during the sample period for a given acquisition. While this measure is left censored, the sample period starts in the early stage of the acquisition wave. Further, even during the sample period, the mean number of previous acquisitions is close to zero. This is consistent with Roll's claim that on average managers make very few major acquisitions.[15]

Target Market Value/Book Value (Tmvbvt). This is the implicit market value (equity) to book value ratio at the effective date of the acquisition.

Diversification Strategy (Dist4). The literature on acquisitions has considered the relatedness of a particular acquisition but not the overall diversification strategy of the new combined firm. I control for the potential effects of a new level of diversification measured using a continuous four-digit SIC product count of the combined firm. That is, Dist4 represents the number of distinct four-digit SIC codes in which the new combined firm operates. This unweighted measure converges to Rumelt's measures of relatedness and has empirical support.[16]

Multiple Bidders (Multb). Singh and You et al. find that the presence of multiple bidders has a negative effect on the performance of the eventual acquirer, so I control for this effect.[17] This control variable is measured as a dichotomous variable indicating the presence of other competing bidders (1 = multiple bidders).

Time (Time and Time^2). This control variable is designed to measure any linear or square time trends present over the period of the study. Time is defined as the merger year minus 1978.

Changes in Risk Taking Following Acquisition

Prior research has used the standard deviation of past return on assets (ROA) to assess risk taking by managers.[18] This has been challenged by Bromiley and by Baucus, Golec, and Cooper. Bromiley argues that the variance of ROA measures only ex-post variance of returns and may result in businesses with predictable but rapidly growing returns being classified as "high risk." Baucus, Golec, and Cooper show how traditional measures of ROA using end-of-period (compared with beginning-of-period) asset values can result in highly inconsistent variance measures.[19] Further, two firms can have the same ROA but quite different capital structures and weighted average costs of capital such that ROA itself across firms may have little meaning with regard to performance. For these reasons, I do not consider variance in accounting measures for changes in risk taking.

The objective here is to get as close to the nature of the gambles facing managers as we can. One method would be to ask managers about the gambles they faced. Alternatively, we could examine analysts' impressions of the risk-taking behavior of the management they follow. For example, Bromiley examines the divergence of analysts' forecasts as a measure of risk-taking behavior of managers.[20]

Unfortunately, analysts rarely make the actual investment decision. In addition, analyst forecasts can change daily such that, depending on when the variance of these forecasts is measured, we can get widely varying results for any period of study. Our interest is not in a snapshot dispersion of analyst opinions, but rather the changes or variability over time in these opinions. Further, we are interested in what these investment decisions actually are—not simply impressions. Rather than consider the dispersion of analyst forecasts, we want to go to the horses' mouth (one might say) and examine the aggregate changes in the performance expectations of market participants. This is represented by the variability of stock returns and is firmly rooted in revealed preference theory.[21] Simply stated, revealed preference theory judges preferences by observing actions or choices.

Specifically, I examine the changes in variance of both monthly raw returns and monthly market-adjusted returns of the firms in the sample. Market-adjusted returns are used because of possible effects of the variance of the market on any given security. The changes in variance for the two return measures are estimated for each security for four time periods (one-year change, two-year change, three-year change, and four-year change) as follows:

$$\frac{\sigma_i^2}{\sigma_j^2}$$

where $i = 1,2,3,4$ years post-acquisition, $j = 1,2,3,4$ years pre-acquisition, and $i = j$. Thus, the change measure is defined as the ratio of the post-acquisition variance divided by the pre-acquisition variance for each of the four time periods.[22]

Empirical Techniques

Aggregate Results on Acquisitions

Following contemporary strategy and financial economics literature, I use announcement effects to test the first hypothesis.[23] Further, conditioning on the announcement effect, I also examine the long-term performance of the acquiring firms. Thus, we are implicitly testing the well-known assertion by Porter doubting the usefulness of announcement effects to gauge longer-term performance in acquisitions. Porter has claimed, "The short-term market reaction is a highly imperfect measure of the long-term success of diversification, and no self-respecting executive would judge a corporate strategy this way."[24] Given the billions of dollars of shareholder value that has been destroyed on announcement, this is a very important claim to explore.

Although this assertion may be true ex post for individual firms, it is subject to testing in the concept of large-sample research. Thus, based on the market reaction to acquiring firms at announcement, I split the sample into a positive reaction portfolio and a negative reaction portfolio and tracked these two portfolios over time. If Porter is correct, the negative announcement portfolio should turn around over time, and the positive announcement portfolio should fall over time.

I used a binomial test for whether there are more negative than positive effects of corporate acquisition strategies. For this hypothesis, the Z-test is:

$$Z = \frac{\text{NEG} - \dfrac{N}{2}}{\sqrt{\dfrac{N}{4}}}$$

where the denominator is the standard deviation of the number of successes (in this case, the number of negative) in a binomial distribution (variance = {Npq}) where p and q are .5 and N is the sample size.

Preliminary Tests and Replications of Evidence on Relatedness

Preliminary tests are conducted in the context of the traditional methods in the literature. Consistent with the prior strategy literature, I use announcement effect returns to examine the hypotheses (2, 3a, and 3b) and the conjectures on relatedness. (I also test these hypotheses, in the context of the full model, with regressions described in the next section.) Traditional t-test methodology is used to replicate past conflicting results on relatedness. I do this by conditioning on other strategic variables that have not been considered before in this literature, in particular, the acquisition premium. T-tests and two-way ANOVA are used to examine the main effect and moderating effect relationships between the premium, relatedness, and performance in the context of the existing literature.

Testing the Acquiring Firm Performance Model

Consistent with prior cross-sectional studies of acquiring firm performance, I use ordinary least squares methodology to estimate the parameters of the model.[25] Parameters of the model are estimated for each of the twenty-eight measures (four return generation methods over seven time periods) of the dependent variable for four model specifications:

1. Control variables only.
2. All main effect variables with contested dummy and controls.
3. All main effect variables with tender dummy and controls.
4. All main effect, interaction effect variables, and controls.

This is a concise method of testing the model and the importance and stability of the parameters. The general structure of the model specifications follows the suggestions of Leamer for classical ordinary least squares regression specification searches. The analysis of interaction effects follows Jaccard, Turrisi, and Wan, and Aiken and West.[26]

I test each regression for heteroskedasticity using White's direct test.[27] This test is a large-sample Lagrange multiplier (LM) test that does not depend on the normality assumption required by other LM tests (e.g., Breusch-Pagan test).[28] In addition, the White direct test does not require a prior knowledge of what might be causing the heteroskedasticity. The null hypothesis is that of homoskedasticity.[29]

Tests for Changes in Risk Taking

I apply both parametric and nonparametric tests to study changes in risk taking. Because I have measured the change in variance as a variance ratio, the natural test for a significant change in variance is an F-ratio test (the ratio of two independent chi-squares).[30] This is done for each period and return measure. A chi-square test is then performed on the number of significant increases in variance for the high-premium and low-premium samples. I also perform a one-way ANOVA for each time period and measure for the difference in variance changes between the high-premium and low-premium samples.

Drazin and Kazanjian have discussed problems with the chi-square statistic in management research and recommend alternative parametric statistics. The major limitation of using parametric tests in this type of setting is that although they may be sensitive to differences in the two means, they may not detect differences in variances.[31]

Therefore, I apply a nonparametric test of the differences in the empirical distribution functions of the high-premium and low-premium variance ratios. The test used is the Kolmogorov-Smirnov two-sided test.[32] This test makes no assumptions about the shape or moments of the distribution. The null hypothesis is that the empirical distribution of high-premium variance ratios ($F_1(x)$) is equal to the empirical distribution of low-premium variance ratios ($F_2(x)$). The test statistic is the greatest vertical distance between the two empirical distribution functions,

$$D = \max_i \left| F_1(x_i) - F_2(x_i) \right|$$

where $i = 1, 2, 3, \ldots, n$ (the variance ratios). If this distance is large enough to reject the null, then this would support the expectation that the distribution of variance changes is different for high-premium versus low-premium acquisitions.

Detailed reporting of the results is contained in Appendix B. Chapter 7 provides a thorough discussion of these results.

7

Discussion of Results

The motivation behind this research grew from a desire to move beyond the largely bivariate nature (related versus unrelated) of the management literature on acquisition performance and the accompanying stream of conflicting evidence, which has offered managers little guidance in maximizing the chances of success in acquisition programs.

Management research on acquisitions consists of two distinct categories: the empirical performance literature and the post-merger integration literature (see Appendix A for a detailed review). The empirical performance literature focuses on explaining the variance in acquiring firm performance. The post-merger integration literature, largely anecdotal, describes potential problems in the acquisition process that may hinder performance. The empirical literature is troubled by conflicting evidence on the major variables (shown in Figure 5.1), and the process literature does not yet offer a method of predicting a distribution of payoffs available to acquiring managers where there are no process problems.

Rather than focus directly on explaining the conflicting evidence in the literature, I took a fresh look at the nature of the acquisition performance problem from the perspective of the requirements of top management by focusing on the fundamentals of the unique business gamble an acquisition represents. The literature is consistent on the idea that managers should seek synergy in acquisitions. But not even the most recent work offers specific requirements of managerial performance in acquisitions or any economic conditions behind the synergy concept.[1]

I asked why an executive team would make the decision to buy another company when a shareholder can simply buy the shares of each company without all the costs of combining the two companies. In answering this question, we must first recognize the performance improvements that may already be built into stock prices. In other words, we might observe improvements in business performance following an acquisition that were *already* expected to occur if the firms had remained independent. This concept has been overlooked in the literature and has led some researchers to suggest a "performance paradox."[2]

Managers can destroy value even though short-term accounting-based returns seem to be improved. It is no wonder that definitions of synergy have been vague.

Thus, an executive team should make an acquisition only where there is synergy, but now we have a clear definition of the term: the increase in performance of the combined firm above what the two firms are already required or expected to accomplish as independent firms. This definition rests on fundamentals of value and focuses on the nature of the performance changes that constitute real synergy.

The academic management literature examines proposed factors that might affect synergy, or post-acquisition management, but does not explicitly consider the nature of the acquisition decision. This is the major void in the literature, and it presents the opportunity for a meaningful contribution. In fact, acquisitions have not previously been approached as decisions (i.e., gambles) that have explicitly embedded and measurable ex-ante (up-front) risk. As a consequence, the literature has lacked a fundamental framework for analyzing the components of an acquisition strategy.

Since the challenge for executive teams in acquisitions is to accomplish what shareholders cannot accomplish on their own, I approach the acquisition performance problem as a game where the decision to play inherently carries up-front risk. The objective has been to carefully consider the *nature* of this up-front risk, which led to developing the concept of the acquisition game.

The acquisition game is best described as a game with some distribution of payoffs and an up-front price to play the game. Recall my previous illustration of the nature of the business gamble: You are invited to play a game with the following payoff distribution: a fair coin will be flipped where heads (H) = $20,000 and tails (T) = $0. Further, it will cost you $9,000 to play the game. Thus,

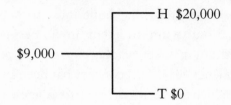

The inherent risk of the decision to play this one-shot game is obvious. Most major acquisitions are one-shot games because acquirers generally make very few of them. But once we separate the distribution of payoffs from the price to play the game, we have an extremely useful framework for understanding the nature of the acquisition decision facing senior executives and the acquisition performance problem. This is the acquisition game.

Assuming that prior expectations can be achieved, strategy formulation and post-acquisition integration will yield an uncertain stream of actual payoffs or synergies, and the acquisition premium is the price to play the game.

With this description of the acquisition game, we can clearly view the dimensions that comprise acquisition performance. The focus is on the ex-ante predictive power of the acquisition premium and the likely distribution of payoffs. My method has been to show exactly what the decision to pay premiums translates to in terms of required performance and to consider what a reasonable distribution of realized synergies may be in a competitive economy.

Chapter 2 established the necessary contestability conditions an acquisition must meet and the necessary cornerstones that must be in place for there to be any chance of synergy. This challenge is very much like running on a treadmill faster than you are already expected to while competitors supply a strong head wind. Chapter 3 simply asked, "Do you feel lucky?" The required performance improvements (RPIs) embedded in an acquisition premium become so intense so quickly that we must challenge whether the premium in most cases actually reflects potential value.

My proposal is that there is a misalignment between the distribution of payoffs in acquisitions and the payoff requirements dictated by most acquisition premiums. Surprisingly, neither of these issues has been addressed in the literature, perhaps as a result of the explicit competitive markets assumptions embedded in the resource-based view of the firm.[3] As Barney states, "Bidding firms that complete a merger or acquisition in [a perfectly competitive market] will not obtain abnormal returns, even if they are completely successful in exploiting anticipated relatedness with a target, for the value of relatedness will be reflected in the price of a target, and thus distributed as abnormal returns to the shareholders of acquired target firms."[4]

The resource-based view is an equilibrium model where factors are presumed, on average, to be priced at their fair value. Thus, the only way to earn excess returns (in the resource-based world) is if there exist ex-ante limits to competition such that factors do not get bid up to their fair value.[5] For any given acquisition, we have:

$$P_0 \dashrightarrow P_T$$

where P_0 is the pre-acquisition price of the target firm and P_T is the acquisition price. Using the resource-based framework in acquisitions, P_T represents the fair value of the target to the acquiring firm and thus, $P_T - P_0$ must represent potential synergy. The acquisition literature has largely subsumed this tenet of the resource-based view in its analysis of acquisition performance. If an acquisition does not produce synergy, then the focus is on the possible factors that did not allow (or disrupted) the potential synergy. These factors have included strategic relatedness, culture problems, executive departure, relative size, method of acquisition, whether the acquiring firm had made previous acquisitions, and various post-merger management problems.

Virtually no theory has accompanied these factors with respect to how or why real performance improvements (synergy) would result. In other words, no model has been offered to suggest the magnitude of how well the firm should do if the acquisition were related, for example, or if there were no "problems." Although post-acquisition issues such as executive departure or culture clashes might certainly damage the expected performance of the independent operations, it is not clear how the absence of these problems will generate synergy and in what degree. The assumption has been that the potential synergy could be realized.

Given the preceding discussion, we can articulate the difference between an ex-post and ex-ante interpretation of what it means to "overpay." Ex post, if an acquisition results in losses, then by definition, the acquiring firm overpaid—the price was too high. But by challenging the competitive markets assumption from the arguments I have presented, we can make *predictions* about the probability and degree of failure (ex ante), given knowledge of the premium, even under the best of post-acquisition circumstances. This obviously would not be predicted by the competitive markets assumption within the resource-based view.

In the framework provided by a competitive markets approach, the premium and potential synergy are highly correlated, and thus the premium would have little predictive power of post-acquisition performance. I have emphasized this point with the following illustration of five acquisition scenarios:

Premium	Synergy A	Synergy B
100%	80%	15%
80	60	15
60	40	15
40	20	15
20	0	15

Overpayment occurs in each scenario. In fact, *systematic* overpayment occurs in each scenario. However, under synergy scenario A, the level of the premium gives no information about the likely amount of acquisition losses. It is merely a winner's curse, and synergy is highly correlated with the premium, as would be predicted by the assumption of the resource-based view. On the other hand, if synergy does not occur or there are limits to the realization of synergy as shown in synergy scenario B, then the up-front predictive power of the premium becomes very meaningful. That is, the level of the acquisition premium predicts the amount of losses.

In this research I have challenged the assumption of the resource-based view (with regard to acquisitions) by arguing that there are severe limits to attainable synergies (i.e., a low expected value) in a competitive market relative to what most acquisition premiums would require. We need to consider the nature of these limits. Ironically, it is the challenge of creating valuable nontradeable assets that develop and accumulate within the firm, embedded in resource-based theory, that sets the stage for what I call the synergy limitation view.[6]

In addition, the resource-based view explicitly assumes no agency problems. In acquisitions, acquiring firm executive teams may do much better than shareholders. There is ample evidence that executive salaries are not correlated with the performance of the acquisition; they simply get larger as the company gets larger.[7] Markets do, however, provide us with a worldwide consensus assessment of the decisions made by these executive teams.

Consider the headline, "In Paramount Battle, the Winners Lost $4.1 Billion."[8] The article measures the destruction in the market value of Viacom (the winner) from announcement of the strategy (first bid) to "winning" the takeover battle. Market professionals have been down this road before and have little confidence in the ability of the Viacom executive team to generate the required performance improvements.

My claim is *not* that synergies do not occur at all. Rather, we need a better understanding of the meaning, probability, and value of synergy. There are, on average, severe limits to realizing synergy because of the difficulty of satisfying the contestability conditions and putting the cornerstones of synergy in place in an already competitive environment with substantial prior expectations. Or as a partner in mergers and acquisitions at Goldman Sachs put it, "Two plus two equals 4.1."[9]

In addition to the new definition of synergy, we also considered other previously unexplored dimensions to the synergy problem. For example, research in acquisitions has not yet developed an understanding of the underlying distribution of payoffs (synergy). There is a wealth of work on potential problems, but no theory or evidence that suggests what form this distribution of payoffs might take. I have suggested that this distribution for any given acquisition is exponential in nature. Although the premium is known with certainty, synergy results from playing a competitive game. Thus, at the minimum, proposing a likely distribution of payoffs forces the consideration of reasonable limits to performance improvements.

Synergy is also limited by the fundamental economics of the industry structure. As synergy is improvements over what firms would have accomplished independently, the probability of realizing synergy will largely be a function of the ability of acquiring firm management to change the economics of competition in the firms' industries. To illustrate this idea, consider the following passage:

> It was, said the utility chief executive, "the opportunity of a lifetime" and the ideal diversification. Applauding the strategic move, eager investors leaped into the stock. To be sure, the utility was paying a premium price, but it was getting into a growth business. "It clearly gives them more muscle and makes them more competitive," an analyst said.
>
> The above paragraph is not about last week's announcement that Bell Atlantic, once viewed as a safe and stodgy utility, was getting into the exciting cable television business by acquiring Tele-Communications Inc., although it might well be. Rarely has a deal been more eagerly embraced by Wall Street.
>
> Instead, it describes the reaction in 1986 when AZP Group, parent of Arizona Public Service, the state's largest electric utility, got into the hot new field of financial services by buying Merabank. Within four years, the bank went under. AZP, renamed Pinnacle West, has yet to see its stock regain 1986 levels.[10]

Perhaps a better-known example of a failed acquisition is the Time Warner marriage. After turning down the $200 per share offer from Paramount and acquiring Warner, J. Richard Munro (Time's chairman) stated, "We have a shared vision of our industries facing a global battle." The economics supporting this "vision" is still a mystery. Over six years after the decision, there is little evidence of synergy from the combination. As Roll has argued with the hubris hypothesis, "Takeover gains may have been overestimated if they exist at all."[11]

Finally, we have also considered the intertemporal nature of synergy as an important factor limiting the value of performance improvements. Synergies tomorrow are not as valuable as synergies today. Further, synergies expected in the future give competitors more time to compete them away before they even occur (and this is more fuel for the consideration of a distribution). Figures 3.4 and 3.5 gave a graphic illustration of the dynamic managerial performance requirements created by the possibility that synergy cannot be generated immediately. Many strategic post-acquisition plans simply cannot be accomplished overnight. Rushing the integration of companies with very different systems can spell disaster. We now term this phenomenon the *synergy paradox*.

Performance improvements may take years to develop, for very good reason.[12] But given the RPIs embedded in most acquisition premiums, these gains need to begin immediately; otherwise value will be destroyed. This is the real performance paradox. If these "improvements" occur far down the road, they may have little value.

In summary, the acquisition premium is an unexplored factor in the acquisition literature, with very important implications. The discussion thus far has reviewed the framework I developed for conceptualizing and increasing our understanding of the acquisition performance problem. By separating the management imperative of realizing RPIs and the probability of achieving these from the resource allocation decision to play the acquisition game, I have provided some insight into the risk of failure in acquisition decisions. By developing this foundation, I can better consider why and how other previously proposed factors affect components of the value of performance (NPV = Synergy − Premium).

The numerical simulations presented in Chapter 3 allow a visual examination of the preceding arguments. This exercise served four major purposes:

1. To show that resource commitments in acquisitions translate into specific required performance improvements.
2. To show that these RPIs can be dynamic ex-ante.
3. To motivate an estimation of the probability of realizing these improvements (synergies).
4. To supplement the theory development in motivating the hypotheses on other strategic factors of potential importance for acquiring firm performance.

The real power of the numerical simulations is that I have used very conservative yet realistic assumptions. The simulations can be reestimated for a variety of assumptions (discount rate, time period, etc.) or customized for industry-specific issues (industry structure, regulatory constraints, environmental liability, etc.). This makes this method of analysis a potentially very useful tool for illuminating the managerial challenge of post-acquisition management.

In addition to the realism in the simulations, the basic results are robust to different assumptions—the pictures will look the same. This is not a minor result and provides graphical support for the claim of performance improvement limits. At the minimum, we have sufficient reason to subject the theory—the synergy limitation view—to empirical testing.

Developing this framework for studying acquisitions—separating the problem into expectations and realizations—allows us to link the strategy literature on acquisitions to the important literature in organizational behavior on escalation of commitment. The starting point in research on the escalation of commitment is the allocation of resources by a decision maker.[13] Because I have modeled the required performance improvements that are dictated by the resource allocation decision, we have an objective target reference point that we can use to predict where managers will observe a failing course of action.

Whether we approach the potential escalation of commitment problem in acquisitions with self-justification theory or prospect theory, this literature can yield insights into future actions of managers in the post-acquisition environment.[14] There are important implications for strategy here.

If managers begin to escalate commitment by allocating additional funds to make a failing acquisition work, there may exist a strategic inertia that prevents the firm from responding to competitive changes in other parts of the company.[15] This inertia may be reinforced by the multitude of side bets that accompany the tremendous organizational change in major acquisitions.[16] Clearly the allocation of an acquisition premium has the potential to create the "failing course of action" environment described so vividly in the literature.

The discussion of results that follows corresponds to the structure of the detailed results presented in Appendix B.

Aggregate Results on Acquisitions

Hypothesis 1: On average, corporate acquisition strategies reduce the value of the acquiring firm.

The results provide strong support for this hypothesis. Using two different techniques (event study and binomial test), I found that corporate acquisition strategies, on average, destroy value of the acquiring firm. This result is consistent with most of the other studies conducted on acquiring firm performance (see Table A.1 in Appendix A).

The managerial significance of these results is important. One of the important propositions of the field of behavioral decision theory is cognitive heuristics and judgment biases.[17] The representativeness bias is basically the failure of the decision maker to consider the base rate of a given event (i.e., condition their distribution of outcomes on the base rate).[18] Acquisitions that represent a major component of corporate strategy (like those considered in this research) are likely to fail; approximately 66 percent of the acquisitions in this sample destroy value. Managers need to condition their acquisition decisions and the formulation of strategic plans on this and similar evidence. Our objective is to understand those factors that determine whether a given acquisition is likely to fail or succeed. Fortunately, 33 percent of the acquisitions in my sample created value, so there is a distribution of positive and negative returns from acquisitions to explain.

I also addressed an issue of concern about the worth of the short-window event studies that dominate the strategy literature on acquisitions. From a large-sample research perspective, I found this concern not to be warranted. By splitting the sample into positive and negative reaction effect portfolios and tracking them over time, I found that initial reactions by the market are representative of longer-term performance measures, respectively. The portfolio of acquirers hit with negative returns on announcement do not turn positive over time, and the positive announcement portfolio does not turn negative over time. This is reassuring, given the widespread use of event study methodology.

Traditional Tests and Replications of Evidence on Relatedness

The motivation behind this part of the research is from the stream of conflicting evidence in the literature about the performance effects on acquiring firms of strategically related versus unrelated acquisitions. The majority of the acquisition literature in management is a series of papers that are essentially bivariate tests of the announcement effects of related versus unrelated acquisitions on acquiring firms. Thus, this is a very important part of this research because of the opportunity to suggest and test propositions to reconcile this conflicting evidence. Also, because this methodology has been the mainstay of the acquisition literature, it is an accepted method of comparing the effects of premiums versus relatedness in addition to replicating the evidence.

Using the traditional methodology, I found strong support for the premium hypothesis and could not reject the proposition of the null hypothesis of no main effect of relatedness. Further, I found a significant positive moderating effect of relatedness on the relationship between premiums and performance, as predicted. Given the significance of the relatedness hypothesis and this methodology in the literature, these are very interesting results. At the minimum, I have documented the importance of considering the ex-ante importance of the premium concept, as well as noting the need for more questioning of the belief that related acquisition strategies should outperform unrelated acquisition strategies. These ideas will be discussed further in the context of the general model in the next section.

Given that the premium concept dominates relatedness in the context of these tests, we can begin to see the writing on the wall for support of the first conjecture on relatedness.

Conjecture 1 on Relatedness: The conflicting evidence about relatedness can be replicated by conditioning on the proposed effects of other strategic factors—in particular, the acquisition premium.

I found very strong support for this conjecture. By conditioning the effect of relatedness on the level of the premium, I found both an insignificant negative effect of strategic relatedness *and* a significant positive effect of strategic relatedness. Further, when I conditioned on method of payment along with the premium, I found a strongly negative effect on the acquiring firm if the acquisition was strategically related. In other words, by simply conditioning on other theoretically driven factors, I was able to manipulate the effects of relatedness and replicate the conflicting evidence in the literature.

Why are these results important? Beyond showing how it might be possible for so much conflicting evidence in the literature, we need to question why the relatedness concept—that is, related acquisitions create more value than unrelated acquisitions—continues to be entrenched in the literature. This issue goes back to the argument concerning the difficulty of generating real synergy in acquisitions. Again, the claim is not that all acquisitions fail or that no acquisition generates synergy. The focus on relatedness may have caused a lack of research attention on important factors that are affecting the value of acquiring firms. There continues to be little evidence (if any) of relatedness resulting in operating synergies.

The second conjecture is closely related to the preceding discussion:

Conjecture 2 on Relatedness: There will be no relationship between the relatedness of the acquisition and the acquisition premium.

I found support for this conjecture. Although related acquisitions had a higher mean premium, it was not significant. Acquisition premiums are driven externally by the market for corporate control. The most common valuation technique is to examine how comparable acquisitions (*compaqs*) have been valued. In a similar vein, Haunschild found that the premium paid by acquirers is related to those paid by companies using the same investment bank.[19] The correlation table (see Table B.1 in Appendix B) shows almost zero correlation between the premium and the relatedness index (the degree of relatedness).

The purpose of these conjectures and this section was to allow us to focus on why relatedness might matter in addition to replicating past conflicting evidence. My proposal was that relatedness would be meaningful as a signal about the future prospects of the current lines of business, where it interacts with the premium. For example, an unrelated acquisition strategy done at a high premium is a "double whammy" to the acquiring firm: overpayment plus a strong signal about the value of current investment opportunities. I found evidence supporting this proposition as well as suggesting a reconciliation of the empirical literature on acquisition relatedness.

Testing the Acquiring Firm Performance Model

The Acquisition Premium

Hypothesis 2: The larger the premium paid for an acquisition, the worse the subsequent returns for the acquiring firm.

This hypothesis—the synergy limitation hypothesis—represents the core of the research. I found consistently strong support for the ex-ante importance of the acquisition premium across twenty-eight different measures of acquiring firm performance (and doubled previous R^2's). Recall that these twenty-eight measures of the dependent variable represent seven different time periods across four return generation models. Part of the strength of these results is that the operationalization of the premium derives directly from my theory and simulations, and thus the results are readily interpretable. The premium is a resource allocation decision with important managerial significance that must be considered in research on acquiring firm performance.

Care was given to control for variables that have "proxied" for the premium in past strategy research on acquisitions: the target market value/book value and the presence of multiple bidders. With respect to the target market value/book value, I found the same insignificant results as did Kusewitt.[20] The market prices securities based on expectations of future performance, so an acquisition premium dictates the same required synergy and ex-ante risk independent of the market/book ratio.

The results are also reinforced by the finding that the effect of the acquisition premium is independent of the presence of a multiple bidder auction. Consistent with past research, I found the presence of multiple bidders to have a negative effect on acquiring firm performance.[21] These authors have referred to winning in a multiple bidder situation as the winner's curse. As Varaiya describes, "In any bidding situation, a party which unknowingly overestimates the value of a given object tends to bid higher than its competitors and is, therefore, more likely to win it."[22]

However, the results strongly suggest that the blind spots in competitor analysis leading to a winner's curse do not only apply to multiple bidder situations.[23] This also makes me hesitate to call the negative effects of multiple bidders a winner's curse in an acquisition context because all firms are potential bidders. In fact, it may be even more worrisome when other firms—in the same industry, for example—are not bidding on particular acquisitions.

More important, my results go well beyond a winner's curse. A winner's curse only predicts overpayment—not how much. This evidence suggests the importance of the acquisition premium as an ex-ante measure of risk in an acquisition decision. In other words, across acquisitions, the level of the premium is a significant factor in predicting the likelihood and degree of failure of a given acquisition strategy.

My theory argues that when executive teams choose to play the acquisition game, they pay a premium for a distribution of returns that typically has a low expected value in a competitive economy. Simply stated, higher premiums require better performance, which is unlikely to occur.

I have developed the managerial importance of the acquisition premium by considering the dynamics of required performance improvements and challenging whether, even under the best conditions, potential synergies are correlated with these required improvements. The simulations and corresponding empirical evidence provide support and an underlying explanation for the claims of scholars that acquisition success or failure, at the company level, is generally apparent by the end of the fourth year.[24] As the dynamics of RPIs (dictated by the premium) set in, the ability to defend the initial decision rapidly becomes more difficult.

Further, it is conceivable that paying premiums may also be a signal of the poor quality of other decisions made throughout the company. It is surprising that a game that has accounted for close to $3 trillion of gambles over the past fifteen years has received so little research attention in terms of the managerial significance behind these gambles.

The importance of the premium from a day-to-day operating manager perspective can be shown by considering the capital approval process. Paying a premium amounts to a mark-up of the costs of office furniture, training programs, manufacturing plants and machinery, warehouses, and so forth. We can imagine how difficult it would have been for capital requests to be approved if they had been marked up 40 to 50 percent or more for the same projects. And this does not include the additional investments that may be required to integrate the acquisition, which would drive down free cash flows.

In the theory development, I focused on what the company must accomplish for a given premium. The company, however, does not earn synergies—the operating managers do. Using the example of capital approval at the operating manager level helps to illustrate the claim that the acquisition premium is a resource allocation decision with important managerial significance. Research on post-acquisition integration must begin to address the likely payoffs from similar cultures, the retainment of executives, strategic renewal, and other post-acquisition management issues. It will then be possible to begin to link these and other important post-acquisition issues to value and the resource allocation decision.

For example, recent work on the effects of executive departure has suggested that departure will cause disruption in the acquired firm that will damage post-acquisition accounting performance.[25] Given the required performance improvements that are dictated by the premium decision, it may be the case that smooth transitions can spell disaster.

Suppose an executive team allocates a 75 percent premium for an acquisition and does not begin earning performance improvements until the third year. In my simulation framework, I found that in this case return on equity would have to be increased 22 percent in the third year and be maintained for the following seven years just to break even; if the initial ROE were, say, 10 percent, the required

ROE would increase to 32 percent. Further, this increase is over those the acquired firm would have had to achieve as an independent firm. Perhaps this managerial scenario of required tripling of ROE will require tremendous disruption, such as human resource and physical asset redeployment and cuts. What I can suggest is that it is not clear *how* smooth transitions through the retainment of executives will generate the required synergies or affect the distribution of performance improvements.[26]

Another possibility concerning the empirical evidence on the effects of executive departure on acquisition performance is that departure is correlated with the level of the premium decision. This would give the appearance of the effects of departure where negative performance may actually be the result of impossible required performance improvements even where there was no departure. We will consider an antecedent to both of these factors when I discuss the results on contestedness in acquisitions.

The literature has assumed that the premium represented potential synergy and that it must be post-acquisition management failures that resulted in losses. My theory and results suggest that this potential is limited and that post-acquisition management may have more to do with preventing diseconomies from corporate combinations than the achievement of synergy.[27]

Strategic Relatedness

Hypothesis 3a: Acquisition relatedness will not have a main effect on acquiring firm performance.

Hypothesis 3b: Acquisition relatedness will have a positive moderating effect between the acquisition premium and acquirer performance. That is, the negative effect of the acquisition premium will be less for related acquisitions than for unrelated acquisitions.

I could not reject the null hypothesis of no main effect of acquisition relatedness on acquiring firm performance (consistent with the bivariate tests). After correcting for collinearity, for only one measure out of twenty-eight is the relatedness parameter significant (and even before the correction, the parameter was inconsistent and unstable). The view that related acquisitions should be more beneficial than unrelated acquisitions continues to be widely held in the literature, even in the shadow of a great amount of inconsistent evidence. Perhaps this is so because there remains an "intuitive" component of this belief. Why did we find these insignificant results on the effect of relatedness?

Beyond the method of operationalization, there are some plausible explanations for these results. It could be that related acquisitions are expected to generate more synergy than unrelated acquisitions, so the premiums are higher, respectively. Under this scenario the benefits would be priced in the acquisition premium, and we would find relatedness (as well as the premium) to be insignificant (i.e., the resource-based view).[28] The relatedness index would have to be highly correlated with the premium; but in fact, the correlation is close to zero (.03), as I predicted.[29]

In the analysis, the benefits derived from acquisitions are generally quite limited, and they are dwarfed by the required improvements distributed across related and unrelated acquisitions. Although the insignificance of the parameter estimates supports this view, it should be noted that the point estimates for relatedness are consistently positive.

I proposed that where acquisition relatedness would have a significant positive effect was in moderating the relationship between the premium and performance. I found some support for the significance of relatedness in the context of the acquisition premium. In other words, the effect of the acquisition premium is amplified as the relatedness of the acquisition decreases. Thus, although there may be a degree of ambiguity in the meaning of related versus unrelated acquisitions at low premiums, high premiums for unrelated acquisitions may indicate a degree of desperation by executive teams about the state of current reinvestment opportunities, in addition to bringing a high degree of risk to the acquisition.

Perhaps the most important issue that arises in this discussion is that of the operationalization of the relatedness concept. My operationalization of acquisition relatedness follows the increasing trend in the literature to focus on the output markets of the firm.[30] The construction of a relatedness index was an attempt to provide a measure of the degree of relatedness in a given acquisition rather than the traditional binary variable. However, we still may be ignoring the real meaning of relatedness with respect to the creation of value—the role of strategy. Although this issue is beyond the scope of this study, it deserves a brief discussion.

The approach to relatedness here considered the information about the prospects of the current businesses that may be embedded in the acquisition decision. Broadly speaking, value can be created and competencies can exist in the input markets, processes (e.g., systems, structures, and procedures), and output markets of a firm. Although a stream of work on the dominant logic of a firm emerged in the literature to address the way the firm was being conceptualized by management, the trend in the literature remains in the direction of categorizing the firm by its output markets.[31]

By categorizing firms or the relatedness of acquisitions based on their output markets, we allow a distribution of strategies in processes and input markets. For example, Cooper Industries, Tenneco, Hanson, and ITT are all diversified firms based on their SIC codes, but they could not be more different in terms of the dominant logic of the management. Thus, the value creation from an unrelated (or related) acquisition made by these firms would likely result from very different sources.

My findings of null results about the effect of relatedness in acquisitions could be the result of a distribution of other strategic components across this measure—or we can say that relatedness at the product level does not appear to be meaningful in predicting the success of an acquisition. Rather than suggest that relatedness is a dead concept, the theory, results, and discussion here highlight the importance of moving ahead to a richer consideration of the concept of a related versus unrelated strategy.

Method of Payment

Hypothesis 4: The payment of cash for acquisitions will result in better performance for acquiring firms than the payment of stock (issuing equity).

I found consistent strong support for this hypothesis, predicting a positive effect for the payment of cash versus the payment of equity for an acquisition across all twenty-eight measures of the dependent variable. The strategy literature on acquisitions has yielded conflicting evidence regarding the performance effects of this factor. Given the strength of the evidence and its consistency with the financial economics literature, we can begin to settle this issue.

In his exploratory work, Kusewitt interpreted his finding of a negative effect for cash acquisitions by proposing that the use of cash poses a threat to liquidity and should result in poorer performance than using equity financing. This claim ignores that the majority of cash acquisitions are debt financed (as in my sample) and should not in general affect the liquidity position. More important, embedded in the statement is the common misperception that equity is somehow "free" because there are not the intermediate payments that accompany debt. But equity has a cost of capital just as debt does, and the firm will simply be disciplined by the equity markets rather than by bankers and creditors when it does not earn this cost of capital.

The results support both of the approaches to motivating the hypothesis. First, because cash acquisitions are generally debt financed, managers must meet intermediate interest and principal payments to avoid default. In addition, the use of debt limits the amount of cash that can be wasted through organizational inefficiency. Second, and perhaps more important, a stock acquisition sends a powerful signal about the current value of the company. Given that the interest on debt is tax deductible and dividends are not, managers presumably will issue equity when the company is overvalued or when operations are not sufficiently strong to handle the debt.

Method of Acquisition

Hypothesis 5a: The implementation of an acquisition through a contested process will result in the payment of a higher premium than through an uncontested process.

Hypothesis 5b: The implementation of an acquisition through a tender offer will not result in the payment of a higher premium than through a merger.

Hypothesis 5c: The implementation of an acquisition through a tender offer versus a merger will not have an independent effect on performance.

There has been a continuing focus and stream of conflicting evidence on the performance effects of mergers versus tender offers. For example, while Fowler and Schmidt find that acquirers using tender offers perform significantly worse than those using mergers (i.e., no tender offer), Datta et al. find exactly the reverse. Similarly, Jemison and Sitkin argue that mergers should outperform tender offers, while Cannella finds no empirical justification for this claim and concludes that the method of acquisition negotiation has no implications for post-acquisition performance.[32]

I found no significant difference in the premium paid in mergers versus tender offers and no effect of tender offers on acquirer performance. Contested acquisitions, however, resulted in higher premiums than uncontested acquisitions, and contested tender offers resulted in higher premiums than uncontested tender offers. The results provide support for the hypotheses and for my claim that the arbitrary distinction between the effects of mergers and tender offers does not address the underlying performance implications. My argument is that the important factor in this issue is not whether an acquisition is made with a tender offer or a merger but whether the transaction is a contested process that would drive a higher premium. In other words, in the tender offer versus merger debate, the issue is contestedness, and the managerial nature of the problem is the premium involved.

Jemison and Sitkin's argument of the superiority of mergers was based on the belief that mergers would have a longer planning period in addition to being "friendlier" than tender offers. This ignores the fact that there are friendly tender offers (planned in great detail) that are just as friendly as mergers and also may have some advantages over mergers. For example, the waiting period for the required antitrust clearance under the Hart-Scott-Rodino law for tender offers can be as much as one-half the waiting period for mergers.[33] This can serve to minimize the chance of competing bidders' entering the game, potentially leading to a contested process.

The findings support the two major objectives of this analysis. First, it is the contestedness of the process that affects the acquisition premium. Second, whether the acquisition is implemented through a contested process (versus uncontested) or through a tender offer (versus merger) has no significant independent effect on acquiring firm performance. Thus, my findings suggest that the method of acquisition does have implications for post-acquisition performance but only to the extent that it influences the resource allocation decision (the premium) of executive teams of acquiring firms.

Finally, these results may also have some implications for recent work on executive departure in acquisitions.[34] I conjectured that if executive departure were correlated with the acquisition premium, an alternative hypothesis to the current literature might be that negative effects are actually the result of the premium. I have found that contested processes are accompanied by higher acquisition premiums. On the other hand, several authors have documented that contested processes also increase the likelihood of departure significantly more than uncontested processes.[35] Rather than rule out the negative effects of executive departure on performance, the analysis presented here may provide an opportunity for an even richer understanding of the post-acquisition performance problem.

Relative Size of the Acquisition

Hypothesis 6: The relative size of an acquisition negatively moderates the relationship between the level of the acquisition premium and acquiring firm performance. That is, the greater the relative size, the more damaging the effect of the premium on acquirer performance.

The strategy literature on acquisitions has also yielded conflicting evidence regarding the effect of the relative size of the acquisition on acquiring firm performance. We had no theory to suggest why relative size should affect acquiring firm performance. The financial economics literature has simply proposed that the relative size matters to the extent positive or negative effects of the acquisition will "show up" in the abnormal returns.[36]

The findings on the interaction effect of relative size with the acquisition premium suggest a negative moderating effect as proposed. The negative moderating effect is significant in eleven time periods of study, particularly in the short and long time periods. Because this study focuses on large relative size acquisitions in general, it may be that the premium parameter reflects some of the information embedded in large relative size acquisitions that suggest the quality of other decisions being made by executive teams.

While not expected, I did find a significant main effect of the relative size of the acquisition. However, the sign of the effect changes from positive to negative as we move to longer time periods of performance. Perhaps the reason for conflicting evidence on this factor is that past studies have used different time periods to measure performance (generally one time period). I simply report this finding as an empirical observation.

Tests for Changes in Risk Taking

Hypothesis 7: Higher acquisition premiums will be associated with increases in managerial risk taking following the acquisition.

I did not find support for this hypothesis. However, there may be some important reasons for these results, and because of the profound effect that strategic resource commitments may have on future strategies, they deserve discussion. Besides the obvious empirical reason that we may have a poor operationalization of changes in risk taking, there are some theoretical possibilities.

First, it is possible that executive teams do not understand the underlying economics and managerial requirements behind acquisition premiums. Consequently, they do not observe a target reference point of required performance improvements. Although this explanation might be plausible, it should be unlikely because of the in-depth spreadsheet analysis and "fairness opinions" of investment banks that support the premium decision.

Second, the managers making the initial resource allocation decision may not be those ultimately responsible for managing the acquisition.[37] Staw found that individuals are significantly more likely to escalate the investment of resources when they are personally responsible for the initial investment decision.[38] Thus, as in the preceding explanation, the actual acquisition manager may not view the required performance improvements as the target reference point.

Finally, perhaps executive teams do not really expect acquisitions to be successful and have objectives other than performance improvement.[39] Consider the necessary (but not sufficient) condition for escalation described by Brockner: "The decision maker allocates some resources—their money, time, even their self-identities—in the hope of attaining some goal or goals."[40] If these goals are nonpecuniary or in general are not aligned with managing the value of the firm, the effect of being in the domain of losses (i.e., failing course of action) may not have an effect on future risk taking.

Rather than admit defeat on this issue, the potential explanations for the results raise testable implications that can be pursued in future research. Large losses from a given acquisition have the potential to decimate prior strategic planning, thus yielding a suboptimal emergent strategy.[41] I have offered a starting point in considering what managerial processes might unfold given the acquisition premium and the corresponding post-acquisition challenge.

8

—

Implications of the Analysis

What does finding the right price mean if it isn't the right thing to do?
In mergers and acquisitions, failing to make the distinction between
price and value is like turning your back on reality.

—J. P. Morgan advertisement, late 1980s

This project began in response to the massive amount of corporate strategic decisions that involved acquisition strategies with often disappointing and even disastrous results. The management literature on this topic has been exploratory in nature and has offered a continued stream of conflicting empirical evidence on proposed factors affecting acquiring firm performance. I took a new approach to acquiring firm performance by focusing on the strategic and financial nature of the acquisition decision and the gamble it represents. Further, I presented extensive empirical work on acquirer performance that provided strong support for the core theory of the synergy limitation view and the up-front risk of the acquisition premium, as well as a potential reconciliation of a wealth of conflicting evidence on strategic relatedness in the acquisition literature.

This work represents an important step in developing an understanding of the acquisition game and the performance nature of the post-acquisition challenge. By introducing an unexplored dimension to the literature, I have created an important opportunity for a greater understanding of a management problem associated with trillions of dollars of decisions. The discrete nature of the acquisition decision allows us to clearly consider, both theoretically and empirically, the implicit assumptions of prior literature and the inherent challenge to executive teams in formulating and implementing an acquisition strategy. This research contains important contributions and implications for theory, public policy, and practice.

Theoretical Contributions

When I began this work, I approached acquisitions as a method of implementing corporate strategy. Then I found that if I approached acquisitions as a strategy in its own right, I could begin to spotlight assumptions that have been driving the literature and real decisions. An illustration of these two approaches would be to compare "managing acquisitions" to "managing acquisition strategies." By focusing on the acquisition as a strategic decision, we can separate the problem into expectations (requirements) and realizations of performance. The integration of concepts and methods from both strategy and finance has yielded several broad implications for theory.

First, by treating an acquisition as a strategic alternative and asking what an executive must accomplish to create value, I am able to develop a more formal and usable definition of synergy than that offered in prior strategy literature. Then, because synergy must be performance gains over what the firms are already expected to accomplish independently, we can consider its expected value in a competitive industry and the alignment with the requirements of the choice variable—the acquisition premium. The analysis of these issues has profound managerial implications.

Past literature on acquisitions implicitly assumed that the price paid represents the potential value of the target to the acquiring firm. With this approach, it is tautological to claim that if acquisition performance is negative, then the acquiring firm overpaid. I develop a framework for understanding and predicting overpayment *up front,* by challenging the competitive markets assumption of the resource-based view in the context of acquisitions.

My view is that synergy is very difficult to achieve and thus has a low expected value in a competitive context. I support this claim by defining precisely what synergy is and developing the cornerstones of synergy that must be in place if there is to be any chance of performance gains. Further, I illustrate this claim by using numerical simulations and developing the concept of dynamic required performance improvements (RPIs) for the executive team of the acquiring firm.

Perhaps the most important contribution to theory is the characterization of an acquisition as a game with a *distribution* of payoffs resulting from the strategy. Executive teams commit resources and make a strategic decision to play this game. This framework is important because it forces a consideration of *potential* value and the degree of uncertainty of performance improvements. Future research must examine the factors that might affect this distribution.

Second, I have presented a reconciliation of the empirical relatedness debate and also considered the meaning of relatedness from another perspective in an acquisition context. By conditioning on the acquisition premium, different results were obtained for relatedness using the common bivariate method of testing the relatedness concept. More important, an unrelated acquisition may not perform worse than a related acquisition (because of the difficulty of earning synergies in either case) but may signal a problem in the current lines of business. I found some evidence of a positive moderating effect of relatedness between the premium and performance. Finally, I suggested that the current trend in operationalizing relatedness at the product level may be missing the strategic richness (both content and process) of operating strategies.[1] Given the framework advanced in this work, there is a great opportunity for more finely grained research in acquisitions that transcends SIC codes.

Third, this research has important implications for the study of post-acquisition accounting performance. By examining the performance expectations that are already built into pre-acquisition share prices, we can begin to approach the issue of benchmarking in post-acquisition performance studies. Improvements in accounting returns will not be the result of the acquisition (synergy) if they were already expected. Because the premium is paid above these pre-acquisition share prices, the valuable performance expectations embedded in these prices must be considered in future research.

Fourth, this research has important implications for the post-acquisition integration literature. Some post-acquisition integration scholars have argued that detailed long-term planning is not very realistic.[2] These authors claim that executives become caught in a chain of events that makes detailed planning difficult to implement. This important work is even further evidence of the difficulty of achieving synergy and the imperative of discipline in post-acquisition planning and implementation. Although this process literature is still in the theory-building stage, given the theory and evidence presented here, we can ask how such factors as executive departure, transition management, or culture might affect performance improvement versus performance preservation.

For example, after one year, the Burroughs and Sperry creation of Unisys was touted as a highly successful massive change effort, particularly with regard to organizational development. As Stum states, "Unisys avoided the pitfalls that plague so many mergers and acquisitions, such as high turnover, low productivity, and destructive culture clashes."[3] Yet within four years after the acquisition, over 90 percent of the shareholder value of Unisys had been destroyed. There is a need for theory and evidence concerning how well an acquisition will perform even when there are none of the commonly described post-acquisition problems. The contestability conditions and cornerstones of synergy are an important step in that direction.

Finally, the fifth implication for theory is the opportunity to link the strategy literature on acquisitions with the extensive organizational behavior literature on escalation of commitment. It is well known from the organizational behavior literature that managers may exhibit an escalation of commitment to a failing course of action. Thus, under my framework, as managers miss what may actually be unachievable performance targets, they may increase their level of risk taking to attempt to meet these targets in the future. In other words, the payment of a large acquisition premium has the potential of changing the planned value-creating strategies the firm had in place. This can cause even more value destruction for all stakeholders in acquiring firms. Although the methods did not yield support for this proposition, this is an area ripe for content and process issues to be integrated, particularly in the acquisitions arena.

Public Policy Implications

Throughout the 1980s acquisition wave, there was constant concern over the rights of shareholders of the target firm. The concern was, and still is, whether boards of directors are properly exercising their fiduciary duty to their shareholders. This concern, however, may be somewhat misdirected. Virtually all empirical research on acquisitions has shown that target firm shareholders do well—very well. The findings presented here suggest that the rights of the shareholders of the acquiring firm may require some attention. Although the academic debate over what motivates executives to make value-destroying acquisition decisions will continue, suffice it to say, from a policy perspective, that managers make these decisions *because they can*. Executives of acquiring firms have tremendous discretion over the resources of these firms, and, given the potential for agency problems and the present evidence, the rights of the shareholders of the acquirer are at least as great a concern as the rights of the shareholders of the target firm. Perhaps this book can pave the way for standards of informed acquisition decisions.

Practical Implications

This research yields several important practical implications. First, my findings, in accordance with a large amount of prior research, suggest it is more likely than not that any given acquisition will fail. Executives should understand—right from the beginning—the odds are that their acquisition strategy will fail. The implications of providing executives with this type of information is to temper the up-the-ante philosophy and the overconfidence created by "fairness opinions" and seductive valuation models that so often drive acquisition decisions (and their accompanying strategic resource commitments). Given the finding that acquirers do not have to participate in multiple bidder contests to predictably overpay, executive teams should revise downward their estimates of what they can accomplish.

Second, acquisitions require resource commitments that can have dramatic effects on acquiring firm performance. This research offers crucial insights on the improvements in performance that managers must achieve to ensure that corporate value is not lost when making acquisitions. Moreover, because of the dynamics of required performance improvements, managers can "lock in" poor post-acquisition performance even where integration yields substantial improvements. It is not surprising that CEOs who were stingy about paying acquisition premiums during the 1980s are now considered very wise.[4]

Third, executives too often focus on the total price of an acquisition rather than the premium required to play the acquisition game. Investment bankers and outside advisers generally use comparable acquisitions (*compaqs*) as a valuation technique, and it becomes very easy for executives to lose sight of what it is that they are claiming they can accomplish. Executives need to be clear about how acquisition prices are derived and exactly what they represent. Through the use of numerical simulations, I have shown a picture of the post-acquisition performance environment based on the premium. This can help executives focus on the up-front risk of the acquisition decision and the incremental benefits they must accomplish when they play the acquisition game.[5]

Fourth, the numerical simulation methodology utilized in this research uncovered a common myth about acquisition management. Boards of directors are routinely presented "hockey stick" performance forecasts by CEOs, with the accompanying logic that the specific acquisition is a long-term investment and needs time to generate the required returns. If synergies do not begin to accrue immediately following the up-front payment of the acquisition premium, they can quickly become unmanageable with respect to avoiding a negative net present value investment. Moreover, managers need to be careful not to make matters worse in desperate attempts to achieve what are likely unachievable performance improvements.

Finally, and perhaps most important, is the need for specific strategies and plans for the acquired firm. Synergies are increases in economic rents being earned from a business and thus are unlikely to occur without an identifiable strategy. Because of the immediacy of the need to begin achieving these increases in economic rents, this pre-acquisition work must include detailed due diligence and post-acquisition planning. Recall that an acquisition premium normally represents a significant amount over what millions of market participants around the world were previously willing to pay for the acquired firm.

As Warren Hellman, the former head of Lehman Brothers, has said, "So many mergers fail to deliver what they promise that there should be a presumption of failure. The burden of proof should be on showing that anything really good is likely to come out of one."[6] The research, tools, and conclusions presented in this book can enable managers to do just that.

Appendix A:
Review and Critique
of Prior Research
on Mergers and Acquisitions

This appendix provides a brief review of the acquisition literature from the financial economics, industrial-organization economics, and strategic management fields. The focus is on the issues that are the subject of the empirical study in Part 2 of this book: aggregate acquirer performance, factors affecting acquirer performance, and risk taking following acquisitions. This appendix closes with an assessment of the literature and a theoretical motivation for the synergy limitation view of acquirer performance. The Bibliography provides a comprehensive inventory of acquisition research.

The Financial Economics and Industrial-Organization Economics Evidence

The research issues that have emerged fall into three categories:

1. What is the aggregate (on average) stock market response (effects on shareholder value) to the announcement of acquisitions?
2. As the event window is expanded beyond announcement, do the aggregate stock market results systematically change over time?
3. What is the actual ex-post aggregate performance (profitability, market share, etc.) of acquisitions?

Financial economists have been the key players offering, as they call it, the "scientific" empirical evidence on the consequences of merger and takeover activity (Jensen and Ruback, 1983). Reviewing studies using event study methodology, Jensen and Ruback (1983) report that target firm shareholders in mergers and takeovers earn risk-adjusted excess returns of 20 percent and 30 percent, respectively, while acquiring firms earn 0 percent and 4 percent, respectively.

These classic event study results assume market efficiency and rational expectations (Muth, 1960, 1961) of market participants and are based on stock price reactions during a few days around the announcement date. Based on this evidence, these authors claim that mergers and takeovers create social welfare by allowing the most efficient redistribution of corporate assets (Jensen and Ruback, 1983).

These results, however, were confronted by a barrage of results from studies finding negative returns to the shareholders of acquirers in the 1980s. Table A.1 lists ten major empirical studies documenting the value-destructive effects of acquisitions to the shareholders of acquirers, in terms of both mean returns and as a percentage of the samples that met with positive versus negative stock market response. Overwhelmingly, the mean returns to acquirers pursuing acquisition strategies are significantly negative, with only about 35 percent of acquisitions being met with positive stock market returns on announcement. Table A.2 documents that the returns to acquirers have gotten progressively worse, on average, for acquisitions occurring in the 1960s, 1970s, and 1980s, respectively.

Further, as the event window is expanded, the returns to acquiring firms deteriorate significantly. Jensen and Ruback (1983) review seven studies that used a 240-trading-day (one year) event window that showed significant average abnormal returns to acquiring firm shareholders of −5.5 percent. Magenheim and Mueller (1988), using event study methodology with a three-year post-takeover event window, find abnormal returns of between −16 percent and −42 percent to shareholders of bidding firms. Ruback (1988b:262) states, "Reluctantly, I think we have to accept this result—significant negative returns over the two years following a merger—as a fact." Finally, Agrawal, Jaffe, and Mandelker (1992) report statistically significant

TABLE A.1

Stock Market Reaction to Acquirers in the 1980s

Study	Sample Period	Sample Size	Event Window	Average Acquirer CAR[a]	% Positive Acquirer CAR[a]
Sirower (1994)	1979–1990	168	(−1,+1)	−2.3% ($t = -5.01$)	35% ($z = -4.02$)
Byrd and Hickman (1992)	1980–1987	128	(−1,0)	−1.2% ($z = -6.78$)	33% ($z = -4.14$)
Banerjee and Owers (1992)	1978–1987	57 (white knights)	(−1,0)	−3.3% ($z = -11.75$)	21% ($z = -5.36$)
Jennings and Mazzeo (1991)	1979–1985	352	(day 0)	−0.8% ($z = -8.11$)	37% ($z = -5.08$)
Servaes (1991)	1981–1987	366	(day 0, closing)	−3.35% (96% conf.)	n.a.
Morck, Shleifer, and Vishny (1990)	1980–1987	172	(−1,+1)	−1.78% ($t = -0.86$)	37% ($z = -2.12$)
Bradley, Desai, and Kim (1988)	1981–1984	52	(−5,+5)	−2.9% (99% conf.)	35% ($z = -5.08$)
Asquith, Bruner, and Mullins (1987)	1973–1983	343	(−1,0)	−0.85% ($t = -8.42$)	41% ($z = -3.35$)
Varaiya and Ferris (1987)	1974–1983	96	(−1,0)	−2.15% ($z = -8.67$)	n.a.
You, Caves, Smith, and Henry (1986)	1975–1984	133	(−1,+1)	−1.5% (n.a.)	33% ($z = -4.15$)

[a]CAR = cumulative abnormal returns during the day(s) surrounding announcement.

TABLE A.2
Historical Evidence of Returns to Acquirers

Study	Transaction Type	1960s	1970s	1980s
Loderer and Martin (1990)	Tender offers and mergers	1.7% ($z = 8.73$)	0.6% ($z = 5.49$)	−0.07% ($z = −0.34$)
Jarrell, Brickley, and Netter (1988); Jarrell and Poulsen (1989)	Tender offers	4.4% ($t = 4.02$)	1.2% ($t = 2.12$)	−1.10% ($t = −1.54$)
Bradley, Desai, and Kim (1988)	Tender offers	4.1% ($z = 5.88$)	1.3% ($z = 1.58$)	−2.93% ($z = −2.79$)
Asquith, Bruner, and Mullins (1983)	Mergers	4.6% (n.a.)	1.7% (n.a.)	n.a.

Source: Ronald Gilson and Bernard Black, *The Law and Finance of Corporate Acquisitions*, 2d ed. (Westbury, NY: Foundation Press, 1995).

losses of 10 percent over a five-year post-merger period for acquisitions made in the period 1955–1987 (–19 percent for mergers made in the period 1980–1987).

This evidence of significant negative abnormal returns to acquiring firms, as the event window is expanded, has been unsettling and controversial in the finance literature because it suggests that initial market expectations may not be consistent with realizations and, thus, is a direct challenge to the rational expectations hypothesis. It may be that market participants make systematic mistakes in initially assessing the effects of acquisition decisions on acquiring firms (Shleifer and Vishny, 1991).

The preceding results, however, are not without controversy. Bradley and Jarrell (1988) use the same sample but a different methodology from Magenheim and Mueller (1988). They do not find significant negative returns to acquiring firms. Nor do Franks, Harris, and Titman (1991), using various multifactor benchmark portfolios for three years following the acquisition for acquisitions during the time period 1975–1984. Finally, in a comprehensive sample of acquisitions by NYSE and AMEX firms during the period 1966–1986, Loderer and Martin (1992), find negative abnormal returns in the three years but not the five years following the acquisition. The negative performance found in the second and third years following the acquisition is most significant in the 1960s, to a lesser extent in the 1970s, and not significant at all in the 1980s. Clearly the measurement of acquiring firm performance remains a difficult issue.

The industrial-organization literature, which has examined ex-post accounting-based and market share performance evidence, suggests that many of these mergers and takeovers are not achieving gains in performance (reviewed in Caves, 1989, and Mueller, 1995). Ravenscraft and Scherer (1989), using performance data for the years 1975–1977 on 2,732 lines of business of U.S. manufacturing firms acquired in the period 1957–1977, found substantial deterioration in the profitability of acquired lines of business relative to their pre-merger levels following acquisition. Mueller (1986) found that firms engaging in acquisition activity for the years 1950–1972 experienced lower on average profitability than firms making no acquisitions. This evidence is consistent with the findings of Wernerfelt and Montgomery (1988) that large firms' values of Tobin's q decreased with their diversification activity during the period 1960–1977. After finding a 56.5 percent sell-off rate for pre-1976 acquisitions of thirty-three diversification-prone U.S. corporations, Porter (1987:43) concluded, "The corporate strategies of most companies have dissipated instead of created shareholder value."

A McKinsey & Company study (Copeland, Koller, and Murrin, 1994) found that of 116 merger programs studied, 61 percent were failures; the acquiring company was unable to earn back its cost of capital or better on the funds invested in the merger. Herman and Lowenstein (1988) found that acquiring firms executing hostile tender offers during the period 1981–1983 suffered sharp declines in profitability. Mueller (1985, 1986) found significant declines in the market shares of a sample of 209 manufacturing companies over an average of eleven years following the acquisition.

The above evidence is consistent with Michael Jensen's comments to the U.S. House of Representatives (1987a:137) that managers with large free cash flow and borrowing power have engaged in "low-benefit or even value-destroying diversification mergers." Even Ivan Boesky made money on the poor performance expectations of acquiring firms. Although Boesky bought the shares (preannouncement) of target firms on inside information, he often shorted the shares of the acquiring firms (Scherer, 1988).

In summary, the weight of the aggregate evidence from the financial and industrial-organization literatures is toward negative returns for acquisition strategies. Clearly this negative evidence raises serious doubt over the value of the takeover market as a mechanism for disciplining poor-performing or self-dealing managers as proposed by the market for corporate control hypothesis (Manne, 1965; sometimes referred to as the inefficient management displacement hypothesis, Ravenscraft and Scherer, 1989; or the improved-management hypothesis, Malatesta, 1983). Given the massive size and scope of the recent acquisition waves, understanding the factors that drive the distribution of these returns is essential.

Acquiring Firm Performance in the Management Literature

The management literature on the performance of acquiring firms has been largely motivated by the original Rumelt (1974, 1982) stream of research on the link between the generic diversification strategy and performance. Rumelt's original finding was that related diversified firms outperformed those that were unrelated. While Rumelt's findings have been challenged by a variety of management scholars (Montgomery, 1985; Nathanson, 1985; Michel and Shaked, 1984; Dubofsky and Varadarajan, 1987; Varadarajan and Ramanujam, 1987), it is important to distinguish the literature on generic diversification strategy from the literature on the performance of acquiring firms. The diversification strategy literature is content-based research that takes a "snapshot" of a sample of firms and compares their performance (cross-sectionally) according to categories of diversification strategy. Attention is not given to whether businesses were acquired or internally developed or to the marginal effect of the businesses' becoming part of the firm.

The Relatedness Question in Acquisitions

In the tradition of the Rumelt stream, the acquisition literature has almost exclusively focused on whether strategically related acquisitions are more beneficial than strategically unrelated acquisitions. This acquisition literature has been conjecture based because it has relied on the theory from the diversification literature. The basic conjecture is that related acquirers should outperform unrelated acquirers. The empirical work, however, has produced a stream of conflicting evidence.

While Cannella and Hambrick (1993) argue against the use of shareholder return measures, virtually all of this literature has employed the event-study methodology of the financial economics literature. Several authors have found no significant difference (with both positive and negative means) in returns to the shareholders of acquiring firms for strategically related versus unrelated acquisitions (Lubatkin, 1987; Chatterjee, 1986; Lubatkin and O'Neill, 1987; Singh and Montgomery, 1987; Seth, 1990a, 1990b and reviewed in Seth, 1990a). Lubatkin (1987) concludes that his findings do *not* support the popular prescription that product market relatedness improves acquisition performance.

On the other hand, some researchers have found that acquiring firms making conglomerate (i.e., unrelated) acquisitions outperform those making nonconglomerate acquisitions (Elgers and Clark, 1980; Agrawal, Jaffe, and Mandelker, 1992). With a five-year event window, Agrawal, Jaffe, and Mandelker (1992) find acquiring firm returns of −25.5 percent for related mergers and −8.6 percent for unrelated mergers.

Using both total stock returns and accounting returns as the dependent variables, Kusewitt (1985) finds that relatedness (industry commonality) had a positive significant effect on performance, while Fowler and Schmidt (1989) find no significant effect of relatedness on performance. Shelton (1988) combines the values of the acquiring firms and target firms for a three-day event window around the announcement date and reports a positive effect for relatedness. Thus, although the popular conjecture continues to favor related acquisitions, the evidence is mixed, with no consistent support. There is a remarkable intuitive appeal about the importance of relatedness that continues to drive researchers to search for a relatedness measure that will support the significance of the concept—with or without a theoretical motivation.

Value Creation of Acquiring Firms

Just as in the relatedness problem, there is significant disagreement among management scholars about whether acquisition strategies create value. In a review paper, Trautwein (1990:285) claims, "The stock market in general values mergers positively. Almost all of the gains, though, are reaped by the targets' stockholders while the bidders' shareholders gain nothing on average." This statement is consistent with the short-window event studies from financial economics (e.g., Jensen and Ruback, 1983) and strategic management (Chatterjee, 1986; Singh and Montgomery, 1987; Datta, Narayanan, and Pinches, 1992).

Lubatkin (1987:45), however, reports positive and significant abnormal returns for acquiring firms and states, "The fact that acquiring firms do not give away all merger-related benefits to the stockholders of the acquired firm refutes the notions both that the acquisitions market is perfectly competitive, and that managers exploit stockholders in their pursuit of building empires through mergers."

On the other extreme, after examining the effectiveness of corporate strategy implemented through acquisition, Fowler and Schmidt (1988:972) find that, on average, returns decrease significantly in the four years after acquisition and caution that managers have trouble maintaining even adequate post-acquisition performance. These authors conclude:

> From a strategic management perspective, the implementation of a major acquisition especially in the form of a tender offer, does not appear to affect financial performance in a favorable manner. Managers and shareholders of firms contemplating a major acquisition or tender offer should be aware of the empirically demonstrated risks associated with such activity.

This study is consistent with the industrial-organization literature results, but the evidence in the management literature remains mixed.

Factors Affecting the Performance of Acquiring Firms

Surprisingly, given the level of acquisition activity during the past two decades, little cross-sectional research exists that investigates the factors (specifically choice variables other than strategic relatedness) affecting acquisition performance. The following are the major cross-sectional studies that comprise this part of the acquisition literature. As in the previous sections, there is inconsistent and conflicting evidence about the effects of different factors.

Fowler and Schmidt (1989) find significant positive relationships with performance (four-year mean-adjusted stock returns) for acquisition experience (number of other acquisitions made in the four years prior to the specific acquisition) and the percentage of the target firm shares acquired, and a strong negative relationship between contested tender offers and organizational performance. These authors find negative but insignificant relationships for relatedness and the relative size of the acquisition.

Shelton (1988) finds a significant positive relationship for the presence of other bidders and the relative size of the acquired firm. Seth

(1990b) also finds a significant positive effect for the relative size of the acquisition. These two studies are event studies that combine the abnormal returns of both the acquiring and acquired firms and so are difficult to compare to studies considering only the performance of the acquiring firm.

In an exploratory study of strategic acquisition factors, Kusewitt (1985) finds significant negative relationships with performance (one-year raw stock returns) for relative size of the acquisition, the acquisition rate of the acquiring firm (number of acquisitions per year of the study), performance of the stock market, and cash acquisitions (versus stock acquisitions). Price paid (i.e., market value/book value of the target at the time of the acquisition) was found to be insignificant. The relationship between the return on assets of the acquisition and the performance of the acquiring firm was found to be significantly positive.

Another exploratory study on acquiring firm performance was conducted by You et al. (1986) focusing on short event period stock returns. Across three windows (day −20 to +1, −1 to +1, and −1 to +10), only the percentage of the acquiring firm owned by the managers and directors was found to be strongly significant. These significant results, however, were in both directions: positive in the first two windows and negative in the third. Weak support was found for a positive relationship between relatedness and acquiring firm performance. The presence of multiple bidders and the number of insiders on the board of directors had a weak negative relationship with performance. The post-merger integration technique (i.e., integrated versus not integrated) had no relationship with performance. This is a particularly interesting and even troubling result because performance gains presumably should be driven by some type of integration.

Because their study was exploratory, You et al. (1986) offered little reasoning about the nature of the importance of managerial ownership on acquiring firm performance. Amihud, Lev, and Travlos (1990) provide significant evidence that the larger the fraction is of managerial ownership in the acquiring firm, the more likely is the use of cash financing. Given the theoretical development on the importance of the financing decision (method of payment) by top management teams (reviewed in Travlos, 1987), it is perhaps more appropriate to consider this factor in a model of acquiring firm performance, particularly because it is a choice variable for a specific decision.

Finally, in an extensive meta-analysis covering the finance, industrial-organization, and strategy literatures, Datta, Narayanan, and Pinches (1992) find that the most significant explanatory factor is the method of payment. In contrast to Kusewitt (1985), these authors find that acquiring firms should avoid stock-financed transactions. They also find a significant negative effect for the presence of multiple bidders and a weakly significant positive effect for acquiring related acquisitions. While Fowler and Schmidt (1988) find that acquirers that use tender offers perform significantly worse than those that use mergers (i.e., no tender offer), Datta, Narayanan, and Pinches (1992) find exactly the reverse.

Problems in Post-Merger Integration

Another stream of research within the management literature attempts to explain what might be driving acquisition performance. Following the decision to pursue an acquisition as a strategic alternative, there are two distinct phases to the implementation process of the decision, or what I call the acquisition game: (1) top management's commitment of resources to make the acquisition and (2) post-merger management of projected synergies.

This literature focuses on identifying the process problems that may occur in the post-merger integration phase of mergers and takeovers that may prevent the realization of synergies (Shrivastava, 1986; Jemison and Sitkin, 1986a, 1986b; Dundas and Richardson, 1982; Buono and Bowditch, 1989; Napier, 1989; Nahavandi and Malekzadeh, 1988; Shanley and Correa, 1992; and reviewed in Ramanujam and Varadarajan, 1989, and Schweiger and Walsh, 1990). The focus is generally on finding the appropriate integration techniques (e.g., procedural, physical, and sociocultural) given the motives and characteristics and organizational cultures of the acquiring and acquired firms (Shrivastava, 1986). Haspeslagh and Jemison (1991) document an array of problems in both the acquisition decision and integration processes.

This literature is still in the theory-building stage, however, with little empirical evidence. What is generally ignored by these authors is the relationship between amount and timing of potential benefits from post-merger integration and the implicit necessary performance objectives that are created by managers when resources are allocated up front to execute a corporate strategy through acquisition. This literature has not yet offered models or even addressed exactly how much synergy or performance gains would be generated if the various process problems did not occur. This is the major void in the literature. Further, researchers have not yet offered testable propositions regarding the prediction of when problems are more likely to occur or how different managers across firms may react when these problems occur.

Jemison and Sitkin (1986a, 1986b) suggest that disappointing merger performance may result from not enough pre-merger attention given to post-merger integration planning issues because of the pressure to close deals quickly. These ideas were first discussed over twenty years earlier in Keil (1966) and reiterated by Leighton and Tod (1969). As Keil (1966:8) reports, "Most acquisitions are consummated too hastily. Then, too, there's an overdependence on intuition. Another reason is that frequently the acquiring company doesn't know enough about the potential of the company it is buying."

So this is clearly not a recent issue or concern in the literature or in practice. Perhaps a greater problem is that the resource allocation (pricing) decision becomes completely detached from any synergies that may be realizable under *any* conditions, even if all post-merger management issues were thoroughly considered. It is now well known that realizing performance gains can actually take several years, and commonly touted operating synergies such as economies of scale can turn out to be extremely complex and difficult management tasks (Haspeslagh and Jemison, 1991; Kitching, 1967; Mueller, 1980; Finkelstein, 1986) exacerbated by conflict between the acquiring and acquired firm (Marks and Mirvis, 1985). Herein lies the synergy limitation view.

Risk Taking by Managers Following Acquisitions

Very little research has been done in the area of the effect of acquisitions on risk taking. The research focus has been whether there are changes in systematic risk (i.e., the stock beta) following the acquisition. Lubatkin and O'Neill (1987) and Chatterjee and Lubatkin (1990) find larger decreases in systematic risk "than an investor can do on his own" for related mergers than unrelated mergers. Unrelated mergers, however, are found to have lower absolute levels of systematic risk (Chatterjee and Lubatkin, 1990). As with the majority of the management literature on acquisitions, these results are not without controversy. Seth (1990b) finds no significant decreases in systematic risk for either type of merger and concludes that attempting to decrease beta is not a source of value creation.

This is a very important area of research on acquisitions. However, the research thus far suggests that executive teams should be concerned with beta management. This would be a waste of managerial resources because investors can clearly adjust the beta of any given portfolio according to their risk preference and they do not need to pay acquisition premiums in the process. Further, systematic risk is a portfolio concept and simply a weighted average. This method of exploring risk does not address how the risk-taking behavior of managers might change following an acquisition.

The concept of changes in risk-taking behavior has not been considered in the post-acquisition environment. In other words, how might a given manager in two different post-acquisition performance environments react differently to a similar post-acquisition problem? Managerial actions do not lie in isolation of the performance environment, and so it is important to consider how the risk-taking posture of executive teams may emerge post-acquisition.

An Assessment and Motivation of the Synergy Limitation View

The evidence of value destruction to acquiring firms squarely challenges the value of the corporate takeover market. Surprisingly, very little theoretical work has been done on understanding the choice variables that managers control during the acquisition process. The theoretical work that has been done on the economics of the relationship between the relatedness principle and acquiring firm performance (Barney, 1988; Lubatkin, 1983; Chatterjee, 1986) has not been empirically verified. Moreover, empirical studies generally explain less than 10 percent of variance in the shareholder performance of acquiring firms. Haspeslagh and Jemison (1987:55) have argued that "nothing can be said or learned about acquisitions in general." In fact, Barney (1988) concluded that successful bidding firms may simply be "lucky." While this may be partially true, it would be unfortunate if this were the only wisdom we could offer executive teams gambling with shareholder resources.

An important choice variable of management, the payment of acquisition premiums, has received virtually no theoretical or empirical attention. Perhaps this is because the implicit assumptions in the strategic management literature on acquisitions are that synergies are realizable—and realizable in at least the amount predicted by the acquisition premium (Haspeslagh and Jemison, 1991). These assumptions have been reinforced by the emergence of the resource-based view of the firm in the strategy literature (Peteraf, 1993).

Lubatkin (1983) suggests that managers of acquiring firms may make mistakes and acquire the wrong company at the wrong price. No attempt is made, however, to formalize the concept of "wrong company" or "wrong price." By definition, if we destroy value, then we paid the wrong price—it is simply tautological ex post. We need to consider what about price is relevant and develop the ex-ante importance of the concept in the context of the acquiring firm performance environment.

The acquisition premium represents the component of price that executive teams choose to allocate that pre-acquisition shareholders would not have to pay. Thus, this component of the resource allocation decision must inherently be strategic in nature and may be a significant predictor of acquisition success or failure. While Datta, Narayanan, and Pinches (1992) acknowledge that "most strategic decisions are investment decisions (i.e., they describe the pattern of resource allocation needed to enhance shareholder wealth)," their meta-analysis of acquisition research reveals that this potentially critical variable has received no attention.

Penn (1981:32) quotes an investment banker with Dean Witter Reynolds who states, "Any work done to link premiums with variables of strategic importance would be useful. However, progress is likely to be slow since there has been very little prior work in the field, and since the theoretical link between strategic variables and pricing considerations is virtually undeveloped." Clearly there remains a need for continued progress in this area of the management literature.

Recent literature in industrial-organization economics (Alberts and Varaiya, 1989) has used the market value/book value ratio to derive the sustained performance improvement requirements necessary to recapture an acquisition premium and create value for the acquiring company. These authors calculate the uniform annual equivalent (UAE) spread between total return and required rate of return managers must achieve to justify a given stock price. Thus, a premium causes this UAE spread to increase. These authors suggest that, given a competitive economy and historical industrial performance, the premiums being paid (65 percent average premium in the Alberts and Varaiya sample) represent difficult performance objectives to achieve and sustain.

The prices—and particularly, the premiums—that managers are willing to pay and directors are willing to approve for acquisitions represent potentially the largest resource allocation decision available to management. Given the large premiums paid during the 1980s and 1990s along with the incredible volume of acquisition activity, there is a need to understand the economics and potential consequences of this resource allocation decision in the context of the acquisition process. This will allow a more thorough consideration of the relative importance of other choice variables that have yielded disappointing empirical support. We now consider the theoretical motivations behind the consideration of premiums and the limits to synergy.

Theoretical Foundations

What can explain the value-destroying evidence we observe and the apparent failure of the market for corporate control with respect to the ability of acquiring firms to generate net performance gains? From the perspective of the decision makers—managers—there are both rational and irrational decision approaches to this problem. We begin with the rational view.

Growth Objectives and the Agency View. The problem of value-destroying acquisitions, and specifically the problem of overpayment, has its theoretical roots in the separation of ownership and control of the managerial enterprise and the agency theory literature (Berle and Means, 1932; Schumpeter, 1934; Marris, 1963, 1964; Mueller, 1969; Jensen and Meckling, 1976; Fama, 1980; Morck, Shleifer, and Vishny, 1990; and reviewed by Mueller, 1995). As early as 1934, Schumpeter described the leading entrepreneurial goal as founding "a private kingdom" where profits are sacrificed for size. As Mueller (1995:15) notes, "Mergers are the quickest and surest way to grow, and thus may be undertaken by managers even if they do not promise profit and shareholder wealth increases."

Compensation, power, prestige, and job security are likely to be valued by managers, and maximizing size might improve the probability of achieving these goals. There is substantial evidence that the income of top managers rises even with declines in performance of the acquiring firm (Firth, 1991; Fowler and Schmidt, 1989; Mueller, 1969) and, thus, compensation practices may drive acquisition activity. Along these lines, an acquisition premium is a clear example of a decision that shareholders are not likely to make when implementing portfolio decisions. Thus, in pursuing their own objectives, managers pay whatever the acquisition market requires them to pay to make the acquisition they desire. The premium has little to do with value creation opportunities, and managers do not really expect these acquisitions to deliver value to their shareholders.

At the other extreme, an alternative to the agency view for motivating the study of the resource allocation decision in acquisition strategies is the role of managerial hubris (Roll, 1986).

The Hubris Hypothesis of Corporate Takeovers. The hubris hypothesis (Roll, 1986) was advanced as a potential explanation of the negative stock market evidence for acquiring firms and has been the subject of significant debate within the finance literature (Shleifer and Vishny, 1988, Morck, Shleifer, and Vishny, 1990). In Roll's view it is the hubris of a single decision maker—overweening pride and self-confidence to the point of arrogance—that causes a manager to over-pay for an acquisition. In the hubris view, the multitude of players involved in generating and promoting bids and the acquisition itself has no effect on the outcome.

The hubris hypothesis is essentially a special case of the winner's curse from auction theory (Varaiya, 1988). That is, in a common value auction (the asset has the same value to all bidders), the highest bidder will likely have the highest positive valuation error and there-fore win the auction but "not like the prize" (Bazerman and Samuel-son, 1983). In Roll's model, it is assumed that markets are strong form efficient—that is, all potential gains are known by the markets and already impounded in the target firm before the actual bid. So it is hubris that drives managers to pay anything more than the market price. The most important assumption that this hubris view rests on is that the observed bid, and specifically the premium, represents the true underlying beliefs of the decision maker about the value he or she can create with the acquisition.

The hubris hypothesis, while intuitively appealing, suffers from its major underlying assumption: the true beliefs of a single decision maker. Haunschild (1994) found that premiums paid by an acquirer are related to those paid by their board interlock partners and to other firms using the same investment bank. And Mueller (1989) states that whether the premium paid actually represents underlying beliefs is "inherently unanswerable." It is difficult to argue that, with premiums today at levels as much as five times their levels of twenty years ago, managers are now five times more confident or arrogant. Also, the same executive team can make many acquisitions and pay a whole range of premiums.

Alternatively, the hubris hypothesis can be challenged because it rests on strong form market efficiency and therefore, *all* bids involve overpayment (Black, 1989). In a world of heterogeneous resource endowments, the assets embedded in an acquisition target may have different values for different acquirers (Barney, 1986a). Thus, acquisi-tions may not be common value auctions.

Finally, while ego and overconfidence clearly can be a source of problems in a variety of investment decisions, perhaps the real trouble with this approach is best described by *Wall Street Journal* writer Joe Queenan (1995), commenting about managerial hubris:

> All journalism revolves around the attempt to get the word hubris into a story. So, whether you lost $25 billion investing in Japanese futures or you ran the corner grocery store, hubris lies at the fault [*sic*]. And you desperately want stories that are layups, and this is it. Because this is the case where whether the guy wins or loses it's the perfect *Forbes* magazine story. If he wins, it's, "They said it wouldn't work, but Charlie showed them." Or, "They warned him this wouldn't work and Charlie went ahead anyway"—and hubris has claimed another victim.

We now consider two additional approaches to value-destructive acquisitions to show just how involved this debate over motivations—and specifically, the assumptions involved—can become. In doing so, my objective is to create the demand for a view of acquisition performance that focuses on the issues of the economics of performance that might have an impact on decision making: the synergy limitation view.

Other Approaches and Hypotheses: Commitment and Regret. To limit the discussion to only agency or hubris views would exclude the sheer depth of this issue of rational versus irrational behavior. The agency view neglects alternative approaches, and the hubris view does not consider a variety of other emotions that may drive precisely the same "irrational behavior," for example, commitment and regret. In fact, when we truly enter this realm of debate, the issue of rationality versus irrationality becomes less clear (Elster, 1993). Many decisions can be locally rational but globally irrational, particularly in an intertemporal sense.

Consider the problem of commitment in the acquisition process (McCann and Gilkey, 1988; Haunschild, Davis-Blake, and Fichman, 1994). Based on interviews with senior executives and investment bankers, McCann and Gilkey (1988:123) conclude that many bad acquisitions are simply driven by the commitment to making the acquisition:

Commitment refers to the tendency for CEO's and merger-acquisition teams to deepen commitment, to "up the ante" and even rationalize bad news in order to negotiate a deal. Assumptions made later and later in a deal that is encountering difficulties have a way of getting more and more suspect. The bearer of "bad tidings" in a hotly pursued deal has a chance of being executed.

Is this agency or hubris? And if executives trust the fairness opinions of their investment bankers and advisers that, in the aggregate, have cost billions of dollars, is that agency or hubris?

On the other hand, consider the problem of fear or regret. This is similar to the "Wow! Grab it!" decision rule (Janis, 1989) I described in Chapter 4. A particular acquisition opportunity may never come around again so you had better grab it while you have the chance or someone else might get it—and you hate to live with regret. Clearly acquisition activity could be driven by the desire to avoid regret. But is it rational or irrational? Elster (1993:185) provides the following discussion regarding regret as an unresolved problem in the theory of rational behavior:

> Suppose I have the choice between two actions, taking an umbrella or leaving it at home. If I leave it home and it rains, I shall get wet. In addition, I'll feel regret that I didn't take the umbrella. The contingency is, in other words, doubly bad. It can be shown, that by taking account of feelings of regret, over and above preferences about the physical states themselves, some of the anomalous forms of behavior can in fact be explained.

> Does this mean that the anomalous behavior is rational? Once again, intuition is ambiguous. On the one hand, regret seems just like another preference. To include regret in the decision calculus we have to expand the space of outcomes, but there is nothing irrational about that.

> On the other hand, there is something about regret that does seem irrational. Rational choice theory tends to lead to recommendations of the following kind: don't cry over spilt milk, let bygones be bygones, cut your losses, and ignore sunk costs when deciding about the future. To worry about what might have happened seems peculiarly pointless—a needless source of frustration and unhappiness.

Ultimately, the debate regarding what drives value-destructive acquisition behavior must converge to a discussion of rational versus irrational decisions. Unfortunately, while this academic exercise is stimulating and challenging, the debate does not address the issues of acquisition performance.

In the next section, I provide the background literature review of the synergy limitation view. The major issue is why synergy—performance gains in excess of what is already expected for firms to achieve—is inherently limited, with a low expected value. The synergy limitation view is an alternative approach to the study of acquisition performance because it focuses on the issues of performance rather than a debate behind why decisions occur.

In the end, executive teams pursue value-destroying acquisitions because they can (Sirower and Abzug, 1996). The business judgment rule has traditionally protected officers and directors of the acquiring firm from shareholder suits—whether they were pursuing their own objectives or truly believed they could realize the required improvements from the acquisition or anything else.

The Synergy Limitation View

In the synergy limitation view (hypothesis), the issues and assumptions discussed in the preceding sections on motives are not of consequence because we focus on the ex-ante importance of the *actions* of the managers (whether or not they understand) and consider them in the context of *realizing* synergies in intensely competitive product and service markets. This forms the foundation for challenging the competitive markets view that prices represent potential value and using the premium as a predictor of losses in most acquisitions.

Whether synergy or real performance gains occur at all remains subject to question. For example, Reed and Luffman (1986:34) have commented, "While the benefits of synergy are truly legendary . . . as every student knows, those particular benefits show an unshakable resolve not to appear when it becomes time for their release." Other strategy scholars have proposed that administrative costs that accompany post-merger integration may offset the potential benefits of synergy (Lubatkin, 1983; Jones and Hill, 1988).

Headlines such as "When Someone Says Synergy, Feel for Your

Wallet" (Berman, 1984, *Forbes*), "Two Plus Two Doesn't Equal Five" (Davis, 1985, *Fortune*), "Synergy, Redefined, Back in Style" (Lohr, 1989, *New York Times*), with regard to the Time Warner merger, "Synergy, Schmynergy" (Brodie and Robins, 1994, *Variety*), and concerning the QVC-Paramount-Viacom affair, " 'Synergy': The Unspoken Word" (Sims, 1993, *New York Times*) reflect a stream of popular disbelief that synergy occurs.

Scholars in industrial-organization economics have provided the true background for considering the economics of synergy. Several economists have expressed skepticism about the synergy concept. Slusky and Caves (1991) find no operating synergies in their sample. After finding decreases in profitability at the line of business level following merger, Ravenscraft and Scherer (1989) squarely challenge the common hypotheses of scale or scope economies in acquisitions. Federal Reserve Board economist Stephen Rhoades (1983:97) has written, "It is time that synergy and related arguments be put to rest. For far too long they have provided an unfounded justification for the acquisition of thousands of viable independent companies in the U.S. economy. There have been no apparent benefits to the system."

Shleifer and Vishny (1991:53) challenge the evidence of increases in plant productivity following a control change offered by Lichtenberg and Siegel (1989) because the increases may have resulted from reduced investments and not from improvements in the present value of profits. Healy, Palepu, and Ruback (1992) critique the poor profitability evidence of Ravenscraft and Scherer (1987a) and show increases in profitability following acquisition. However, Shleifer and Vishny (1991:53) challenge this evidence because Healy, Palepu, and Ruback (1992) may not have adequately corrected for asset sales and therefore find artificial improvements in profitability.

Alberts (1984) documents the intense competitiveness in product and factor markets by showing that most firms essentially earn economic rents (i.e., return on capital less cost of capital spreads) that are not much different from zero. Further, he shows that to profit maximize in the long run, oligopolists do not charge higher prices—they constrain capital return minus capital cost spreads—specifically to deter *future* entry from potential competitors. He concludes, "Noncompetitive structures do not result in noncompetitive performance," because barriers to entry are not high enough to make earning excess returns in the short run consistent with long-run value maximization (Alberts, 1984:630). You et al. (1986) find no evidence of the importance of financial synergy. Moreover, these authors found that whether the acquisition was integrated into the acquirer had no effect on performance. *So much for synergy.*

I close with a comment by industrial-organization economist Dennis C. Mueller (1989:6):

> The market for corporate control seems to be vulnerable to the same kinds of fads that affect the stock market and lead to over optimism about stock prices. At the time of this writing (October, 1988), the acquisition of food companies is all the rage in the United States. Thus, one finds that each merger wave spawns its own new set of buzz words to characterize it and set it off from its predecessors ("synergy," "strategic diversification"). That these buzz words often find their way into the academic lexicon only shows how attractive these fads are.

Appendix B:
Detailed Results of the Analysis
in Part 2

This appendix begins with a summary of the empirical findings. Table B.1 reports descriptive statistics and correlations of the independent variables. Table B.2 reports means and standard deviations of the twenty-eight measures of the performance dependent variable, and Table B.3 reports the correlations of these twenty-eight distributions. The sample size is 168. The average size of the acquiring firms is $2.31 billion, with a range from $27 million to $34 billion. The average size of the targets is $753 million, with a range of $17 million to $8.3 billion. The average size of the targets relative to their acquirers is 45.6 percent. The premium ranges from −6.9 percent to 107 percent, with an average of approximately 30 percent.

The empirical results are summarized as follows:

1. Acquisition strategies, on average, reduce the value of the acquiring firm (supporting Hypothesis 1). Announcement effects are indicative of long-term performance.
2. Strong support is found for a negative relationship between acquisition premiums and acquiring firm performance (supporting Hypothesis 2).
3. Strategic relatedness is found to have a moderating effect, but no main effect, using traditional analysis. In the context of the general model, no support is found for a main effect of relatedness

167

TABLE B.1

Descriptive Statistics and Correlations of Independent Variables

Variable	Mean	S.D.	Fre-quency	1	2	3	4	5	6	7	8	9	10	11	12	13
1. Premium	30.106	21.146	—	1												
2. Relindx	0.141	0.229	—	0.03	1											
3. Relsize	0.456	0.415	—	−0.03	0.09	1										
4. Cash	0.530	0.501	89	0.21***	0.01	0.02	1									
5. Contest	0.226	0.438	43	0.18***	0.02	0.19***	0.09	1								
6. Tender	0.560	0.497	94	0.12	−0.03	0.19***	0.39***	0.38***	1							
7. Tmvbvt	2.419	1.529	—	0.05	0.06	−0.15	−0.05	−0.09	−0.15	1						
8. Prev	0.256	0.766	28	−0.09	−0.12	−0.06	−0.04	−0.04	0.11	−0.02	1					
9. Dist4	8.905	4.180	—	0.04	−0.51***	0.08	0.04	0.09	0.17**	−0.10	0.29***	1				
10. Bmv1	2.316	4.388	—	0.04	−0.00	−0.17*	−0.03	0.15**	−0.00	0.19***	0.02	0.21***	1			
11. Multb	0.274	0.447	46	−0.04	−0.06	0.23***	0.10	0.47***	0.30***	−0.12	0.02	0.18**	−0.02	1		
12. Time	5.042	2.943	—	0.04	0.09	0.17**	0.25***	0.10	0.13	0.12	0.21***	0.05	0.24***	0.02	1	
13. Time²	34.030	30.796	—	0.05	0.09	0.14*	0.24***	0.09	0.14*	0.16**	0.22***	0.06	0.27***	0.03	0.96***	1

*** $p < .01$, ** $p < .05$, * $p < .1$.

TABLE B.2

Means and Standard Deviations of Performance Measures

Time Period	Market Adjusted (MK)	Market Model (MM)	Mean Adjusted (MA)	Raw Returns (RR)
Day −1,1 (0)	−2.338 (5.907)	−2.295 (5.941)	−2.446 (6.297)	−2.207 (6.241)
Day −5,+5 (01)	−2.658 (8.125)	−2.646 (8.175)	−2.752 (9.300)	−1.878 (9.160)
Day −5,T (T)	−2.483 (16.725)	−0.815 (18.336)	−2.263 (23.579)	3.839 (20.147)
Month 0,12 (1 year)	−1.214 (29.457)	−0.917 (32.836)	−4.487 (37.944)	17.940 (34.409)
Month 0,24 (2 years)	−7.014 (46.350)	−7.097 (53.480)	−16.303 (59.210)	25.929 (51.425)
Month 0,36 (3 years)	−8.224 (56.075)	−8.795 (68.325)	−24.572 (74.181)	35.599 (62.740)
Month 0,48 (4 years)	−6.173 (60.261)	−6.091 (78.967)	−27.403 (86.399)	48.959 (70.151)

Note: Raw returns are unadjusted total shareholder returns (TSRs); standard deviations are given in parentheses; day T is the effective date of the acquisition.

(I could not reject the null Hypothesis 3a), and weak support is found for a moderating effect of relatedness. Where significant support is found, the interaction effect is positive, as proposed (supporting Hypothesis 3b).

4. Conditioning on other strategic factors, namely, the acquisition premium, the conflicting evidence on relatedness is replicated (supporting Conjecture 1 on relatedness).

5. No significant difference is found for premiums paid for related versus unrelated acquisitions (I could not reject the null Conjecture 2 on relatedness).

6. Strong support is found for a positive relationship between the payment of cash for acquisitions (relative to equity) and performance (supporting Hypothesis 4).

7. Contested acquisitions result in the payment of significantly

TABLE B.3

Correlations of the Twenty-Eight Performance Measures

	MK0	MK01	MKT	MK1	MK2	MK3	MK4	MM0	MM01	MMT	MM1	MM2	MM3	MM4
MK0	1.00													
MK01	0.79	1.00												
MKT	0.49	0.54	1.00											
MK1	0.38	0.42	0.58	1.00										
MK2	0.40	0.30	0.46	0.72	1.00									
MK3	0.35	0.24	0.35	0.59	0.86	1.00								
MK4	0.28	0.18	0.29	0.55	0.77	0.92	1.00							
MM0	0.99	0.77	0.48	0.36	0.38	0.32	0.25	1.00						
MM01	0.77	0.96	0.51	0.39	0.29	0.20	0.15	0.79	1.00					
MMT	0.41	0.43	0.83	0.49	0.34	0.18	0.16	0.44	0.50	1.00				
MM1	0.35	0.36	0.51	0.88	0.63	0.51	0.48	0.35	0.38	0.52	1.00			
MM2	0.35	0.25	0.36	0.61	0.84	0.73	0.65	0.36	0.28	0.37	0.78	1.00		
MM3	0.28	0.17	0.25	0.48	0.70	0.82	0.76	0.28	0.19	0.23	0.68	0.89	1.00	
MM4	0.21	0.11	0.17	0.42	0.58	0.70	0.76	0.22	0.14	0.20	0.66	0.83	0.94	1.0
MA0	0.97	0.75	0.46	0.37	0.41	0.36	0.28	0.95	0.74	0.38	0.35	0.37	0.30	0.
MA01	0.76	0.92	0.48	0.40	0.32	0.28	0.21	0.75	0.87	0.38	0.36	0.28	0.22	0.
MAT	0.42	0.43	0.76	0.47	0.43	0.38	0.30	0.42	0.41	0.66	0.49	0.41	0.36	0.
MA1	0.31	0.34	0.47	0.80	0.58	0.50	0.47	0.30	0.33	0.44	0.87	0.67	0.61	0.
MA2	0.33	0.25	0.36	0.58	0.81	0.73	0.66	0.33	0.26	0.35	0.72	0.93	0.86	0.
MA3	0.27	0.19	0.25	0.46	0.66	0.80	0.74	0.26	0.17	0.21	0.64	0.84	0.95	0.
MA4	0.18	0.09	0.16	0.39	0.54	0.67	0.74	0.18	0.10	0.18	0.60	0.75	0.88	0.
RR0	0.97	0.76	0.46	0.37	0.40	0.35	0.28	0.95	0.74	0.37	0.34	0.35	0.28	0.
RR01	0.76	0.93	0.49	0.39	0.30	0.26	0.20	0.74	0.86	0.36	0.33	0.24	0.18	0.
RRT	0.45	0.48	0.86	0.51	0.44	0.36	0.30	0.44	0.43	0.68	0.48	0.35	0.28	0.
RR1	0.33	0.38	0.53	0.86	0.64	0.54	0.51	0.30	0.33	0.42	0.77	0.53	0.44	0.
RR2	0.36	0.29	0.44	0.63	0.92	0.82	0.73	0.34	0.26	0.33	0.58	0.80	0.69	0.
RR3	0.30	0.23	0.33	0.50	0.76	0.91	0.84	0.26	0.18	0.18	0.46	0.67	0.77	0.
RR4	0.20	0.14	0.24	0.43	0.64	0.78	0.87	0.17	0.10	0.15	0.41	0.57	0.68	0.

Note: Where correlation > .2, $p < .01$.

higher premiums than uncontested acquisitions but have no independent effect on acquiring firm performance (supporting Hypothesis 5a).

8. The tender offer method of acquisition does not result in the payment of higher premiums and does not have an independent effect on acquiring firm performance (I could not reject the proposed null hypotheses Hypothesis 5b and Hypothesis 5c, respectively).

MA0	MA01	MAT	MA1	MA2	MA3	MA4	RR0	RR01	RRT	RR1	RR2	RR3	RR4	
														MK0
														MK01
														MKT
														MK1
														MK2
														MK3
														MK4
														MM0
														MM01
														MMT
														MM1
														MM2
														MM3
														MM4
1.00														MA0
0.79	1.00													MA01
0.44	0.50	1.00												MAT
0.35	0.40	0.62	1.00											MA1
0.37	0.31	0.50	0.73	1.00										MA2
0.31	0.27	0.45	0.67	0.89	1.00									MA3
0.21	0.17	0.36	0.64	0.82	0.93	1.00								MA4
1.00	0.79	0.42	0.33	0.34	0.29	0.20	1.00							RR0
0.78	0.99	0.44	0.35	0.26	0.22	0.13	0.78	1.00						RR01
0.45	0.50	0.88	0.55	0.40	0.34	0.26	0.45	0.49	1.00					RRT
0.35	0.41	0.60	0.92	0.59	0.50	0.44	0.34	0.38	0.59	1.00				RR1
0.38	0.32	0.48	0.61	0.88	0.72	0.61	0.37	0.29	0.46	0.67	1.00			RR2
0.32	0.28	0.42	0.52	0.74	0.83	0.69	0.32	0.26	0.40	0.57	0.86	1.00		RR3
0.22	0.18	0.33	0.48	0.68	0.75	0.77	0.22	0.17	0.33	0.52	0.77	0.90	1.00	RR4

9. Consistent with past studies, the presence of multiple bidders (a control variable) is found to have a negative effect on performance, but this effect is independent of the size of the premium. Further, only 27 percent of the sample represented multiple bidder auctions, and they are not found to generate significantly higher premiums than single bidder auctions.

10. Relative size is found to have a significant main effect, although the sign changes from positive to negative over time. Moderate support is found for a negative interaction effect of relative size

on the relationship between premiums and performance (supporting Hypothesis 6).

11. No relationship is found between the acquisition premium and changes in risk taking by acquiring firm managers (not supporting Hypothesis 7).

The description of results will correspond to the discussion of empirical techniques in Chapter 6 and will proceed as follows: (1) aggregate results on acquiring firm performance, (2) traditional tests and replications of evidence on relatedness, (3) tests of the acquiring firm performance model, and (4) tests for changes in risk taking in acquiring firms.

In reporting the results, market-adjusted, market-model, mean-adjusted, and raw returns are denoted MK, MM, MA, and RR, respectively. For each of the four return generation methods, returns for short-term performance windows 1, 2, and 3 are denoted 0, 01, and T, respectively, and returns for the longer-term performance windows 4, 5, 6, and 7 are denoted 1, 2, 3, and 4 (to correspond to the number of years). For example, the market-adjusted return for day −1 through +1 is denoted MK0, the market-adjusted return for day −5 through +5 is denoted MK01, the market-adjusted return for day −5 through day T (the effective date of the acquisition) is denoted MKT, the market-adjusted return for month zero through month 12 (i.e., one year) is denoted MK1, and so on for twenty-four-month (2 year, MK2), thirty-six-month (3 year, MK3), and forty-eight-month (4 year, MK4) returns.

Aggregate Results on Acquisitions

Hypothesis 1 states that acquisition strategies will, on average, destroy value for the acquiring firm. Table B.4A reports the market-adjusted, market-model, and mean-adjusted effects for the sample of acquiring firms as described in the empirical techniques section in Chapter 6. The results strongly support the hypothesis that acquisition strategies destroy value of acquiring firms. The market-adjusted, market-model, and mean-adjusted returns to acquiring firms are significantly negative (−2.338, $p < .01$; −2.295, $p < .01$; −2.446, $p < .01$, respectively).

TABLE B.4

Value Effects of Corporate Acquisition Strategies

A. Returns to shareholders of acquiring firms (day −1, +1)

	Mean	T-Statistic	# Negative	Z-Negative
Market adjusted	−2.338	−5.130	107	3.549
Market model	−2.295	−5.008	110	4.019
Mean adjusted	−2.446	−5.035	108	3.703

B. Longer window returns for portfolio of negative announcement effects where MK0 < 0

Return	Mean	T-Statistic
MK01	−6.643	−10.582
MKT	−7.568	−5.269
MK1	−8.536	−2.990
MK2	−19.184	−4.120
MK3	−20.919	−3.628
MK4	−17.188	−2.856

C. Longer window returns for portfolio of negative announcement effects where MM0 < 0

Return	Mean	T-Statistic
MM01	−6.236	−9.810
MMT	−5.731	−3.794
MM1	−8.564	−2.638
MM2	−20.766	−3.937
MM3	−23.144	−3.329
MM4	−19.831	−2.815

In Table B.4: All $p < .01$.

Table B.4A also reports the results of the binomial test for the number of the value-reducing acquisitions for each of the three return measures. These results strongly support the value–destruction hypothesis, showing there are more negative than positive effects of corporate acquisitions strategies.

To examine Porter's assertion that announcement effects do not have long-run performance implications, I split the sample based on the announcement effects (positive or negative) and tracked the long-term performance of these portfolios. Note that I am conditioning ex ante on announcements, and thus longer-term performance is not known when I split the sample.

Table B.4B and B.4C report market-adjusted and market-model results, respectively, for the negative announcement portfolio over the six subsequent time periods. Strong support is found for the announcement effect's being representative of long-term performance. All six periods show significant negative performance ($p < .01$).

Thus, Porter's assertion is subject to question with respect to the success of acquisition strategies. Although his assertion may be true for some particular firms, I caution against its usefulness in the research literature or for executives hoping that the stock market value of their company will rebound. Similar long-term positive results are found for firms in the positive announcement portfolio.

Preliminary Tests and Replications of Relatedness Evidence

This section reports the results of preliminary tests using the traditional methodologies of the acquisition literature to explore the effect of relatedness on acquiring firm performance. The hypotheses tested here are also tested in the full model regressions over seven time periods in the next section.

Table B.5 and B.6A present results of the traditional tests of Hypotheses 2, 3a, and 3b and the conjectures on relatedness, respectively. In this section, I present main effects results on the premium and relatedness (Hypothesis 2 and Hypothesis 3a), results of a 2×2 analysis of Hypothesis 2, Hypothesis 3a, and Hypothesis 3b, and results on tests of the relatedness conjectures. Although I report market-adjusted results, the results using market-model and mean-adjusted returns are very similar.

TABLE B.5

Analysis of Acquisition Relatedness Results

A. Acquirer returns for high- versus low-acquisition premiums (MK)

	N	Mean	T-Difference
HPremium	88	−3.413	2.514★★★
LPremium	80	−1.155	

B. Acquirer returns for related versus unrelated acquisitions (MK)

	N	Mean	T-Difference
Related	79	−1.589	1.554
Unrelated	89	−3.002	

C. ANOVA results of premium-relatedness 2 × 2

	Related	Unrelated
HPremium	−2.111	−4.906
LPremium	−0.823	−1.376

	F-value
Premium	6.45★★★
Relatedness	2.52
Premium × Related	2.82★

D. Acquirer returns for related versus unrelated acquisitions (MK)

	N	Mean	T-Difference
Related	47	−2.111	0.652
Unrelated	48	−1.376	

E. Acquirer returns for related versus unrelated acquisitions (MK)

	N	Mean	T-Difference
Related	32	−0.823	2.843★★★
Unrelated	41	−4.906	

F. Acquirer returns for related versus unrelated acquisitions (MK)

	N	Mean	T-Difference
Related	18	−4.769	3.193★★★
Unrelated	21	0.381	

In Table B.5: ★★★ $p<.01$, ★$p<.10$

TABLE B.6

Analysis of Proposed Determinants of the Premium

A. Acquisition premium for related versus unrelated acquisitions

	N	Mean	T-Difference
Related	79	32.233	1.561
Unrelated	89	27.323	

B. Acquisition premium for contested versus uncontested acquisitions

	N	Mean	T-Difference
Contested	43	44.448	4.017★★★
Uncontested	125	25.799	

C. Acquisition premium for tender offers versus mergers

	N	Mean	T-Difference
Tender	94	33.263	1.438
Merger	74	27.154	

D. Acquisition premium for contested versus uncontested tender offers

	N	Mean	T-Difference
Contested	38	46.864	4.148★★★
Uncontested	56	24.034	

In Table B.6: ★★★ $p < .01$.

Hypothesis 2 predicted an independent negative effect of the acquisition premium on performance. As can be seen in Table B.5A, using traditional t-tests, strong support is found for this hypothesis. High-premium acquisitions yield significantly more negative performance (value destruction) for acquiring firms than do low-premium acquisitions ($p < .01$). Hypothesis 3a proposed the null hypothesis of no independent effect of relatedness on performance. As can be seen in Table B.5B, the difference between the performance effects of related acquisitions versus unrelated acquisitions is insignificant. Thus, in this traditional analysis, the premium dominates relatedness.

Table B.5C presents the results of a traditional 2 × 2 of relatedness and premiums and their effects on performance. In addition to Hypotheses 2 and 3b, Hypothesis 3b predicted a positive moderating effect for relatedness. As proposed, there is a strongly significant main effect for the premium ($p < .01$), no main effect for relatedness, and a significant interaction effect (moderating effect) of relatedness with the premium ($p < .05$, one-tail test). Thus, although relatedness does not have an independent effect on performance, it does moderate the strength of the negative premium relationship. In other words, the negative effects of high-premium acquisitions are worse for unrelated acquisitions than for related acquisitions.

Conjecture 1 proposed that the conflicting evidence on relatedness may have resulted in the literature because of the exclusion of other important factors in the analysis. This analysis attempts to show that such a potentially incomplete model can yield different results by conditioning on other important strategic factors that have not previously been considered or have not been considered in this context in the literature. Tables B.5D–F show how conflicting evidence on relatedness can be found by this method. Tables B.5D–E condition on the premium, and Table B.5F includes the premium and the method of payment.

Thus, given the analysis in Table B.5C, Table B.5D shows a high-premium related sample compared to a low-premium unrelated sample, and Table B.5E shows a low-premium related sample compared to a high-premium unrelated sample. In the former, related acquisitions yield lower but insignificantly different performance than unrelated acquisitions. In the latter, unrelated acquisitions yield significantly lower performance than related acquisitions ($p < .01$).

Table B.5F shows exactly the reverse performance results of Table B.5E by conditioning on both premium level and method of payment. Here we compare a related sample of high-premium, noncash acquisitions to an unrelated sample of low-premium, cash acquisitions. In this case the unrelated acquisitions yield significantly greater performance than related acquisitions ($p < .01$).

Although the preceding analysis may be constructed, the factors I conditioned on were motivated by theory and in the direction I proposed. The main point of the simple analysis in Table B.5 is to introduce the importance of how considering other important strategic factors can improve our understanding of the fragility of the relatedness concept, in addition to acquiring firm performance more generally. Furthermore, given the relatively small sample sizes of most relatedness studies ($N < 100$), it is conceivable there may not have been sufficient heterogeneity of other factors across the related versus unrelated acquisition samples. At the minimum, this analysis supports the need for a more general model of acquiring firm performance.

Table B.6A provides a test of Conjecture 2, which proposed the null hypothesis that there would not be a significant difference in premiums between related and unrelated acquisitions. Although the mean for premiums in related acquisitions is higher than that of unrelated acquisitions, the distribution is such that there is not a significant difference, and we cannot reject the null (which is what was conjectured).

Testing the Acquiring Firm Performance Model

This section reports in detail the market-adjusted cross-sectional results for tests of Hypotheses 2 through 6 in Tables B.7 through B.13. The use of market-adjusted results avoids the potential parameter bias problem that may occur using market-model returns (Magenheim and Mueller, 1988). For each of the seven time periods of study, I present the results for the four model specifications described in the empirical techniques section of Chapter 6. All significance tests of parameter estimates are two-tailed (unless noted) to be conservative (although since most of the hypotheses are directional, I could use one-tail tests; Gibbs, 1993). Where I report parameter estimates in the text, I report the estimate from Model 2 in the tables.

Other results using market-model, mean-adjusted, and raw returns are similar and are summarized in Table B.14. In Table B.14, I report the sign of the coefficient where the parameter is at least significant at the .05 level. I summarize the results for MK, MM, MA, and RR measures across all seven time periods of the study. All regressions are significant ($p < .05$) except for the model specification including only the control variables (see Model 1 in Tables B.7 through B.13), which are not significant. Given the different ways acquiring firm performance can be and has been measured in prior studies, we can observe whether there is consistency in direction and significance across measures.

TABLE B.7

Cross–Sectional Regression Results:
Determinants of Acquiring Firm Performance

Dependent Variable = MK0

Independent Variable	Model 1	Model 2	Model 3	Model 4
Intercept	−0.781	−2.787	−2.612	−3.783*
	(1.843)	(2.012)	(2.018)	(2.100)
Premium	—	−0.053***	−0.053***	−0.029
		(0.020)	(0.020)	(0.032)
Relindx	—	3.598	3.619	1.449
		(2.310)	(2.305)	(3.299)
Premium × Relindx	—	—	—	0.101
				(0.108)
Relsize	—	2.061*	2.182*	4.727**
		(1.159)	(1.162)	(1.962)
Premium × Relsize	—	—	—	−0.089*
				(0.051)
Cash	—	3.982***	4.270***	4.130***
		(0.930)	(0.994)	(0.925)
Contest	—	−0.127	—	—
		(1.178)		
Tender	—	—	−0.815	—
			(1.011)	
Tmvbvt	−0.269	−0.102	−0.123	−0.064
	(0.317)	(0.301)	(0.301)	(0.298)
Prev	0.479	0.773	0.837	0.852
	(0.642)	(0.619)	(0.622)	(0.616)
Dist4	−0.039	0.040	0.046	0.036
	(0.120)	(0.137)	(0.137)	(0.137)
Bmv1	−0.153	−0.077	−0.075	−0.068
	(0.115)	(0.114)	(0.112)	(0.111)
Multb	−1.492	−2.325**	−2.184**	−2.441**
	(1.050)	(1.141)	(1.041)	(1.030)
Time	−0.199	−0.409	−0.428	−0.408
	(0.531)	(0.503)	(0.501)	(0.503)
Time^2	0.032	0.025	0.027	0.024
	(0.052)	(0.049)	(0.049)	(0.049)
R^2	.037	.177	.181	.196
F	0.884	2.783***	2.848***	2.894***

*** $p < .01$, ** $p < .05$, * $p < .10$. Standard errors are given in parentheses.

TABLE B.8

Cross-Sectional Regression Results:
Determinants of Acquiring Firm Performance

Dependent Variable = MK01

Independent Variable	Model 1	Model 2	Model 3	Model 4
Intercept	−0.716	−2.845	−2.731	−2.912
	(2.509)	(2.737)	(2.750)	(2.874)
Premium	—	−0.081***	−0.077***	−0.096**
		(0.029)	(0.028)	(0.044)
Relindx	—	3.585	3.626	−0.888
		(3.142)	(3.141)	(4.516)
Premium × Relindx	—	—	—	0.205*
				(0.128)
Relsize	—	3.291**	3.494**	3.898
		(1.577)	(1.584)	(2.685)
Premium × Relsize	—	—	—	−0.025
				(0.070)
Cash	—	5.267***	5.528***	5.346***
		(1.265)	(1.354)	(1.266)
Contest	—	0.728	—	—
		(1.603)		
Tender	—	—	−0.750	—
			(1.378)	
Tmvbvt	0.124	0.381	0.344	0.379
	(0.431)	(0.409)	(0.410)	(0.408)
Prev	1.326	1.751**	1.800**	1.736**
	(0.874)	(0.842)	(0.848)	(0.843)
Dist4	−0.250	−0.182	−0.180	−0.170
	(0.164)	(0.187)	(0.187)	(0.187)
Bmv1	−0.178	−0.074	−0.057	−0.049
	(0.155)	(0.156)	(0.153)	(0.152)
Multb	−2.051	−3.670**	−3.164**	−3.255**
	(1.430)	(1.553)	(1.418)	(1.381)
Time	0.374	0.040	0.050	0.177
	(0.723)	(0.684)	(0.683)	(0.688)
Time^2	−0.037	−0.042	−0.043	−0.058
	(0.070)	(0.066)	(0.066)	(0.067)
R^2	.057	.195	.196	.209
F	1.390	3.140***	3.149***	3.228***

*** $p < .01$, ** $p < .05$, * $p < .10$. Standard errors are given in parentheses.

TABLE B.9

Cross-Sectional Regression Results:
Determinants of Acquiring Firm Performance

Dependent Variable = MKT

Independent Variable	Model 1	Model 2	Model 3	Model 4
Intercept	−5.111	−9.457★	−9.211★	−7.810
	(5.183)	(5.655)	(5.682)	(5.955)
Premium	—	−0.153★★★	−0.142★★★	−0.190★★
		(0.060)	(0.058)	(0.092)
Relindx	—	5.169	5.270	7.784
		(6.492)	(6.491)	(9.357)
Premium × Relindx	—	—	—	−0.122
				(0.307)
Relsize	—	11.026★★★	11.519★★★	6.665
		(3.258)	(3.272)	(5.563)
Premium × Relsize	—	—	—	0.150
				(0.145)
Cash	—	8.573★★★	9.169★★★	8.324★★★
		(2.613)	(2.798)	(2.624)
Contest	—	1.946	—	—
		(3.311)		
Tender	—	—	−1.723	—
			(2.848)	
Tmvbvt	1.378	1.976★★	1.886★★	1.879★★
	(0.890)	(0.846)	(0.848)	(0.845)
Prev	1.671	2.764	2.873★	2.604
	(1.806)	(1.739)	(1.753)	(1.747)
Dist4	−0.269	−0.234	−0.230	−0.230
	(0.338)	(0.386)	(0.386)	(0.388)
Bmv1	−0.444	−0.166	−0.121	−0.145
	(0.322)	(0.321)	(0.315)	(0.316)
Multb	−2.922	−6.951★★	−5.667★★	−5.955★★
	(2.953)	(3.207)	(2.930)	(2.861)
Time	1.589	0.816	0.848	0.901
	(1.493)	(1.414)	(1.411)	(1.426)
Time^2	−0.144	−0.150	−0.152	−0.155
	(0.145)	(0.137)	(0.137)	(0.139)
R^2	.051	.190	.190	.194
F	1.221	3.024★★★	3.026★★★	2.851★★★

★★★ $p<.01$, ★★ $p<.05$, ★ $p<.10$. Standard errors are given in parentheses.

TABLE B.10

Cross-Sectional Regression Results:
Determinants of Acquiring Firm Performance

Dependent Variable = MK1

Independent Variable	Model 1	Model 2	Model 3	Model 4
Intercept	−8.594	−17.017*	−16.377	−10.237
	(9.175)	(10.216)	(10.256)	(10.637)
Premium	—	−0.318***	−0.302***	−0.532***
		(0.109)	(0.107)	(0.166)
Relindx	—	24.150**	24.284**	23.856
		(11.683)	(11.670)	(16.636)
Premium × Relindx	—	—	—	−0.003
				(0.547)
Relsize	—	4.954	5.810	−11.702
		(5.861)	(5.879)	(9.906)
Premium × Relsize	—	—	—	0.538**
				(0.256)
Cash	—	13.463***	14.733***	12.697***
		(4.707)	(5.028)	(4.675)
Contest	—	2.252	—	—
		(5.991)		
Tender	—	—	−3.653	—
			(5.121)	
Tmvbvt	1.132	1.833	1.684	1.580
	(1.569)	(1.522)	(1.524)	(1.506)
Prev	2.781	3.068	3.322	2.490
	(3.196)	(3.144)	(3.165)	(3.121)
Dist4	−0.020	0.750	0.763	0.820
	(0.604)	(0.704)	(0.703)	(0.698)
Bmv1	−0.468	−0.377	−0.318	−0.371
	(0.571)	(0.580)	(0.570)	(0.565)
Multb	−3.376	−7.720	−5.801	−6.034
	(5.245)	(5.833)	(5.305)	(5.124)
Time	1.855	1.139	1.137	1.577
	(2.632)	(2.546)	(2.538)	(2.541)
Time^2	−0.076	−0.095	−0.093	−0.135
	(0.257)	(0.247)	(0.247)	(0.248)
R^2	.029	.135	.137	.159
F	0.666	1.993**	2.028**	2.206***

*** $p<.01$, ** $p<.05$, * $p<.10$. Standard errors are given in parentheses.

TABLE B.11

Cross-Sectional Regression Results:
Determinants of Acquiring Firm Performance

Dependent Variable = MK2

Independent Variable	Model 1	Model 2	Model 3	Model 4
Intercept	−24.298★ (12.896)	−36.288★★ (15.579)	−35.623★★ (15.448)	−35.309★★★ (15.972)
Premium	—	−0.377★★★ (0.151)	−0.382★★★ (0.150)	−0.555★★ (0.229)
Relindx	—	28.097★ (16.441)	28.109★ (16.440)	−6.665 (23.415)
Premium × Relindx	—	—	—	1.585★★ (0.768)
Relsize	—	8.394 (8.248)	8.526 (8.282)	9.591 (13.943)
Premium × Relsize	—	—	—	−0.108 (0.362)
Cash	—	21.872★★★ (6.624)	22.688★★★ (7.035)	22.404★★★ (6.580)
Contest	—	−2.331 (8.431)	—	—
Tender	—	—	−2.338 (7.214)	—
Tmvbvt	1.401 (2.206)	2.306 (2.142)	2.278 (2.147)	2.418 (2.120)
Prev	3.906 (4.492)	4.721 (4.424)	4.945 (4.459)	4.610 (4.393)
Dist4	0.365 (0.850)	1.189 (0.991)	1.208 (0.991)	1.323 (0.984)
Bmv1	−0.370 (0.802)	−0.060 (0.816)	−0.089 (0.803)	−0.025 (0.795)
Multb	−6.763 (7.372)	−10.507 (8.208)	−10.990 (7.474)	−10.770 (7.213)
Time	5.473 (3.700)	4.514 (3.583)	4.397 (3.575)	5.384 (3.576)
Time^2	−0.376 (0.361)	−0.418 (0.348)	−0.409 (0.347)	−0.521 (0.349)
R^2	.039	.143	.143	.166
F	0.921	2.121★★	2.124★★	2.321★★★

★★★ $p<.01$, ★★ $p<.05$, ★ $p<.10$. Standard errors are given in parentheses.

TABLE B.12

Cross-Sectional Regression Results:
Determinants of Acquiring Firm Performance

Dependent Variable = MK3

Independent Variable	Model 1	Model 2	Model 3	Model 4
Intercept	−28.223*	−34.676**	−35.162**	−43.744**
	(15.968)	(17.877)	(17.966)	(18.618)
Premium	—	−0.528***	−0.530***	−0.330
		(0.191)	(0.187)	(0.285)
Relindx	—	35.446*	35.399*	12.411
		(20.446)	(20.443)	(29.116)
Premium × Relindx	—	—	—	1.077
				(0.955)
Relsize	—	−12.899	−13.225	11.532
		(10.257)	(10.299)	(17.338)
Premium × Relsize	—	—	—	−0.861**
				(0.440)
Cash	—	22.875***	22.128***	24.292***
		(8.237)	(8.808)	(8.182)
Contest	—	0.285	—	—
		(10.485)		
Tender	—	—	2.144	—
			(8.971)	
Tmvbvt	2.961	3.444	3.502	3.781
	(2.731)	(2.664)	(2.670)	(2.636)
Prev	6.656	5.438	5.262	6.083
	(5.562)	(5.502)	(5.544)	(5.462)
Dist4	−0.081	1.282	1.269	1.262
	(1.052)	(1.232)	(1.232)	(1.223)
Bmv1	0.261	0.057	0.051	0.161
	(0.994)	(1.015)	(0.998)	(0.989)
Multb	−8.093	−9.965	−10.362	−10.216
	(9.128)	(10.208)	(9.294)	(8.969)
Time	7.407	7.053	7.103	7.109
	(4.881)	(4.455)	(4.446)	(4.447)
Time^2	−0.625	−0.659	−0.663	−0.685
	(0.447)	(0.432)	(0.432)	(0.433)
R^2	.042	.137	.138	.161
F	0.985	2.032**	2.037**	2.240***

*** $p<.01$, ** $p<.05$, * $p<.10$. Standard errors are given in parentheses.

TABLE B.13

Cross-Sectional Regression Results:
Determinants of Acquiring Firm Performance

Dependent Variable = MK4

Independent Variable	Model 1	Model 2	Model 3	Model 4
Intercept	−27.296	−31.639	−32.308	−38.519★
	(17.889)	(20.099)	(20.196)	(21.023)
Premium	—	−0.582★★★	−0.588★★★	−0.473†
		(0.215)	(0.210)	(0.322)
Relindx	—	45.101★	45.022★	17.718
		(24.290)	(24.980)	(32.878)
Premium × Relindx	—	—	—	1.270
				(1.078)
Relsize	—	−23.163★★	−23.688★★	−3.621
		(11.532)	(11.577)	(19.578)
Premium × Relsize	—	—	—	−0.671†
				(0.508)
Cash	—	16.260★	16.179★	17.514★
		(9.261)	(9.901)	(9.239)
Contest	—	−0.076	—	—
		(11.788)		
Tender	—	—	3.105	—
			(10.085)	
Tmvbvt	3.249	3.397	3.490	3.686
	(3.059)	(2.995)	(3.001)	(2.976)
Prev	6.665	3.867	3.621	4.339
	(6.231)	(6.186)	(6.233)	(6.186)
Dist4	0.095	1.953	1.938	1.973
	(1.179)	(1.385)	(1.385)	(1.381)
Bmv1	0.762	0.220	0.203	0.317
	(1.113)	(1.141)	(1.122)	(1.116)
Multb	−13.696	−13.423	−14.219	−13.545
	(10.226)	(11.476)	(10.448)	(10.127)
Time	8.036	8.271★	8.329★	8.621★
	(5.132)	(5.009)	(4.998)	(5.021)
Time^2	−0.758	−0.785	−0.790	−0.834★
	(0.501)	(0.486)	(0.486)	(0.489)
R^2	.045	.134	.135	.150
F	1.068	1.979★★	1.988★★	2.069★★

★★★ $p<.01$, ★★ $p<.05$, ★ $p<.10$; † $p<.10$ (one-tailed). Standard errors are given in parentheses.

TABLE B.14

Cross–Sectional Summary of Significance

Independent Variable	MK0	MK01	MKT	MK1	MK2	MK3	MK4	MM0	MM01	MMT	MM1	MM2	MM3	MM4
Premium	–	–	–	–	–	–	–	–	–	–	–	–	–	–
Relindx				+	+		+							
Premium × Relindx			+											
Relsize		+	+	+				+	+	+				
Premium × Relsize	–			+		–	–						–	–
Cash	+	+	+	+	+	+		+	+	+	+	+	+	+
Contest														
Tender														
Tmvbvt			+	+										
Prev		+												
Dist4														
Bmv1														
Multb	–		–					–	–					

Note: Significance at $p < .05$.

TABLE B.14 (continued)

Cross-Sectional Summary of Significance

Independent Variable	MA0	MA01	MAT	MA1	MA2	MA3	MA4	RR0	RR01	RRT	RR1	RR2	RR3	RR4
Premium	−	−	−	−		−		−	−	−		−	−	−
Relindx											+			+
Premium × Relindx														
Relsize		+	+						+	+				−
Premium × Relsize	−					−		−			+		−	
Cash	+	+	+	+	+	+	+	+	+	+	+	+	+	+
Contest														
Tender														
Tmvbvt										+				
Prev		+							+					
Dist4														
Bmv1														
Multb	−	−						−	−					

Note: Significance at $p < .05$.

Acquisition Premiums

Hypothesis 2 predicts that there will be a negative relationship between the acquisition premium and acquiring firm performance.

Market-Adjusted Returns. Tables B.7 through B.13, Models 2 and 3, present results of the tests of this hypothesis. Very strong support is found for the synergy limitation hypothesis. The parameter estimate for this continuous variable is negative and strongly significant across all seven time periods (b = $-.053$, $p < .01$; b = $-.081$, $p < .01$; b = $-.153$, $p < .01$; b = $-.318$, $p < .01$; b = $-.377$, $p < .01$; b = $-.528$, $p < .01$; b = $-.582$, $p < .01$; from Model 2, respectively). Because synergies are limited (have a low expected value) across acquisitions, the acquisition premium is a strong predictor of losses in acquisition strategies. The acquisition premium is a resource allocation decision with embedded ex-ante risk and extremely important managerial significance.

Other Measures. Table B.14 provides a summary of regression results using all measures of performance and shows the strong negative significance of the acquisition premium across twenty-six of the twenty-eight measures of performance ($p < .01$). In the MM2 and MA2 performance measures, the coefficients for premiums are negative and significant at the $p < .062$ and $p < .087$ levels, respectively (and all are two-tailed tests).

Past Evidence on Acquisition Premiums. Travlos (1987) regressed acquiring firm announcement returns on a measure of premium (defined as the bid premium as a percentage of the bidding firm's stock price) and found negative but insignificant results. I replicated the Travlos measure and found the same results (approximately the same coefficient). I also found that this measure was virtually a proxy for relative size of the acquisition ($r = .85$, $p < .0001$) and was not theoretically motivated in the Travlos study (this measure does not represent post-acquisition required performance improvements). Given that my measure derives directly from the theory and simulations, I have a high degree of confidence in my results.

Kusewitt (1985) operationalized the premium as the target market value/book value (MV/BV) ratio (Tmvbvt) when acquired. This author regressed one-year raw acquiring firm returns on this measure and found insignificant results. I included this variable as a control variable in the ordinary least squares analysis and discussed an implicit null hypothesis this variable tests in the operationalization section in Chapter 6. I found the same positive but insignificant results as Kuse-witt (who studied RR1) in all but two measures of performance (MKT and RRT; $p < .05$). This variable has little to do with required improvements in post-acquisition performance, and I conclude that I cannot reject the null that expectations reflected in pre-acquisition market pricing are accurate on average. In other words, I find support for the principle that the market appropriately prices companies at high (low) MV/BV multiples.

Strategic Relatedness

Hypothesis 3a proposes the null hypothesis of no main effect for re-latedness on performance, and Hypothesis 3b predicts a positive moderating effect for relatedness with premiums on performance.

Market-Adjusted Returns. In the context of the general model, I find mixed support for Hypothesis 3a. The coefficient for relatedness is positive but insignificant for performance measures MK0, MK01, and MKT. The coefficient for relatedness is positive and significant for MK1 (b = 24.15; $p < .05$) and weakly significant for MK2, MK3, and MK4 (b = 28.097, b = 35.446, b = 45.101; $p < .10$ for each). Thus, using market-adjusted returns, I observe a weak long-term positive main effect for related acquisitions.

Weak support is found for Hypothesis 3b. Relatedness has a positive and significant moderating effect with premiums in MK01 (b = .205, $p < .10$) and MK2 (b = 1.585, $p < .05$). Recall that in the regressions I operationalized relatedness as a continuous index rather than dichotomous, as I did in the traditional tests in the previous section. For completeness and to check for consistency, I used the dichotomous relatedness variable in the regression for announcement effect returns (the period examined in the traditional tests). The results are consistent. Relatedness has a positive and significant interaction effect with premiums for MK0 and MK01 ($p < .1$ and $p < .05$, respectively;

two-tailed) but an insignificant main effect. This premium × relatedness interaction is positive but not significant for MK0, MK3, and MK4. In MKT and MK1 the parameter estimate is slightly negative but with almost a zero significance level.

Other Measures. Table B.14 gives an indication of the inconsistency of the significance of the relatedness variable. The raw return measures exhibit a similar pattern of significance as the market-adjusted measures in the longer-term periods (RR1, $p < .05$; RR3, $p < .10$; RR4, $p < .05$). This evidence of significance, however, disappears in the market-model and mean-adjusted measures of performance. Market-model and mean-adjusted returns adjust performance for individual firm characteristics (past performance and risk, and past performance, respectively), where market-adjusted and raw returns do not. More troubling, though, is that in addition to losing significance, the sign of the related parameter estimate switches to negative for the MM2, MM3, and MM4 and MA2, MA3, and MA4 performance measures. Before giving a judgment on whether we can reject the null Hypothesis 3a, I consider a potential collinearity problem in the next section, which will serve as an important example of why collinearity problems must be carefully considered.

In contrast to the results for the relatedness parameter, the premium × relatedness interaction results show a consistent pattern across the performance measures. The sign of this interaction is slightly negative, with approximately a zero significance level for only the same two periods across the four groups of performance measures (T and 1). In all other cases, the sign is positive. The parameter estimate shows statistical significance in MM2 ($p < .10$), MA01 ($p < .10$, one-tail test), RR01, and RR2 (both $p < .10$, one-tail test). As in the case of the relatedness variable, before giving a conclusion on the interaction, I examine a potential collinearity problem.

Diagnostics. Examining the correlation among the independent variables in Table B.1, we observe that there may be a possible collinearity problem between relatedness (Relindx) and the diversification strategy control variable (Dist4, the number of distinct four-digit SIC codes in the new combined firm) ($r = .51$; $p < .01$). Because the parameter estimates for Dist4 are consistently insignificant, we can justifiably drop this variable from the ordinary least squares regressions and assess the effects of collinearity (Leamer, 1979; Kmenta, 1986).

The parameter estimates of the relatedness variable are the only estimates that are significantly affected. *After removing Dist4, all significance of the relatedness parameters disappears except for RR1* ($p < .05$). Moreover, in the six cases where the sign for the relatedness parameter was negative, only MM4 remains negative with close to zero significance. Therefore, with regard to Hypothesis 3a, I conclude that we cannot reject the null hypothesis of no main effect of relatedness on performance.

Removing the Dist4 variable has no effect on the signs or significance of the parameter estimates of the premium × relatedness interaction term. Given the pattern of signs and significance described above, I conclude that there is, at best, weak support for a positive moderating effect of relatedness on performance.

Method of Payment

Hypothesis 4 predicts that the payment of cash for acquisitions will result in better performance than for the payment of equity.

Market-Adjusted Returns. Tables B.7 through B.13 present results that strongly support this hypothesis. The parameter estimates for cash are positive and strongly significant across all seven time periods of the market-adjusted measures ($b = 3.982$, $p < .01$; $b = 5.267$, $p < .01$; $b = 8.573$, $p < .01$; $b = 13.463$, $p < .01$; $b = 21.872$, $p < .01$; $b = 22.875$, $p < .01$; $b = 16.260$, $p < .10$). Kusewitt (1985:160) has claimed that using cash for acquisitions poses a threat to liquidity and should result in poorer performance than using equity financing. My evidence strongly challenges this proposition. This is discussed further in Chapter 7.

Other Measures. Table B.14 shows the strong positive significance of using cash as the method of payment in acquisitions in all twenty-one of the other measures of acquiring firm performance. The parameter estimate for cash is significant at $p < .01$ or better in all but MM4,

MA4, and RR4, where it is significant at the $p < .05$ level (two-tailed test).

Method of Acquisition

Hypothesis 5a proposes that the implementation of an acquisition through a contested process will result in the payment of a higher acquisition premium than through an uncontested process. No main effect of contestedness is proposed.

Hypothesis 5b proposes the null hypothesis that the implementation of an acquisition through a tender offer will not result in the payment of a higher acquisition premium than through a merger. Hypothesis 5c proposes the null hypothesis that the implementation of an acquisition through a tender offer versus a merger will not have an independent effect on performance.

Results. Table B.6B presents results of the test of Hypothesis 5a. Strong support is found for the hypothesis that contested processes yield significantly higher acquisition premiums than uncontested processes ($p < .01$). I present tests of a main effect of contestedness on performance in the next section.

Table B.6C presents results of the test of Hypothesis 5b. It provides no support for rejecting the null hypothesis that tender offers do not command significantly higher premium payments than mergers. Further, Table B.6D shows that the difference in means between the acquisition premium paid in tender offers versus mergers can be explained by contestedness. This is one of the two major objectives of this analysis (the other is discussed in the following section). The nature of the tender offer versus merger problem is contestedness. Contested tenders command significantly higher premium payments than uncontested tenders ($p < .01$).

Independent Effects of Contestedness and Tender Offers. I have claimed that the only effect of contestedness of an acquisition on acquiring firm performance is its effect on the premium; this is implicit in Hypothesis 5a. Hypothesis 5c explicitly proposes the null hypothesis that there are no independent effects of tender offers versus mergers on acquiring firm performance.

Tables B.6 through B.14 provide strong support for both of these assertions. This was the main purpose of running model specifications 2 and 3 in the cross-sectional regressions, in addition to being able to observe the stability of other coefficients. For each of the twenty-eight measures of performance, Model 2 tests for an independent effect of contestedness, and Model 3 tests for an independent effect of tender offers. In no case is the contestedness or tender offer variable significant in the cross-sectional analysis.

I also conducted (but do not report) simple t-tests of contested versus uncontested acquiring firm performance and tender offer versus merger acquiring firm performance and found no significant difference for either category. Cannella (1991) finds the same results, and thus, we both challenge the assertions of Jemison and Sitkin (1986) that mergers should outperform tender offers. However, I disagree with the claim of Cannella (1991:143) that "pre-acquisition negotiations have no implications for post-acquisition performance." To the extent that these negotiations drive the acquisition premium, they can have *dramatic* implications for post-acquisition performance, as evidenced by my simulations and empirical findings.

Relative Size of the Acquisition

Hypothesis 6 predicts that the relative size of the acquisition will have a negative moderating effect on the relationship between the level of the acquisition premium and acquiring firm performance. No main effect of relative size is proposed.

Market-Adjusted Returns. Tables B.7 through B.13 present results giving moderate support for a negative moderating effect of relative size on the relationship between the acquisition premium and performance. The parameter estimate for relative size is negative in five of seven time periods. The parameter estimate is negative and significant for MK0, MK3, and MK4 ($b = -.089$, $p < .10$; $b = -.861$, $p < .05$; $b = -.671$, $p < .10$, one-tail). For MK1, the parameter estimate is positive and significant ($b = .538$, $p < .05$). However, I caution the interpretation of the positive moderating effect because the parameter for premiums increases in a negative direction over 77 percent when the interaction term is added. Overall, the evidence generally gives support for the negative moderating effect of relative size.

Contrary to my expectations, relative size has a significant main effect in four of the seven time periods of study. However, the signs of the parameter are contingent on the time period of measure. The parameter for relative size is positive and significant in MK0, MK01, and MKT ($b = 2.061$, $p < .10$; $b = 3.291$, $p < .05$; $b = 11.026$, $p < .01$) but negative and significant in MK4 ($b = -23.163$, $p < .05$). The trend is clearly toward a negative effect of relative size in the longer periods of performance measurement. Where the parameter for relative size is insignificant, the parameter is positive in MK1 and MK2 and then negative in MK3. From this analysis, we observe that the conflicting evidence of the effect of relative size of the acquisition in the acquisition literature is perhaps a function of the different time periods that have been studied.

Other Measures. Table B.14 reports results that are generally support-ive of a negative moderating effect of relative size. The parameter esti-mate for the interaction term with the acquisition premium is negative and significant for MM0 ($p < .10$, one-tail), MM3 ($p < .05$), MM4 ($p < .10$), MA0 ($p < .05$), MA3 ($p < .05$), MA4 ($p < .10$, one-tail), RR0 ($p < .05$), and RR3 ($p < .05$). Thus, across all four groups of perfor-mance measures, relative size has a negative and significant moderat-ing effect in the very short- and long-term periods of study. The parameter estimate is positive and significant only for RR1 ($p < .05$). I conclude that there is moderate support for the proposed moderat-ing effect of relative size.

The results for the main effect of relative size are very similar across the four groups of performance measures. Consistently, the relative size parameter is positive and significant in time periods 0, 01, and T. Also, the sign is positive and insignificant in time periods 1 and 2 (i.e., one-year and two-year returns) and negative and insignificant in time period 3 (i.e., three-year returns). Although the parameter estimate for relative size is negative for MM4, MA4, and RR4, it is statistically significant only for RR4. We cannot dismiss a main effect for relative size, but the sign of the parameter depends on the time used for per-formance measurement.

Control Variables

The only control variable for which I find any pattern of consistent significance is the presence of multiple bidders. The parameter estimate for the presence of multiple bidders is negative and significant in the short-term windows only (MK0, MK01, MKT, MM0, MM01, MMT, MA0, MA01, RR0, RR01, RRT; all are $p < .05$, except for MMT and RRT, which are $p < .10$). The short-window findings are consistent with Singh (1984) and You et al. (1986). Over 72 percent of the acquisitions in the sample, however, are single bidder auctions, and the results for the effect of the presence of multiple bidders are independent of the level of the premium. Further, while not reported, no significant difference is found in the premiums paid for multiple-bidder versus single-bidder auctions.

I find the parameter estimate for the number of previous acquisitions positive and significant in a few cases (see Table B.14).

Tests for Changes in Risk Taking

Hypothesis 7 proposed that the higher the acquisition premium, the greater would be the subsequent risk-taking behavior of managers of acquiring firms. I conducted twenty-four separate tests of this hypothesis. I examined the change in variance for two measures over four time periods using two parametric tests and one nonparametric test.

Table B.15 reports the results of the chi-square tests (parametric) for significant increases in variance and the Kolmogorov-Smirnov tests (nonparametric) for any differences in the empirical distribution function of the variance ratio. The latter is a two-sided test that would detect significant increases or decreases in variance based on the premium. No support is found for this hypothesis. The other parametric test run was a one-way ANOVA looking at the change in variance based on the premium. The results were very similar to the chi-square tests. Although not proposed, I conditioned this analysis by manipulating other strategic factors such as size and relatedness and found similar results.

TABLE B.15

F-Tests and Kolmogorov-Smirnov Tests of
Changes in Risk Taking

A. Tests of one-year change in variance

	RR	MK
High Premium	18	12
Low Premium	19	8
K-S test:	$\chi^2 = 0.027$ $D = 0.11$	$\chi^2 = 0.8$ $D = 0.085$

B. Tests of two-year change in variance

	RR	MK
High Premium	25	16
Low Premium	23	19
K-S test:	$\chi^2 = 0.083$ $D = 0.065$	$\chi^2 = 0.257$ $D = 0.137$

C. Tests of three-year change in variance

	RR	MK
High Premium	20	17
Low Premium	25	23
K-S test:	$\chi^2 = 0.56$ $D = 0.107$	$\chi^2 = 0.9$ $D = 0.126$

D. Tests of four-year change in variance

	RA	MK
High Premium	25	20
Low Premium	24	22
K-S test:	$\chi^2 = 0.02$ $D = 0.098$	$\chi^2 = 0.095$ $D = 0.123$

In Table B.15: RR = raw returns, MK = market-adjusted returns.

Summary

Other than the findings for changes in risk taking (Hypothesis 7), my results are generally very supportive of the hypotheses:

1. Acquisition strategies destroy value on average (Hypothesis 1).
2. The level of the acquisition premium has a strong linear negative effect on performance across acquisitions (Hypothesis 2).
3. Some support is found for a positive moderating effect of relatedness between premiums and performance, but no main effect of relatedness is found (Hypotheses 3a and 3b).
4. Conflicting findings of the relatedness literature are replicated by conditioning on the premium, and no significant difference is found for the premiums paid in related versus unrelated acquisitions (Conjectures 1 and 2 on relatedness).
5. The payment of cash for acquisitions has a strong positive effect on performance (Hypothesis 4).
6. Contested acquisitions result in the payment of higher premiums than uncontested acquisitions, whereas this is not found for tender offers versus mergers (Hypotheses 5a and 5b). Further, tender offers versus mergers are not found to have an independent effect on performance (Hypothesis 5c).
7. Moderate support is found for a negative interaction effect of relative size on the relationship between premiums and performance (Hypothesis 6).

Limitations and Future Research

There are a number of important limitations to the research design on acquiring firm performance. Four concerns are prominent: (1) the use of publicly available data, (2) acquisition size, (3) measures of performance and risk taking, and (4) coarse-grained research.

First, this research uses only publicly available acquisition data. Consequently, I exclude a tremendous amount of acquisition activity involving privately owned companies. Given the size, scope, and random nature of my sample, I believe I am capturing a representative sample of corporate strategic acquisitions that occurred during the period. However, public companies are likely to suffer from agency problems compared to private companies where there is a tighter alignment between the interests of the shareholders and the managers. Future research should attempt to examine the difference in acquisition decisions and performance between public and private companies.

Second, I considered only acquisitions that were relatively large enough to be thought of as a significant component of corporate strategy. Admittedly this was an arbitrary designation. There are many acquiring firms that have active acquisition programs of very small acquisitions (relative to the acquiring firm) such as CPC International, pre-1979 Beatrice, and thousands of privately held buyout groups with intricate operating strategies. Given my research design, including these very small acquisitions would have lowered the signal-to-noise ratio and hampered the testing of the major issues at hand. In the future, it will be important to test whether I can generalize the results to acquisitions regardless of their relative size.

Third, I relied solely on shareholder measures in this research. This has been the predominant measure of performance used in the acquisition literature in strategy and is increasingly becoming the standard by which executive compensation contracts are constructed (Rappaport, 1986). Shareholder measures reflect changes in the value of the firm as a result of changes in expectations of future operating performance.

Although little acquisition research in strategy has examined accounting performance, it can be the subject of fruitful research. When accounting performance has been examined, only aggregate measures such as return on assets or return on equity have been used, without controls for accounting treatments. The challenge for acquisition strategy scholars will be to break down these traditional measures into their component parts (tax effects, efficiency, profitability, leverage, etc.). I believe the use of four return generation models over seven time periods is a satisfactory attempt to overcome the traditional criticisms of the short-term nature of shareholder measures of performance. The use of accounting information may also allow us to get a better idea of escalation in resource allocation decisions (i.e., changes in risk taking) that is difficult to detect in shareholder measures.

Finally, this research design was very coarse-grained in nature. This research and much of the acquisition literature in general lacks a fine-grained examination of the economics (both micro and organizational) behind most of the managerial decisions that occur in the management of acquisition strategies. Nevertheless, I have developed a framework that can be used in future research on individual acquisition strategies by describing the nature of strategic resource commitments in acquisitions, the low expected value of synergy, and the acquisition game.

Appendix C:
Sample and Descriptions of Targets
and Acquirers Used in the Analysis

Note: All business descriptions in Appendix C are at the time of acquisition; they are derived from the journal *Mergers and Acquisitions*, various dates.

TARGET		ACQUIRER	
Company Name	Business Description	Company Name	Business Description
Adams-Russell Inc.	Manufactures microwave ovens and electronic products	M/A-COM Inc.	Manufactures semiconductors and circuits
Advanced Systems Inc.	Manufactures and markets multimedia training courses	National Education Corp.	Operates vocational and technical schools; provides training system programs and services
Allied Maintenance Corp.	Provides office cleaning services; dispenses aviation fuel at airports	Ogden Corp.	A transportation, industrial products, and services concern
AMEDCO Inc.	Manufactures caskets, burial garments, hospital beds and related health care equipment	Service Corp. International	The largest operator of funeral homes in the United States
American Broadcasting Cos. Inc.	Engages in broadcasting, publishing, and the operation of leisure attractions	Capital Cities Communications Inc.	Operates radio and TV broadcasting stations; publishes newspapers and magazines; has franchise to construct and operate cable TV systems
American Hospital Supply Corp.	Manufactures and distributes healthcare products to hospitals, laboratories, and medical specialists	Baxter Travenol Laboratories	Manufactures a variety of medical care products for hospitals, clinics, blood and kidney dialysis centers, and in-house patient care
American Motor Inns Inc.	Operates motels, restaurants, and telephone systems	Prime Motor Inns Inc.	Operates motels, gas stations; acts as general contractor for construction
American Natural Resources Inc.	Operates natural gas pipeline system and regional trucking services; processes coal and synthetic fuel	Coastal Corp.	An integrated oil and gas company that operates a pipeline system from Texas to Wyoming
American Stores Co.	Operates 936 food stores, drugstores, and restaurants	Skaggs Cos.	Operates 227 retail super drug and food centers

Company	Description	Company	Description
Anchor Hocking Corp	Manufactures packaging products and household products	Newell Co.	Manufactures and markets household products
Anderson Clayton & Co.	Manufactures and markets food products; provides life and automobile insurance services	Quaker Oats Co.	Manufactures and markets food products; operates hard-to-find tools and gift stores, men's and women's clothing stores, and eyewear products stores
Anderson, Greenwood & Co.	Manufactures safety-relief valves, hand valves, instrument manifolds, and related safety valves	Keystone International Inc.	Manufactures butterfly valves and actuators
Aro Corp.	Manufactures air-powered equipment such as hoists, valves, and aeronautical life support products	Todd Shipyards Corp.	Engages in commercial and defense shipbuilding
Associated Dry Goods Corp.	Operates 440 retail stores in the United States	May Department Stores Co.	Operates 145 department stores in 15 states
Avco Corp.	Manufactures propulsion systems; provides financial and management services	Textron Inc.	Manufactures industrial and consumer products, aerospace and electronic products
Bangor Punta Corp.	Manufactures light aircraft and boats	Lear Siegler Inc.	Manufactures systems for commercial and military aerospace industries, machine tools, automotive products, and electronics
Beckman Instruments Inc.	Manufactures industrial and scientific instruments, specialty chemicals, and precision electronics parts	SmithKline Corp.	Manufactures ethical pharmaceuticals, over-the-counter medicines, veterinary and eye care products, and operates clinical laboratories

Table continues

	TARGET		ACQUIRER
Company Name	Business Description	Company Name	Business Description
Beech Aircraft Corp.	Engages in private aircraft, aerospace, and defense business	Raytheon Co.	A diversified electronic concern
Belco Petroleum Corp.	Engages in the exploration, production, and sale of natural gas and crude oil	InterNorth Inc.	Owns and operates natural gas business; engages in the production, transportation, and marketing of liquid fuels and petrochemicals; engages in the exploration and production of oil and gas
Buffalo Forge Co.	Manufactures machine tools, pumps, and other equipment	Ampco-Pittsburgh Corp.	Produces railroad freight cars, forging, and fabricated parts
Bunker-Ramo Corp.	Manufactures electrical parts	Allied Corp.	Manufactures chemicals, plastics, fibers, electrical and electronic products
C&K Petroleum Inc.	Engages in oil and gas operations in the United States	Alaska Interstate Co.	Engages in oil and gas exploration and development
Caldor Inc.	Operates a regional chain of discount department stores	Associated Dry Goods Corp.	Operates department stores and wholesalers
California Computer Products Inc.	Produces computer peripheral equipment	Sanders Associates Inc.	Develops, manufactures, and sells high-technology electronic and electromechanical systems and products
Cameron Iron Works Inc.	Designs, manufactures, and markets oil field tools and equipment	Cooper Industries Inc.	Manufactures electrical and electronic components, commercial and industrial products, and compression and drilling products
Campbell Taggart Inc.	The second largest U.S. producer of bread and bread-related products	Anheuser-Busch Inc.	Produces and distributes beer and sells yeast and snack foods

Celeron Corp.	A natural gas transmission company
Cessna Aircraft Co.	Designs and manufactures aircraft and fluid power components
Champion Spark Plug Co.	Manufactures automobile components and cold-drawn steel
Chicago Pacific Corp.	Produces washers, dryers, refrigerators, dishwashers, and microwave ovens; manufactures floor care products and furniture
Chilton Corp.	Provides consumer credit reports, related data processing services, and collection of past-due accounts
Clausing Corp.	Engages in industrial distribution and plastics engineering; manufactures press controls
Cluett, Peabody & Co. Inc.	Produces and markets men's and women's apparel and accessories
CoastAmerica Corp.	Franchises and operates hardware stores
Goodyear Tire & Rubber Co.	Manufactures tires, chemicals, vehicle wheels, and industrial roofing
General Dynamics Corp.	Builds submarines, fighter planes, commercial aircraft, space systems, and tactical missiles
Cooper Industries Inc.	Manufactures electrical and electronic components, commercial and industrial products, and compression and drilling products
Maytag Corp.	Produces appliance, vending, and ventilation equipment
Borg-Warner Corp.	Manufactures automatic and manual transmission systems and components, air-conditioning equipment, industrial seals and valves, and chemicals and plastics
Rexnord Inc.	Manufactures mechanical and hydraulic power transmission components and water pollution control equipment
West Point-Pepperell Inc.	Produces industrial, apparel, and household fabrics of cotton and synthetic fibers
American Hoist & Derrick Co.	Manufactures industrial products and distributes hardware products

Table continues

	TARGET		ACQUIRER
Company Name	Business Description	Company Name	Business Description
Colonial Penn Group Inc.	An insurance holding company that engages in administering, insuring, and reinsuring life, health, automobile, and home owners' insurance policies	FPL Group Inc.	A holding company with interests in utilities, financial services, real estate development, and cable television
Columbia Pictures Industries Inc.	A major motion picture studio active in television, cable television, and home video	Coca-Cola Co.	Bottles soft drinks and makes other beverage products
Computervision Corp.	Develops, manufactures, and services computer-aided design and manufacturing systems	Prime Computer Inc.	Manufactures a broad line of computers
Conoco Inc.	Produces petroleum, crude oil, natural gas, coal, and chemicals	E. I. du Pont de Nemours & Co.	The nation's largest chemical firm
Contel Corp.	Provides telephone operations and information systems	GTE Corp.	Provides telephone operations; manufactures telecommunication products and electrical products
CP National Corp.	Supplies electric, gas, and telephone service; markets electronic equipment and makes electronic signal processing equipment and graphic display terminals	ALLTEL Corp.	Provides local service and toll service access to customer lines and sells telecommunication equipment

Crouse-Hinds Co.	Manufactures electrical products, including lighting and wiring products
Cooper Industries Inc.	Manufactures consumer and industrial tools and mining and construction equipment; provides aircraft services
Crum and Forster	A property and liability insurance holding company
Xerox Corp.	Manufactures copiers, duplicators, and electronic printers and makes office information system and products
Day International Corp.	Manufactures rubber and plastic products, industrial and transportation products
M. A. Hanna Co.	Extracts oil and gas, mixes polymer compounds, and produces ferrosilicon and silicon metals
Development Corp. of America	Engages in residential and commercial real estate development, title insurance and mortgage financing services, and a coal mine operation
Lennar Corp.	Engages in residential and commercial real estate development and cable TV services
Dillon Cos Inc.	Operates supermarket and convenience stores
Kroger Co.	The nation's second largest supermarket chain
Dyco Petroleum Corp.	Engages in oil and gas exploration; manages public drilling investment programs
Diversified Energies Inc.	Engages in gas distribution
E-II Holdings Inc.	Engages in consumer products and specialty foods businesses
American Brands Inc.	Engages in tobacco printing, foil laminating, and insurance operations; produces food products
E. F. Johnson Co.	Manufactures mobile communications parts and electronics parts
Western Union Corp.	Provides telecommunication systems and services to business, government, and the public

Table continues

	TARGET	ACQUIRER	
Company Name	Business Description	Company Name	Business Description
Earth Resources Co.	Refines and markets petroleum; operates retail gasoline stations; transports crude oil; manufactures and sells paving materials	Mapco Inc.	Produces oil, gas, and gas liquids; operates coal properties
Eltra Corp.	Manufactures electrical products, consumer and industrial products	Allied Chemical Corp.	Manufactures chemicals
Emery Air Freight Corp.	Provides worldwide air cargo services	Consolidated Freightways Inc.	Engages in common and contract carrier trucking of commodities; offers motor carrier and specialized truckload and rail piggy–back services
Emhart Corp.	Manufactures door locks and gardening tools	Black & Decker Corp.	Manufactures power tools and household appliances
Esmark Inc.	Manufactures food, chemicals, and personal products; provides auto leasing	Beatrice Cos. Inc..	Manufactures processing and distributes food, consumer, industrial, and chemical products
Ex–Cell–O Corp.	Manufactures agricultural and industrial machine tool and equipment, and automotive replacement components	Textron Inc.	Manufactures industrial and commercial equipment and parts and specialty consumer products; provides financial services
Fairchild Industries Inc.	Manufactures space and space defense electronics, industrial products, and aerospace fasteners; engages in communications services	Banner Industries Inc.	Conducts operations in the aerospace industry and the wastewater treatment industry
Felmont Oil Corp.	Engages in exploration and production of oil and gas	Homestake Mining Co.	Operates gold, silver, lead-zinc, and uranium mines

Fisher Scientific Intl. Inc.	Manufactures laboratory and hospital equipment	Allied Corp.	Makes chemicals, plastics, fibers, electrical and electronic products
Flintkote Co.	Manufactures building materials	Genstar	Involved in production of building materials, venture capital investment, housing, land development, financial services, construction, tug and barge transportation, shipbuilding and ship repair
FoxMeyer Corp.	A drug and personal care product wholesaler	National Intergroup Inc.	Manufactures and markets aluminum and finished aluminum products
G. C. Murphy Co.	Operates 383 discount stores in 19 states	Ames Department Stores Inc.	Operates 184 discount stores in 11 northeastern states
G. D. Searle & Co.	Manufactures and markets pharmaceuticals, consumer products, and NutraSweet	Monsanto Co.	Manufactures and markets a variety of industrial and agricultural chemicals, plastics, and fibers
Gardner-Denver Co.	Manufactures drilling equipment, other industrial equipment, and electronic wiring tools	Cooper Industries Inc.	Manufactures hand tools; provides aircraft services and energy services
Garfinckel, Brooks Brothers, Miller & Rhoads, Inc.	Operates retailing clothing store chain	Allied Stores Corp.	Operates department and specialty stores
General American Oil Co. of Texas	Produces crude oil and natural gas	Phillips Petroleum Co.	Refines, transports, and markets crude oil, natural gas liquids, and petroleum products
General Care Corp.	Operates seven hospitals	Hospital Corp. of America	Operates 158 hospitals

Table continues

| TARGET | | ACQUIRER | |
Company Name	Business Description	Company Name	Business Description
General Foods Corp.	Processes and packages grocery and meat products	Philip Morris Companies. Inc.	Manufactures and markets cigarettes, printing and specialty papers, beers and soft drinks; engages in real estate development
General Steel Industries Inc.	Manufactures cast-iron and steel rolls, heavy-duty vibrating screens, conveyors, feeders, and foundry shakeouts	Lukens Steel Co.	Produces plate steel and plate steel shapes
Getty Oil Co.	The fourteenth largest integrated oil company in the United States	Texaco Inc.	The third largest integrated oil company in the United States
Gray Drug Stores Inc.	Operates a chain of drugstores	Sherwin-Williams Co.	Manufactures chemicals, paints, and other coatings
Great Northern Nekoosa Corp.	Produces paper products, lumber, plywood, coal and by-products; engages in railroad business	Georgia-Pacific Corp.	Manufactures and distributes forest products
Gulf Corp.	The fifth largest oil company in the United States	Standard Oil Co. of California	The fourth largest oil company in the United States
Gulfstream Aerospace Corp.	Designs, sells, and services fan-jet and turboprop aircraft	Chrysler Corp.	Manufactures and markets passenger cars, trucks, related automotive parts and accessories, and inboard marine and industrial engines; provides financial services
H. Miller & Sons Inc.	Builds and sells single- and multi-family homes on company-developed land	Lennar Corp.	A national real estate developer

Company	Description	Company	Description
Hammermill Paper Co.	Markets hardwood and softwood lumber, engages in paper business, and operates a railroad company	International Paper Co.	Engages in paper business, oil and gas drilling, mineral development, and industrial real estate
Harrah's Inc.	Operates casinos and hotels in Reno and Lake Tahoe, Nevada	Holiday Inns Inc.	The largest concern in the lodging industry in the United States
Heublein Inc.	Markets wine, spirits, and grocery products and operates KFC franchises	R. J. Reynolds Tobacco Inc.	A tobacco, food, energy, and shipping company
Hoover Universal Inc.	Manufactures plastic parts and seating for automobiles, consumer components, and industrial products and systems	Johnson Controls Inc.	Designs, manufactures, installs, and services automated control systems of heating and air-conditioning
Houston Natural Gas Corp.	Engages in transmission and sale of natural gas, exploration and production of oil and gas, and operation of gas-gathering systems	InterNorth Inc.	Engages in wholesale, retail, and transportation of natural gas; produces and markets liquid fuels and petrochemicals
Houston Oil & Minerals Corp.	An oil and gas exploration firm	Tenneco Inc.	A holding company with interests in chemicals, packaging, petroleum products, land use, and manufacturing
Hughes Tool Co.	Manufactures and markets oil field, mining, and construction tools and products	Baker International Corp.	Manufactures petroleum and mining equipment
Inexco Oil Co.	Engages in oil and gas exploration and production	Louisiana Land & Exploration	Explores for, develops, and sells oil, gas, natural gas liquids, and minerals (primarily copper)

Table continues

	TARGET		ACQUIRER	
Company Name	Business Description	Company Name	Business Description
Integon Corp.	An insurance holding company	Ashland Oil Inc.	A diversified oil marketer, refiner, and chemical concern
Interpace Corp.	Manufactures industrial machinery, building products, and insulators for electric utility poles	Clevepak Corp.	Manufactures fans and blowers, cardboard boxes and tubes, and industrial products
Iowa Beef Processors	The nation's largest beef packer	Occidental Petroleum Corp.	The nation's thirteenth largest energy company
Jonathan Logan Inc.	Manufactures women's dresses, blouses, and sportswear and girls' underwear and sleepwear	United Merchants & Manufacturers Inc.	Manufactures rayon, cotton, print cloth, nylon, silk, wool, Dacron, glass, and plastic fabrics
Kennecott Corp.	The nation's largest copper producer	Standard Oil Co. (Ohio)	An integrated petroleum company
Kenner Parker Toys Inc.	Manufactures toys, including action figures, trucks, stuffed animals, and staple toys, and board and card games (e.g., Monopoly)	Tonka Corp.	Manufactures toys, including toy robots, trucks, action figures, and plush and soft fabric puppies
Key Pharmaceuticals Inc.	Manufactures ethical drug products	Schering–Plough Corp.	Manufactures pharmaceutical and consumer health products
Kraft Inc.	Manufactures and distributes consumer foods and food services; specializes in cheeses and dressings	Philip Morris Cos. Inc.	The largest tobacco company in the United States; owns Miller Beer and General Foods Corp., a major food processor

Lanier Business Products Inc.	Manufactures office automation products
Lifemark Corp.	The fifth largest hospital management company in the United States, with major business in the South
Lucky Stores Inc.	Operates 483 supermarkets, primarily in California
M. Lowenstein Corp.	Manufactures Wamsutta household goods; makes finished fabrics for consumer textile products and operates 19 plants
Magic Chef Inc.	Manufactures and markets household and commercial appliances
Manhattan Industries Inc.	Manufactures and markets men's and women's apparel
Maryland Cup Corp.	Manufactures and distributes a variety of single-use paper and plastic products for food and beverage services, and other packaging and food products
Masonite Corp.	Has interests in timber, building materials, furniture parts, flooring, and paneling
Harris Corp.	Manufactures information processing and communication equipment
American Medical International Inc.	The third largest hospital management company in the United States
American Stores Co.	Operates 1,593 food and drug stores in 40 states
Springs Industries Inc.	Manufactures finished fabrics and home furnishing products
Maytag Co.	Manufactures and markets household and commercial appliances
Salant Corp.	Manufactures men's slacks, men's and boys' jeans, children's sleepwear and playwear
Fort Howard Paper Co.	Manufactures disposable paper products
U.S. Gypsum Co.	Manufactures building materials and gypsum products

Table continues

TARGET		ACQUIRER	
Company Name	Business Description	Company Name	Business Description
Mass Merchandisers Inc.	Distributes health and beauty products, housewares, hardware, and non-food items to supermarkets	McKesson Corp.	Manufactures and distributes drugs and health care products, food, liquors, wire products, and chemicals
McGraw–Edison Co.	Manufactures electric energy–related products for industrial, commercial, and utility use	Cooper Industries Inc.	Manufactures compressors for the oil and gas industry, and electrical and electronic products, tools, and hardware
MetPath Inc.	Operates clinical testing laboratories	Corning Glass Works Inc.	Manufactures glass products, medical instruments, and diagnostic products
MGM Grand Hotels Inc.	Operates casinos and hotels	Bally Manufacturing Corp.	Operates amusement parks, health clubs, and a casino; manufactures and distributes video games
Michigan Energy Resources Co.	Engages in gas utility business, cable TV, and radio broadcasting operations	UtiliCorp United Inc.	Supplies electrical utility services in north-central and west-central Missouri and a portion of Kansas City, Missouri
MidCon Corp.	Operates natural gas pipelines; explores for and develops oil, gas, and other mines	Occidental Petroleum Corp.	Engages in oil and natural gas exploration and production; operates coal mines; manufactures and markets industrial chemicals; beef processing
Miller–Wohl Co. Inc.	Operates women's specialty stores	Petrie Stores Corp.	Operates a chain of women's apparel stores
MITE Corp.	Manufactures fasteners, time stamps, and rotary dies	Emhart Corp.	Manufactures a variety of commercial, industrial and component products
Modern Merchandising Inc.	The nation's largest operator of catalog showrooms	Best Products Co. Inc.	The nation's largest catalog showroom merchandiser

Moore McCormack Resources Inc.	Produces cement, concrete products, and aggregates
Moran Energy Inc.	Engages in oil and gas exploration and production
NCR Corp.	Manufactures, markets, installs, and services business information processing systems
Nevada Savings & Loan Association	A state-chartered stock association in Nevada with interests in real estate development, mortgage banking, and mobile home and recreational vehicle loans
NLT Corp.	An insurance holding company that owns insurance operations, radio stations, and the Grand Ole Opry
Northwest Energy Co.	Engages in natural gas pipeline system operation, oil and natural gas exploration
Oscar Mayer & Co.	Produces processed meat
Overnite Transportation Co.	A trucking company with operations in the Northeast, Southeast, and Great Lakes regions
Southdown Inc.	Produces cement and ready-mixed concrete
Kaneb Services Inc.	Engages in contract drilling, coal production and marketing, and pipeline transportation
American Telephone & Telegraph Inc.	Provides products, services, and systems for the movement and management of information
Southwest Gas Corp.	A natural gas company operating in California, Nevada, and Arizona
American General Corp.	An insurance holding company with interests in insurance, finance, and mutual funds
Williams Cos.	Engages in fertilizer, energy, and metal processing businesses
General Foods Corp.	A coffee and packaged food company
Union Pacific Corp.	Has interests in railroads, natural resources, energy, and real estate development

Table continues

TARGET		ACQUIRER	
Company Name	Business Description	Company Name	Business Description
Ozark Holdings Inc.	Provides scheduled air transportation services to 66 cities in the United States, with businesses centered in the Midwest	Trans World Airlines Inc.	Provides domestic and international passenger and cargo air services
Peavey Co.	Produces flour, merchandises grain, and operates fabric stores and commodities brokerages	ConAgra Inc.	Processes and merchandises grain and produces feeds, fertilizers, and foods
PennCorp Financial Inc.	Provides life insurance, supplemental accident and health coverage, credit and student accident insurance	American Can Co.	Engages in packaging, financial services, and specialty retailing
Petrolane Inc.	Markets liquified petroleum gas; operates retail automotive products outlets; provides petroleum services	Texas Eastern Corp.	Operates natural gas pipeline and supplies liquid-petroleum products
Piedmont Aviation Inc.	Provides domestic airline services; sells aircraft and related parts and supplies	USAir Group Inc.	Provides airline services for 83 airports with 147 aircraft
Planning Research Corp.	A technology-based professional company for computer software design, integration of hardware, telecommunications, system engineering, and civil and aerospace engineering	Emhart Corp.	Produces hardware, industrial and commercial adhesives, fastening systems, and electronic and consumer products

Prentice-Hall Inc.	Publishes college and professional textbooks
Primerica Corp.	A financial services and specialty retailing company
Purolator Courier Corp.	Delivers commodities and documents; makes filters, caps, and other products for automotive and specialized filtration markets
RCA Corp.	A diversified manufacturer and marketer of electronic products
Republic Airlines Inc.	Provides scheduled air transportation services to 98 cities in the United States, Canada, and the Caribbean; provides charter flights, mainly in the United States
Republic Steel Corp.	The fourth largest steelmaker in the country
Gulf & Western Industries Inc.	Engages in financial services, movie and television production, music and book publishing; manufactures industrial equipment and controls; manufactures and distributes automotive parts, electronics, machinery, food and consumer products
Commercial Credit Group Inc.	Provides consumers with lending and savings products and credit-related insurance; engages in property and casualty and financial services insurance
Emery Air Freight Corp.	Provides domestic and international air cargo services
General Electric Co.	A diversified manufacturer and marketer of electronic products
NWA Inc.	Provides scheduled air transportation services to 74 cities in the United States, Canada, Guam, Western Europe, and the Far East
LTV Corp.	The third largest steel producer in the country

Table continues

TARGET		ACQUIRER	
Company Name	Business Description	Company Name	Business Description
Richardson Co.	Makes specialty chemicals and engineered metals and products	Witco Chemical Corp.	Manufactures specialty chemicals and petroleum products
Sanders Associates Inc.	Makes electronic equipment and systems	Lockheed Corp.	Designs and produces aircraft, missiles, spacecraft, electronic systems, and ocean vessels; provides related repair and maintenance services
Sargent-Welch Scientific Co.	Manufactures and distributes analytical instruments and related products	ARTRA Group INC.	Manufactures and distributes costume and fashion jewelry, medical diagnostic ultrasound devices, and household products
Sav-On Drugs Inc.	Operates 145 drugstores in California, Texas, and Nevada	Jewel Cos. Inc.	A diversified food and drug retailer
Sea-Land Corp.	Engages in containerized freight shipping	CSX Corp.	Has interests in railway operations, pipeline systems, commercial barge operations, real estate development, coal mining, and aviation
Shearson Loeb Rhoades Inc.	The nation's second largest securities firm	American Express Co.	Provides travel, insurance, and international banking services
Signal Cos. Inc.	A diversified high-technology concern with interests in aerospace, electronics, information processing, engineering, and construction services	Allied Corp.	Has interests in oil and gas, chemical, and automotive, aerospace, industrial, and technological products
Sikes Corp.	Manufactures glazed ceramic wall, floor tile, and trim	Premark International Inc.	Manufactures Tupperware, food equipment, and consumer and decorative products

Silo Inc.	Sells appliances, television sets, and audio products
Cyclops Corp.	Produces steel and steel-fabricated products of industrial and commercial construction; sells retail construction products
Simmonds Precision Products Inc.	Designs, manufactures, and sells fuel gauging and management systems, engine ignition systems, electrical power systems, and motion control systems used mainly in aerospace applications
Hercules Inc.	Manufactures a diversified line of chemicals and allied products
Southwest Forest Industries	Manufactures and markets paper, packaging, and building products; engages in railroad operation
Stone Container Corp.	Manufactures packaging products and machinery systems
Spectro Industries Inc.	Wholesales pharmaceutical and toiletry items; manufactures hospital beds and other medical, laboratory, and health care equipment
McKesson Corp.	Manufactures and distributes drugs and health care products, food, liquors, wire products, and chemicals
Sperry Corp.	Manufactures, sells, rents, and services computer systems
Burroughs Corp.	Designs, manufactures, and markets computer systems and related equipment
Squibb Corp.	Manufactures and sells pharmaceutical and medical products
Bristol-Myers Co.	Manufactures toiletries and beauty aids, pharmaceutical, medical, nonprescription health, and household products
St. Joe Minerals Corp.	Produces lead, zinc, coal, and other minerals
Fluor Corp.	An international construction and engineering concern

Table continues

TARGET		ACQUIRER	
Company Name	Business Description	Company Name	Business Description
St. Regis Corp.	Has interests in paper, packaging, insurance, and energy	Champion International Corp.	A forest products company
Sterchi Bros. Stores Inc.	Operates retailing home furnishing and consumer electronic equipment stores	Heilig-Meyers Co.	Operates retailing, home furnishing, and consumer electronic equipment stores
Sterling Drug Inc.	Manufactures and markets medicinal and pharmaceutical preparations; makes household and other products	Eastman Kodak Co.	Manufactures and markets camera, film, photofinishing equipment, video equipment, and copiers
Stokely–Van Camp Inc.	Processes and markets food products	Quaker Oats Co.	Has interests in food, toys, and specialty retailing
Studebaker Worthington	Manufactures equipment and provides services for raw materials processing and energy industries	McGraw Edison	Manufactures products used in transmission of energy
Suburban Propane Gas Corp.	Markets propane and engages in oil and gas operations	National Distillers & Chemicals Corp.	A beverage and chemical company
Sunbeam Corp.	Manufactures consumer appliances and industrial and commercial equipment	Allegheny International Inc.	Produces specialty metals, piping, components, industrial gases, and industrial, consumer, and other products
Superior Oil Co.	Engages in oil and gas exploration for and production of oil and gas	Mobil Corp.	Engages in petroleum operations, retail merchandising, and paperboard packaging
Technicon Corp.	Manufactures automatic systems that analyze blood samples and medical information systems	Revlon Inc.	Produces beauty and health products

Teleprompter Corp.	A cable television operator
Texas Eastern Corp.	Engages in oil and gas exploration and refining operations
Texas Gas Resources Corp.	Operates gas transmission, inland waterways, oil and gas, and development
Thiokol Corp.	Produces specialty chemicals, defense and space-related rocket propulsion systems, and motors
Ticor Inc.	The largest real estate title insurance business in the United States
Tiger International Inc.	An international carrier of freight and mail; provides specialty trucking services
Trane Co.	Manufactures air-conditioning equipment
UniDynamics Corp.	Produces defense systems, engineered materials, factory automation systems, and merchandising systems
United Financial Corp. of California	Engages in financial services and savings and loan services
Westinghouse Electric	Manufactures electric equipment; provides network broadcasting services
Panhandle Eastern Corp.	Engages in natural gas transportation and coal and gas processing
CSX Corp.	Engages in railroad freight operations and natural resources development
Morton-Norwich Products Inc.	Produces salt, household products, and specialty chemicals
Southern Pacific Co.	Engages in diversified railroad operations
Federal Express Corp.	Provides overnight, door-to-door delivery services for packages and documents
American Standard Inc.	Manufactures plumbing and other building products, railway and automotive braking devices, and graphic products
Crane Co.	Produces steel, cement, and other building products, pollution-control devices, and aircraft systems
National Steel Corp.	One of the major steel manufacturers in the United States

Table continues

	TARGET		ACQUIRER	
Company Name	Business Description	Company Name	Business Description	
Universal-Rundle Corp.	Manufactures bathroom fixtures and cabinets	Nortek Inc.	Manufactures building supplies and metal products; engages in dyeing, finishing, and printing textile materials	
Varo Inc.	Manufactures navigational and night-viewing systems and other military gear; makes power conversion products, weapon delivery systems, reflective metal optics, and optical assemblies	Imo Delaval Inc.	Supplies analytical and optical instruments; makes instruments and controls such as tank level, indicators and transducers, screw-type fuel pumps, worm gear sets, steam turbines, compressors, and steam condensers	
VSI Corp.	Manufactures precision metal products; distributes hardware and electronics components to wholesalers and retailers	Fairchild Industries Inc.	A diversified aerospace, industrial and commercial products, and communications company	
Wallace Murray Corp.	Manufactures and sells plumbing products, engine components, tools, gears, heating and ventilating equipment, and electronic products	Household International Inc.	A diversified concern with interest in financial services, merchandising, manufacturing, and transportation	
Western Air Lines Inc.	The ninth largest carrier in the United States with routes covering the West	Delta Air Lines Inc.	The sixth largest carrier in the United States with routes covering most of the East and Southeast	
Western Publishing Co. Inc.	Produces and distributes adult and juvenile books and games, puzzles and craft products; provides commercial printing services	Mattel Inc.	Manufactures toys and hobby products; provides leisure and entertainment services	

Signal Cos. Inc.	Manufactures audio and video products; engages in aerospace and petroleum-related businesses
Sunshine Mining Co.	Operates silver and gold mines
Square D Co.	Manufactures electrical equipment
Wheelabrator Frye Inc.	An engineering and construction company; manufactures pollution control equipment
Woods Petroleum Corp.	Owns oil and gas reserves
Yates Industries Inc.	Manufactures electro-deposited copper foil

Notes

Chapter 1: Introduction: The Acquisition Game

1. Terence P. Pare, "The New Merger Boom," *Fortune,* November 28, 1994, p. 96.
2. *Securities Data Company.*
3. Consult Mueller (1995) for a review and discussion of recent merger and acquisition activity.
4. Recent research by Steven Kaplan of the University of Chicago, in Zangwill (1995).
5. See, for example, Magenheim and Mueller (1988), Agrawal, Jaffe, and Mandelker (1992), Sirower (1994), and Mueller and Sirower (1996) for a discussion of the evidence of longer-term declines in the wealth of the shareholders of acquirers.
6. See Copeland, Koller, and Murrin (1994), Chapter 14, for a complete description of the study by the McKinsey & Company's Corporate Leadership Center.
7. See, for example, Sirower and Harrigan (1996) on the issues of dominant logic and organizational learning in acquiring firms and Zollo (1996) on organization learning from an evolutionary economics perspective.
8. See Zangwill (1995) for a description of the study. The Boston Consulting Group found that less than 20 percent of companies had considered, prior to the acquisition, the steps needed to integrate the acquisition into their company. This statistic alone should bring almost any acquisition premium we observe under serious scrutiny.
9. See Phillip L. Zweig, "The Case Against Mergers," *Business Week* Special Report, October 30, 1995, p. 125.
10. See *Mergerstat Review* (1996): p. 8.
11. See *Wall Street Journal,* November 20, 1991, p. C1.

12. See Miller and Modigliani (1961). It should be emphasized that V represents the value of the firm, not necessarily the value of the assets. Only when the firm does not pay taxes will the value of the firm equal the value of the assets. I introduce the $V = D + E$ concept here to develop the idea of an economic balance sheet and value transfer.

13. From *GSB Chicago* (Autumn 1986), as quoted in Ross, Westerfield, and Jaffe (1993:435).

14. G. Bennett Stewart III, *The Quest for Value* (New York: Harper Business, 1991), p. 383.

15. G. Pascal Zachary, "Novell Pact with WordPerfect Followed a Secret Bidding War Initiated by Lotus," *Wall Street Journal,* March 24, 1994, p. A3; Rosanna Tamburri and Don Clark, "Corel to Acquire Novell's WordPerfect for $124 Million in Cash and Stock," *Wall Street Journal,* February 1, 1996, p. A3.

16. See Appendix A of this book and the accompanying tables for a review.

17. See Appendix A of this book and the accompanying tables for a review of returns to acquirers in the 1980s.

18. For example, consult Magenheim and Mueller (1988) for evidence and Ruback (1988b) for a comment on this issue.

19. On profitability results, consult Ravenscraft and Scherer (1987a, 1987b, 1988, 1989); on market share declines, consult Mueller (1985). For a thorough review of this literature, see Mueller (1995) and Jarrell (1995).

20. Consult Roll (1986). The hubris hypothesis has been the subject of significant debate within the finance literature (Shleifer and Vishny, 1988; Morck, Shleifer, and Vishny, 1990). Morck, Shleifer, and Vishny, in particular, present results that support the hypothesis that managers are simply pursuing their own objectives (e.g., salary, growth) at the expense of their shareholders. The hubris hypothesis is essentially a special case of the winner's curse from auction theory (Varaiya, 1988). That is, in a *common* value auction (the asset has the same value to all bidders), the highest bidder will likely have the highest positive valuation error. In Roll's model, it is assumed that markets are strong form efficient, meaning all potential gains are known by the markets and already impounded in the target firm before the actual bid. The most important assumption that this hubris view rests on is that the observed bid represents the true underlying beliefs of the decision maker. Given the multitude of players involved in generating and promoting this bid and the acquisition itself (Haspeslagh and Jemison, 1991), this assumption is easily challenged from a practical perspective.

21. See Mueller (1989:7), a wonderful review and critique. It is required reading for managers and researchers interested in acquisitions.

22. Consult Rumelt (1974). This research remains one of the most influential works in the field of strategic management.

23. Consult, for example, Seth (1990a, 1990b) and Appendix A of this book for a review of this literature.

24. In a competitive market, factor prices are bid up to their value to the buyer (Barney, 1986a; Peteraf, 1993).

25. Given the existence of a competitive market for corporate control where bids represent their value to the acquirer, only when firms are lucky (Barney, 1986a, 1988) or when there are limits to this competition (Peteraf, 1993) will there be excess returns to bidders. The post-acquisition integration process literature has implicitly assumed this competitive markets view. Because prices represent potential, it must be post-acquisition problems that prevent performance gains from being "released." See Haspeslagh and Jemison (1991) for a thorough review of this literature.

26. Consult Jemison and Sitkin (1986a, 1986b) and Haspeslagh and Jemison (1991). This important research develops and describes the problems of fragmented perspectives, ambiguous expectations, multiple motives, and increasing momentum surrounding the acquisition decision. It is this research that drives home the importance of understanding the fundamentals of the acquisition game.

Chapter 2: Can You Run Harder? Synergy

1. Anne B. Fisher, "How to Make a Merger Work," *Fortune,* January 24, 1994, p. 66. Warren Hellman's statement is in stark contrast to Barry Diller's quotation in the epigraph. See Elizabeth Jensen, Mark Robichaux, and Greg Steinmetz, "Larry-Barry Show: Is CBS in Play Now? If Merger Is 'Strategic,' What Is the Strategy?" *Wall Street Journal,* July 1, 1994, p. A1.

2. Consult Haspeslagh and Jemison (1991:Ch. 6) for an excellent conceptual overview of the organizational situations where this type of problem is common.

3. The assumptions in this analysis for Lotus Development, Scott Paper, Wal-Mart and Microsoft, respectively, are as follows: (1) 1994 year-end market values (millions): $2,113, $7,645, $61,555, $35,689; (2) 1994 year-end invested capital (millions): $1,349, $4,852, $26,559, $5,785; (3) capital growth rate assumption (one-third of trailing five-year compounded capital growth rate): 3.9 percent, 0.4 percent, 10.6 percent, 16.1 percent; (4) projected market value at 2004 year end (millions): $4,793, $12,078, $142,551, $86,303; (5) weighted average costs of capital: 17.87 percent, 10.80 percent, 9.64 percent, 14.37 percent.

4. Consult Mahoney and Pandian (1992) and Peteraf (1993) for thorough discussions of the resource-based view and the classic Prahalad and Hamel (1990) for a discussion of core competence.

5. Consult Jacobson (1992) for an "Austrian" economics approach to strategy and the similarities between this approach and the resource-based view of the firm. Although these approaches are invaluable in understanding business success or failure ex post, they offer little in the way of differentiating between strategic alternatives ex ante.

6. For a detailed description, consult Porter (1985:Ch. 2).

7. The use of the word *contestability* is not an attempt to bring contestability theory (Baumol, Panzar, and Willig, 1982) into the fold. My objective here is to emphasize the synergy problem as a problem of competitiveness and establish necessary conditions to move away from treating synergy as some mysterious occurrence that is to be "released" because of a given acquisition. Competitive advantage for any business as a stand-alone is a fleeting concept, and synergy must be increases in this advantage (Sirower and Harrigan, 1996). Ghemawat (1991) is an excellent source for a motivation of this argument. Also consult the important research on action and response of competitors (Chen and MacMillan, 1992) and the nature of the resources involved in driving competitor reactions (Chen, 1996).

8. Richard A. Melcher, "How Eagle Became Extinct," *Business Week,* March 4, 1996, pp. 68–69.

9. Tim Smart, "Defying the Law of Gravity," *Business Week,* April 8, 1996, p. 124.

10. Ibid., p. 127.

11. Jeff Cole, "McDonnell Plans to Shift Its Purchases," *Wall Street Journal,* April 18, 1996, p. A3.

12. See Introduction and Chapters 1–4 of D'Aveni (1994). The idea that competitors will not sit idle while acquirers attempt to generate synergies at their expense cannot be overemphasized.

13. John J. Keller, "Disconnected Line: Why AT&T Takeover of NCR Hasn't Been a Real Bell Ringer," *Wall Street Journal,* September 19, 1995, p. A1.

14. Cynthia A. Montgomery, *Sears, Roebuck and Co. in 1989,* Harvard Case 9-391-147, p. 6.

15. Glenn Collins, "Quaker Oats to Acquire Snapple," *New York Times,* November 3, 1994, p. D1.

16. Greg Burns, "Putting the Snap Back in Snapple," *Business Week,* July 22, 1996, p. 40.

17. Michael Oneal, "I'm Perfectly Willing to Be Run out of Town," *Business Week,* October 9, 1995, p. 38.

18. E. Tatum Christiansen, *Sears, Roebuck & Co. in the 1980's: Renewal and Diversification,* Harvard Case 9-386-029, p. 10.

19. Gregory Patterson, "Sears to Spin Off Allstate; Brennan to Retire in 1995," *Wall Street Journal,* November 11, 1994, p. A3.

20. See Palij (1992:303–323).

21. Keller, "Disconnected Line," p. A1.

22. "Fatal Attraction," *Economist,* March 23, 1996, p. 73.

23. Todd D. Jick, *Northwest Airlines Confronts Change,* Harvard Case 9-491-036.

24. Todd D. Jick, *Unisys: The Merger of Burroughs and Sperry,* Harvard Case 9-489-055, p. 17.

25. James B. Stewart, "Sony's Bad Dream," *New Yorker,* February 28, 1994, pp. 43–51.

26. James Sterngold, "Sony, Struggling, Takes a Huge Loss on Movie Studios," *New York Times,* November 18, 1994, p. A1.
27. See, for example, Marks and Mirvis (1985, 1991).
28. John Brodie and J. Max Robins, "Synergy, Schmynergy," *Variety,* March 21–27, 1994, p. 1.
29. Consult O'Reilly (1989) for an excellent overview of culture in organizations with a managerial approach.
30. Brodie and Robins, "Synergy, Schmynergy," p. 70.
31. Philip M. Rosenzweig and Andrall E. Pearson, *Primerica: Sandy Weill and His Corporate Entrepreneurs,* Harvard Case 9-393-040, p. 12.
32. "Fatal Attraction," p. 74.

Chapter 3: Do You Feel Lucky? The Acquisition Premium

1. By "law of averages" I am referring to the expected value of the payoffs from this gamble. Here, the expected value of the payoffs is $10,000, but you have to play the game several times to realize an expected value. This is one of the underlying problems in most major acquisitions because these are one-shot games for most companies.
2. See Bradley, Desai, and Kim (1983).
3. The issue here is that it is the shareholder who chooses the systematic risk profile of his or her investments. Beta management is not and should not be a concern for managers.
4. See Panzar and Willig (1981), and Teece (1982) for the underlying theory to these means of performance improvement.
5. Even where "competitiveness" may have been improved, unless the result is an increase in current or future free cash flow—the funds available to suppliers of capital—the firm is no more valuable. Said another way, with enough capital investment, many things can be accomplished, but these investments have a cost of capital of their own that must be met.
6. See Ravenscraft and Scherer (1987a, 1987b, 1988, 1991).
7. Accounting treatments (i.e., pooling versus purchase) can make these returns look quite different. In purchase accounting, the acquired assets are stepped up relative to their pre-merger book values. Under pooling of interests accounting, the assets of the acquired firm are recorded at their book value. Thus, for the same premium, the asset bases for a measure such as return on assets will be different when different accounting treatments are in effect.
8. Ravenscraft and Scherer (1991:436).
9. See, for example, Haspeslagh and Jemison (1991). These authors are right on target that the actual performance gains from an acquisition are earned over time. Unfortunately, value can be destroyed right on announcement of the acquisition, particularly if performance gains are not expected to occur until well into the future. What has not been addressed is the expected

value of these performance gains and the ex-ante alignment with a given premium.

10. Consult Hax and Majluf (1984) and Varaiya, Kerin, and Weeks (1987) for the theoretical and empirical importance of the market value/book value ratio.

11. Special thanks to Professor Gailen L. Hite of Columbia University for assistance with this graph.

12. See Fowler and Schmidt (1988) concerning declines in return on equity in acquisitions.

13. *Wolf Bytes No. 7,* First Boston Equity Research, July 10, 1991.

14. The meaning of the acquisition premium with respect to performance gains can also be viewed with a Tobin's q approach. Tobin's q, or the ratio of the total market value of the assets of a company (debt plus equity) divided by the estimated replacement cost of the assets, provides important economic and managerial intuition about the implications of the resource allocation problem. This measure has been used in the strategy literature (Wernerfelt and Montgomery, 1988) to measure the effects of firm focus. We can interpret q as the expectation of economic rents that can be generated by the assets of a firm. Thus, firms with q's below unity may be good takeover candidates because the market value of the assets is less than the replacement cost of the assets. On the other hand, assets are worth only as much as their discounted cash flow generation potential, and, in an efficient market, a low q is a reflection of this. Thus, an acquisition premium implicitly drives up the q of the target, implying an increase in the economic rents that the acquiring firm must now generate with the assets of the acquired firm.

15. In this model, we are solving for a constant return on equity by which beginning book value will be compounded (all earnings are reinvested) over the given investment horizon.

16. Laurie Hays and William M. Bulkeley, "If IBM Acquires Lotus, It May Be Years Before It Earns a Respectable Return," *Wall Street Journal,* June 8, 1995, p. A3.

17. This analysis is extremely practical because the calculations are done on the basis of free cash flow. Thus, the value driver(s) affecting these cash flows can and must be identified. It is the cornerstones of synergy that will determine how and which value drivers will be instrumental in generating performance gains. This type of analysis is vitally important to academic research on post-acquisition integration that must now go well beyond the problems that arise in the management process.

18. Jemison and Sitkin (1986a, 1986b); Nelson and Lagges (1993:12).

19. See Leighton and Tod (1969), Bleeke and Daniels (1985), and Zangwill (1995).

20. Note that in this analysis we are working with percentages. Thus, for a given percentage required increase in performance, a larger acquisition will require greater dollar amounts of synergy generation.

21. Haspeslagh and Jemison (1987:57).

22. This is actually an accounting-based statement. From a market-based perspective, high-premium acquisitions of relative size of 10 percent or more may carry a strong signal of the quality of other investment decisions being made within the company.

23. Conversations with Geoffery Phillips, now an independent consultant in Briarcliff, New York.

24. *Smith v. Van Gorkom,* 488 A.2d 858 (Del. 1985). This was a landmark judgment against Van Gorkom and the directors of the Trans Union Corporation. In a meeting lasting only two hours, the directors approved a leveraged buyout offer presented as fair by Van Gorkom, owner of 75,000 shares of the company. The court found the directors grossly negligent because they did not make an *informed* decision. Specifically, the directors did not seek to inform themselves as to Van Gorkom's motives, they did not adequately inform themselves as to the intrinsic value of the company, and the decision was made in a two-hour meeting in the absence of an emergency situation (Kaplan and Harrison, 1993).

Chapter 4: Tool and Lessons for the Acquisition Game

1. The duty of loyalty requires that directors not act in their personal interest to the detriment of the corporation. This is not to say that directors must be self-denying, but that in conflict of interests, the corporation must come first. The duty of care requires that directors act "carefully" in directing and monitoring the activities of corporate management (American Bar Association, 1978). The Revised Model Business Corporation Act defines the general standard for the duty of care: that a director shall discharge the duties as a director "in good faith; with the care an ordinary prudent person in a like position would exercise under similar circumstances; and in a manner reasonably believed to be in the best interest of the corporation." The business judgment rule is a tool of judicial review rather than a standard of conduct where, after reasonable investigation, informed and disinterested directors adopt a course of action that, in good faith, they honestly and reasonably believe will benefit the corporation (see Gevurtz, 1994; Sirower and Abzug, 1996, for reviews).

2. Janis (1989:196).

3. Consult Ghemawat (1991) for a thorough treatment of the commitment concept.

4. Excerpt from Robert A. Lutz, president of Chrysler Corp, Delivered to the Strategic Management Society's 15th Annual International Conference, October 18, 1995.

Chapter 5: Acquired Performance and Risk Taking

1. Haspeslagh and Jemison (1987) have argued that because of the variety of factors that account for why acquisitions are successful or not, nothing can really

be said in general about acquisitions. In a sense, they have established an important challenge for researchers in the mergers and acquisitions arena.

2. This schematic represents the major managerial choices that have been examined in exploratory studies in the management literature. Other factors that acquiring firm performance has been regressed on include the percentage of target firm shares acquired, the market value/book value ratio of the target at acquisition, the presence of multiple bidders, the number of insiders on the board of directors, and the fraction of managerial ownership in the acquiring firm (finance literature). Our focus here is on those choice variables that have produced a stream of conflicting evidence in the management literature. The major issue here is that we cannot simply ignore past conflicting evidence. This is a literature representing many papers on this topic, and we cannot just walk away from it.

3. See Barney (1986a, 1988) and Peteraf (1993) for discussions of the competitive markets assumption embedded in the resource-based view.

4. See Chatterjee (1986), Lubatkin (1987), Singh and Montgomery (1987) and Seth (1990a).

5. Reviewed in Seth (1990a).

6. Lubatkin (1987:39).

7. For example, with a five-year window, Agrawal, Jaffe, and Mandelker (1991) find acquirer returns of −25.5 percent for related versus −8.6 percent for unrelated mergers.

8. The difficulty of reaching a satisfactory measurement of the relatedness concept alone helps to support this statement. There is a remarkable intuitive quality about the importance of "relatedness" that continues to drive researchers to find a measure that will support the significance of the concept.

9. Consult Lang and Stulz (1994).

10. In an extensive meta-analysis covering the finance, industrial-organization, and strategy literatures, Datta, Narayanan, and Pinches (1992) find that the most significant explanatory factor of acquirer performance is the method of payment (cash versus equity payments). While Kusewitt (1985) finds equity the more favorable method of payment for acquirers, Datta, Narayanan, and Pinches find that acquiring firms should avoid equity-financed transactions. The empirical finance literature is unequivocal on the advantage of cash payments over equity payments (Travlos, 1987).

11. Myers and Majluf (1984). Consult also Lang, Stulz, and Walkling (1991) for a review.

12. See Jensen (1986).

13. Thanks to Professors Modigliani and Miller (1958), Proposition I simplified the problem of the appropriate amount of debt in corporate capital structure to three assumptions: In a world where (1) there are no taxes, (2) debt does not interfere with the operations of the firm, and (3) there are no frictions in implementing a debt policy, the value of the firm will be independent of capital

structure choice. Once we introduce taxes and allow for the potential of debt to interfere with operations, managers should lever up to that point where the company gets maximum advantage of the tax code while not exceeding a level where the debt can damage operations in difficult times (Sirower, 1995).

14. While Fowler and Schmidt (1988) find that acquirers using tender offers for acquisitions perform significantly worse than mergers, Datta, Narayanan, and Pinches (1992) find exactly the reverse. Similarly, Jemison and Sitkin (1986) have argued that because mergers are "friendlier" and may have a longer planning period, they should outperform tender offers. Cannella (1991), however, finds no empirical justification for this claim and concludes that the method of acquisition negotiation has no implications for post-acquisition performance.

15. See Jensen and Ruback (1983).

16. For example, Cannella (1991), Herzel and Shepro (1990), and Fowler and Schmidt (1989).

17. Consult Fowler and Schmidt (1989).

18. See Banerjee and Owers (1992).

19. See Shleifer and Vishny (1991).

20. In a very interesting study, Haunschild, Davis-Blake, and Fichman (1994) find that managers, during the acquisition process, increase their commitment to the deal, particularly when they have personal responsibility for the decision, there is competition from other bidders for the target, and the acquisition decision is public. We can argue that contested processes involve all three of these factors and thus increase commitment to the acquisition and reduce the probability of walking away.

21. See, for example, Lang, Stulz, and Walkling (1991) for a review. In the management literature, Shelton (1988) and Seth (1990b) find positive effects for relative size on acquirer performance where Kusewitt (1985) finds the opposite and Fowler and Schmidt (1989) find no significant relationship.

22. Biggadike (1979). See Fowler and Schmidt (1989), Shelton (1988), Seth (1990b), and Kusewitt (1985).

23. Consult Copeland, Koller, and Murrin (1994:Ch. 14).

24. Consult Fiegenbaum (1990) for a review.

25. Consult Brockner (1992), Staw (1976, 1981), and Brockner and Rubin (1985) for excellent discussions.

26. Brockner (1992:39).

27. See Roll (1986).

28. Consult Duhaime and Schwenk (1985).

29. Consult Kahneman and Tversky (1979) and Fiegenbaum and Thomas (1988) on prospect theory and Brockner (1992) for an excellent review and critique of perspectives on escalation.

30. This would clearly be an example of the "risk-return paradox" reported by Bowman (1980, 1982, 1984).

Chapter 6: Methodology

1. See Singh and Montgomery (1987).
2. See, for example, You et al. (1986), Chatterjee (1986), Singh and Montgomery (1987), and Datta, Narayanan, and Pinches (1992).
3. Consult Cornell and Shapiro (1987) for a discussion.
4. See Watts (1986) and Copeland, Koller, and Murrin (1994:Ch. 1–3).
5. See, for example, Benston (1985) and Higgins (1992); reviewed by Black (1989). See also Baucus, Golec, and Cooper (1993) for an excellent discussion of how the use of different conventions causes radically different results. The most important problem is determining an appropriate benchmark. As I detailed in Chapter 2, stock prices have embedded expectations of future growth and profitability. Future research will need to move toward an appropriate standard for this benchmark.
6. Porter (1987).
7. Consult Cannella and Hambrick (1993) for arguments against the use of shareholder returns in assessing performance in acquisitions—specifically, the problems inherent in the use of the market model for return generation. A potentially more serious problem of the use of shareholder return measures arises in assessing past research. Prior studies have used various return generation techniques over different time periods, which makes comparison very difficult. Here I subject hypothesis testing to the whole range of techniques and time periods.
8. Brown and Warner (1985).
9. There were many cases where companies did not trade on the actual announcement date because the announcement came after the close of trading or trading on the security was halted for as much as three days.
10. For example, if the raw premium is 70 percent and the overall market is up 20 percent, then the market-adjusted premium is 50 percent. In a cross-sectional regression analysis of acquirer performance, Travlos (1987) operationalizes the bid premium as a percentage of the bidding firm's stock price one month prior to the first announcement of the bid. This measure seems illogical to me because it would be possible to pay a large percentage premium for a relatively small acquisition, but, with this measure, it would appear to be a small premium. In other words, this measure would not pick up the size of the performance improvements that management is claiming it can add to the pre-acquisition valuation. I replicated the Travlos measure and found the same insignificant results he found (and almost the identical parameter estimate). Further, I found that this measure (the dollar premium divided by the market value of the bidder) was highly correlated with relative size of the acquisition; it was practically a proxy in my sample.
11. Kusewitt (1985).
12. Consult Hall and St. John (1994) for a discussion of limitations and Lubatkin, Merchant, and Srinivasan (1993) for empirical support.

13. See You et al. (1986). Here, combination methods are minimally 50 percent equity.

14. See, for example, Fama and French (1993) and Boeker and Goodstein (1991).

15. Roll (1986).

16. See Lubatkin, Merchant, and Srinivasan (1993).

17. Singh (1984); You et al. (1986). As a point of interest, I did not propose an effect of multiple bidders on the premium because it is likely that lower prices will attract multiple bidders. No significant difference was found in the premiums paid in multiple versus single bidder acquisitions. This is important because nearly 75 percent of the sample involved single bidder "auctions."

18. See, for example, Kim, Hwang, and Burgers (1993).

19. Bromiley (1991); Baucus, Golec, and Cooper (1993).

20. Bromiley (1991).

21. Consult Samuelson (1948) and Houthakker (1950).

22. See Ohlson and Penman (1985). In the empirical techniques section, I explain in detail the parametric and nonparametric tests using this measure. I considered using the coefficient of variation measure (discussed by Allison, 1978), but this measure would be unstable where the mean return approached zero from either direction.

23. See, for example, Singh and Montgomery (1987) and Jensen and Ruback (1983).

24. Porter (1987:45).

25. See Seth (1990b), Travlos (1987), You et al. (1986), and Kusewitt (1985).

26. Leamer (1978); Jaccard, Turrisi, and Wan (1984); Aiken and West (1991).

27. Consult White (1980).

28. Consult Breusch and Pagan (1979).

29. Simply put, the error term of the regression equation has a constant variance for all observations.

30. See Kalay and Loewenstein (1985) and Ohlson and Penman (1985).

31. Drazin and Kazanjian (1993). Consult Conover (1980) for a thorough treatment of these issues.

32. See Smirnov (1939).

Chapter 7: Discussion of Results

1. See, for example, Goold and Luchs (1993:16). These authors define synergy as: "when the performance of a portfolio of businesses adds up to more than the sum of its parts."

2. See Meyer and O'Shaughnessy (1992). This point is actually an important contribution of this research in considering acquisition performance. While Meyer and O'Shaughnessy (1992) cite Jacobson (1987) as evidence of low correlation between accounting performance and stock market performance, these authors fail to mention that Jacobson states, "Unquestionably, ROI [return on investment] has serious limitations as a measure of business performance." Jacobson

concludes that ROI contains little information about economic rate of return (which is reflected in stock returns). It is important to understand that value-based measures of performance (i.e., shareholder returns) reflect revisions of forecasts of accounting-based measures. Thus, managers can destroy value even though short-term accounting-based returns seem to be improved. This has not been acknowledged in the acquisition literature, and thus, it is not surprising that definitions of synergy have been vague.

3. See Wernerfelt (1984), Barney (1986a), and Peteraf (1993).

4. Barney (1988:73).

5. See Barney (1986a, 1988) and Peteraf (1993).

6. Consult Dierickx and Cool (1989) and Peteraf (1993) for thorough discussions.

7. See Firth (1991) and the classics *The Economic Theory of Managerial Capitalism* (Marris, 1964) and "A Theory of Conglomerate Mergers" (Mueller, 1969).

8. Floyd Norris, "In Paramount Battle, the Winners Lost $4.1 Billion," *New York Times,* February 20, 1994, p. E1. Interestingly, QVC Network, the "losing" bidder, destroyed over $500 million of value for its shareholders during the bidding contest, and this value was not recovered after losing the contest. Beyond the obvious substantial advisory fees and other costs of the acquisition battle, presumably the market is forecasting the propensity of management to make this type of decision again in the future and the accompanying lack of attractive strategic alternatives.

9. Roger Lowenstein, "After 2 Years, Time Warner Marriage Still Has to Bloom," *Wall Street Journal,* June 18, 1991, p. C1. There is a long history of literature that casts doubt on the potential for acquisitions to create substantial synergy. See, for example, Kitching (1967), Rhoades (1983), Lubatkin (1983), Reed and Luffman (1986), Jones and Hill (1988), Mueller (1989), Alberts and Varaiya (1989), and Slusky and Caves (1991). Even the popular press has reported that corporate executives avoid using the word synergy in their discussions of rationale behind corporate acquisition decisions. Rosabeth Moss Kanter has claimed, "Synergies are very difficult to achieve in any industry," (Calvin Sims, " 'Synergy': The Unspoken Word," *New York Times,* October 5, 1993, p. D1), and DeWitt Bowman, former chief investment officer at CalPERS, has stated in a variety of public forums his disbelief in synergy arguments.

10. Floyd Norris, "On Wall Street, Love Can Soon Turn to Hate," *New York Times,* October 17, 1993, p. D1.

11. Roll (1986:198); see also Lowenstein, note 9 in this chapter, regarding J. Richard Munro's vision statement.

12. Consult Haspeslagh and Jemison (1991).

13. Consult Brockner (1992) for an excellent review and critique.

14. Consult Staw (1976) and Fiegenbaum and Thomas (1988).

15. Consult Tang (1988) for an economic approach to this problem.

16. See, for example, Staw and Ross (1987).
17. Consult Bazerman (1990) for an excellent review.
18. Consult Kahneman and Tversky (1972) for the theoretical development of the representativeness bias.
19. Haunschild (1994).
20. Kusewitt (1985).
21. See, for example, Singh (1984) and You et al. (1986).
22. Varaiya (1988:209). Also see Servaes (1991).
23. In the Zajac and Bazerman world (1991), however, there is no distinction between common value and private value auctions. This type of analysis, while informative, does not consider the role of a secondary market. What these authors describe is actually a unique common value auction where public markets play no role. Theoretically, in a private value auction the winning bidder will not, ex ante, "fall prey" to the winner's curse (Varaiya, 1988). The analysis presented in this book does not rely on common value auction assumptions.
24. See, for example, Scherer (1986) and Salter and Weinhold (1979). That failed acquisitions are apparent by the end of the fourth year is clearly illustrated in the simulations presented in Chapter 3.
25. See Cannella and Hambrick (1993).
26. Executive departure and organizational disruptions may have important meaning with regard to acquisition diseconomies. In the simulations, I assumed no diseconomies following acquisitions. That is, I assumed that combined businesses would perform no worse than they would have performed as independent firms. Perhaps losing important executive talent may challenge this assumption in my analysis. The main point here is to motivate a consideration of how departure will affect the distribution of payoffs or improvements.
27. It is important to discuss an alternative interpretation of these results. My argument has centered on considering the limits to potential performance improvements. I did this by defining synergy within a competitive context, in addition to running simulations to show that premiums translate into "outrageous" required synergies. An argument can be made that a problem with my interpretation of the empirical results is that we are making claims about "potential" without being able to observe it.

    Thus, an alternative interpretation of these results is that premiums do represent potential but that premiums are correlated with post-acquisition problems. At higher premium levels, management becomes "shaken up" and less effective. With this interpretation, managers must learn how to be more effective than my evidence shows they have been as premiums move higher. As I have discussed, the major task of this argument would be to show how well the acquisition would perform if the post-acquisition problems did not occur. Required synergy must be driven by improvements in competitive advantage. Systems and procedures are useless without a strategy that satisfies one or both of the contestability conditions.

28. Consult Chatterjee (1990) on the relatedness principle.
29. Slusky and Caves (1991) report similar results.
30. See, for example, Lubatkin, Merchant, and Srinivasan (1993).
31. Consult Prahalad and Bettis (1986) on the concept of dominant logic.
32. See Fowler and Schmidt (1988), Datta, Narayanan, and Pinches (1992), Jemison and Sitkin (1986), and Cannella (1991).
33. Consult Herzel and Shepro (1990:Ch. 12).
34. See Cannella and Hambrick (1993).
35. See, for example, Walsh (1989) and Hayes and Hoag (1974).
36. See Lang, Stulz, and Walkling (1991).
37. See Jemison and Sitkin (1986) and Shanley and Correa (1992).
38. Staw (1976).
39. Consult Mueller (1989) for a review.
40. Brockner (1992:39).
41. Consult Mintzberg (1978, 1987) for a discussion of deliberate versus emergent strategies.

Chapter 8: Implications of the Analysis

1. For an important exception, consult Markides and Williamson (1994) for research on measuring the concept of "strategic" relatedness along the value chain in the context of a diversified firm.
2. See, for example, Jemison and Sitkin (1986).
3. Stum (1987:41). And even with the share price of Unisys at an all-time low (less than $3 per share), Curtis Hessler, Unisys' vice chairman, stated: "The logic of the merger was the correct logic. On either side, Sperry or Burroughs, we would have been worse off if the merger hadn't occurred." Hope springs eternal in mergers. See John Crudele, "Coming Unglued? Power of 2: Too Good to Be True," *St. Louis Post-Dispatch,* November 12, 1990.
4. Phillip L. Zweig, "The Case Against Mergers," *Business Week* Special Report, October 30, 1995, and Brian Bremner, "The Age of Consolidation," *Business Week,* October 14, 1991.
5. These benefits must be incremental after-tax operating cash flows less additional required investments—free cash flows. I cannot overemphasize this concept; the cornerstones of synergy must drive these benefits.
6. Terence P. Pare, "The New Merger Boom," *Fortune,* November 28, 1994, p. 96.

Bibliography

Aaronovitch, S., and Sawyer, M. C. (1975). "Mergers, Growth and Concentration." *Oxford Economic Papers* 27:136–155.

Abell, D. F. (1980). *Defining the Business: The Starting Point of Strategic Planning.* Englewood Cliffs, NJ: Prentice Hall.

Adams, W., and Brock, J. W. (1989). *Dangerous Pursuits.* New York: Pantheon.

Agrawal, A., and Mandelker, G. (1987). "Managerial Incentives and Corporate Investment and Financing Decisions." *Journal of Finance* 42:823–837.

Agrawal, A., Jaffe, J. F., and Mandelker, G. N. (1992). "The Post-Merger Performance of Acquiring Firms: A Re-Examination of an Anomaly." *Journal of Finance* 47:1605–1671.

Aiken, L. S., and West, S. G. (1991). *Multiple Regression: Testing and Interpreting Interactions.* Newbury Park, CA: Sage.

Akerloff, G. A. (1970). "The Market for 'Lemons': Qualitative Uncertainty and the Market Mechanism." *Quarterly Journal of Economics* 84:488–500.

Alberts, W. W. (1984). "Do Oligopolists Earn Non-Competitive Rates of Return?" *American Economic Review* 74:624–632.

Alberts, W. W., and Varaiya, N. P. (1989). "Assessing the Profitability of Growth by Acquisition: A 'Premium Recapture' Approach." *International Journal of Industrial Organization* 7:133–149.

Allison, G. T. (1971). *Essence of Decision.* Boston: Little, Brown.

Allison, P. D. (1978). "Measures of Inequality." *American Sociological Review* 43:865–880.

Amel, D. F., and Rhoades, S. A. (1989). "Empirical Evidence on the Motives for Bank Mergers." *Eastern Economic Journal* 12:605–617.

American Bar Association, Committee on Corporate Laws. (1978). "Corporate Director's Guidebook." *Business Lawyer* 33:1595–1644.

Amihud, Y., Dodd, P., and Weinstein, M. (1986). "Conglomerate Mergers, Managerial Motives and Stockholder Wealth." *Journal of Banking and Finance* 10:401–410.

Amihud, Y., and Lev, B. (1981). "Risk Reduction as a Managerial Motive for Conglomerate Mergers." *Bell Journal of Economics* 12:605–617.

Amihud, Y., Lev, B., and Travlos, N. G. (1990). "Corporate Control and the Choice of Investment Financing: The Case of Corporate Acquisitions." *Journal of Finance* 45:603–616.

Andrews, K. R. (1970). *The Concept of Corporate Strategy.* Homewood, IL: Dow Jones Irwin.

Anslinger, P. L., and Copeland, T. E. (1996). "Growth Through Acquisitions: A Fresh Look." *Harvard Business Review* (January–February): 126–135.

Ansoff, I. (1975). *Corporate Strategy.* New York: McGraw-Hill.

Arrow, K. (1974). *The Limits of Organization.* New York: Norton.

Asquith, P. (1983) "Merger Bids, Uncertainty, and Stockholder Returns." *Journal of Financial Economics* 11:51–83.

Asquith, P., Bruner, R. F., and Mullins, Jr., D. (1983). "The Gains for Bidding Firms from Merger." *Journal of Financial Economics* 11:121–139.

Asquith, P., Bruner, R. F., and Mullins, D. W., Jr. (1987). "Merger Returns and the Form of Financing." Working paper. Boston: Harvard Business School.

Asquith, P., and Kim, E. H. (1982). "The Impact of Merger Bids on the Participating Firm's Security Holders." *Journal of Finance* 37:1209–1228.

Asquith, P., and Mullins, D. (1986). "Equity Issues and Offering Dilution." *Journal of Financial Economics* 15:61–89.

Auerbach, A. J., and Reishus, D. (1988). "Taxes and the Merger Decision." In J. C. Coffee, Jr., L. Lowenstein, and S. Rose-Ackerman, eds., *Knights, Raiders, and Targets: The Impact of Hostile Takeovers,* 300–313. New York: Oxford University Press.

Axelrod, R. (1980). *The Evolution of Cooperation.* New York: Basic Books.

Azzi, C. (1978). "Conglomerate Mergers, Default Risk, and Homemade Mutual Funds." *American Economic Review* 68:161–172.

Backaitis, N. T., Balakrishnan, R., and Harrigan, K. R. (1984). "The Dimensions of Diversification Posture, Market Power and Performance: The Continuing Debate." Working paper, Graduate School of Business, Columbia University.

Baker, G. P., and Wruck, K. H. (1989). "Organizational Changes and Value Creation in Leveraged Buyouts." *Journal of Financial Economics* 25:163–190.

Balakrishnan, S., and Koza, M. (1993). "Information Asymmetry, Adverse Selection and Joint Ventures: Theory and Evidence." *Journal of Economic Behavior and Organization* 20:99–117.

Baldwin, J., and Gorecki, P. (1990). "Mergers Placed in the Context of Firm Turnover." In U.S. Department of Commerce, Bureau of the Census, *1990 Annual Research Conference, Proceedings.* Washington, D.C.: Government Printing Office.

Banerjee, A., and Owers, J. E. (1992). "Wealth Reduction in White Knight Bids." *Financial Management* 21:48–57.

Barney, J. B. (1986a). "Strategic Factor Markets: Expectations, Luck, and Business Strategy." *Management Science* 32:1231–1241.

Barney, J. B. (1986b). "Organizational Culture: Can It Be a Source of Sustained Competitive Advantage?" *Academy of Management Review* 11:656–665.

Barney, J. B. (1988). "Returns to Bidding Firms in Mergers and Acquisitions: Reconsidering the Relatedness Hypothesis." *Strategic Management Journal* 9:71–78.

Bastien, D. T. (1987). "Common Patterns of Behavior and Communication in Corporate Mergers and Acquisitions." *Human Resource Management* 26:17–33.

Bastien, D. T., and Van De Ven, A. H. (1986). "Managerial and Organizational Dynamics of Mergers and Acquisitions." Discussion paper no. 46, Strategic Management Research Center, University of Minnesota.

Baucus, D. A., Golec, J. H., and Cooper, J. R. (1993). "Estimating Risk-Return Relationships: An Analysis of Measures." *Strategic Management Journal* 14:387–396.

Baumol, W. J., Heim, P., Malkiel, B. G., and Quandt, R. E. (1970). "Earnings Retention, New Capital and the Growth of the Firm." *Review of Economics and Statistics* 52:345–355.

Baumol, W. J., Panzar, J. C., and Willig, R. D. (1982). *Contestable Markets and the Theory of Industry Structure.* New York: Harcourt Brace Jovanovich.

Bazerman, M. H. (1986). *Judgement in Managerial Decision-Making.* New York: Wiley.

Bazerman, M. H. (1990). *Managerial Decision Making.* New York: Wiley.

Bazerman, M. H., and Samuelson, W. F. (1983). "I Won the Auction But I Don't Want the Prize." *Journal of Financial Studies* 27:618–634.

Beattie, D. L. (1980). "Conglomerate Diversification and Performance: A Survey and Time Series Analysis." *Applied Economics* 12:251–273.

Bell, R. (1982). *Surviving the 10 Ordeals of the Takeover.* New York: AMACOM.

Benston, G. (1985). "The Validity of Profits-Structure Studies with Particular Reference to the FTC's Line of Business Data." *American Economic Review* 75:37–49.

Berkovitch, E., and Khanna, N. (1990). "How Target Shareholders Benefit from Value-Reducing Defensive Strategies in Takeovers." *Journal of Finance* 45:137–156.

Berkovitch, E., and Narayanan, M. P. (1990). "Competition and the Medium of Exchange in Takeovers." *Review of Financial Studies* 3:153–174.

Berkovitch, E., and Narayanan, M. P. (1993). "Motives for Takeovers: An Empirical Investigation." *Journal of Financial and Quantitative Analysis* 28:347–362.

Berle, A. A., and Means, G. C. (1932). *The Modern Corporation and Private Property.* New York: Macmillan.

Berman, P. (1984). "When Someone Says Synergy, Feel for Your Wallet." *Forbes,* December 3, pp. 38–39.

Berman, R. J., and Wade, M. R. (1981). "The Planned Approach to Acquisitions." In S. J. Lee and R. D. Coleman, eds., *Handbook of Mergers, Acquisitions, and Buyouts.* Englewood Cliffs, NJ: Prentice Hall.

Bettis, R. A. (1981). "Performance Differences in Related and Unrelated Diversified Firms." *Strategic Management Journal* 2:379–394.

Bettis, R. A. (1983). "Modern Financial Theory, Corporate Strategy, and Public Policy: Three Conundrums." *Academy of Management Review* 8:406–415.

Bettis, R. A., and Hall, W. K. (1985). "Diversification Strategy, Accounting Determined Risk, and Accounting Determined Return." *Academy of Management Journal* 45:254–264.

Bettis, R. A., and Mahajan, V. (1985). "Risk/Return Performance of Diversified Firms." *Management Science* 31:785–799.

Bhagat, S., Shleifer, A., and Vishny, R. W. (1990). "Hostile Takeovers in the 1980s: The Return to Corporate Specialization." *Brookings Papers on Economic Activity* 1–84.

Biggadike, R. (1979). "The Risky Business of Diversification." *Harvard Business Review* (May–June): pp. 103–111.

Bing, G. (1980). *Corporate Acquisitions.* Chicago: Gulf Publishing Co.

Black B. S. (1989). "Bidder Overpayment in Takeovers." *Stanford Law Review* 41:597–660.

Blake, R. R., and Mouton, J. S. (1984). *Solving Costly Organizational Conflicts: Achieving Intergroup Trust, Cooperation and Teamwork.* San Francisco: Jossey-Bass.

Blake, R. R., and Mouton, J. S. (1985). "How to Achieve Integration on the Human Side of the Merger." *Organizational Dynamics* (Winter): 41–56.

Bleeke, J. A., and Daniels, L. K. (1985). "After a Deal Is Completed: How Far and How Fast to Move." *California Management Review* 30 (Fall): 9–11.

Boeker, W., and Goodstein, J. (1991). "Organizational Performance and Adaptation: Effects of Environment and Performance on Changes in Board Composition." *Academy of Management Journal* 34:805–826.

Borg, J. R., Borg, M. O., and Leeth, J. D. (1989). "The Success of Mergers in the 1920s: A Stock Market Appraisal of the Second Merger Wave." *International Journal of Industrial Organization* 7:117–131.

Borys, B., and Jemison, D. B. (1989). "Hybrid Arrangement as Strategic Alliances: Theoretical Issues in Organizational Combinations." *Academy of Management Review* 14:234–249.

Bourgeois, L. J. (1981). "On the Measurement of Organizational Slack." *Academy of Management Review* 6:29–39.

Bower, J. L. (1970). *Managing the Resource Allocation Process: A Study of Corporate Planning and Investment.* Boston: Graduate School of Business Administration, Harvard University.

Bowman, E. H. (1980). "A Risk/Return Paradox for Strategic Management." *Sloan Management Review* 21:17–31.

Bowman, E. H. (1982). "Risk Seeking by Troubled Firms." *Sloan Management Review* 23:33–42.

Bowman, E. H. (1984). "Content Analysis of Annual Reports for Corporate Strategy and Risk." *Interfaces* 14:61–71.

Boyle, S. E. (1970). "Pre-Merger Growth and Profit Characteristics of Large Conglomerate Mergers in the United States, 1948–68." *St. John's Law Review* 44 (special edition): 152–170.

Bradley, J. W., and Korn, D. H. (1981). "The Changing Role of Acquisitions." *Journal of Business Strategy* 2:30–42.

Bradley, M. (1980). "Interfirm Tender Offers and the Market for Corporate Control." *Journal of Business* 53:345–376.

Bradley, M., Desai, A., and Kim, E. H. (1983). "The Rational Behind Interfirm Tender Offers: Information of Synergy?" *Journal of Financial Economics* 11:183–206.

Bradley, M., Desai, A., and Kim, E. H. (1988). "Synergistic Gains from Corporate Acquisitions and Their Division Between the Stockholders of Target and Acquiring Firms." *Journal of Financial Economics* 21:3–40.

Bradley, M., and Jarrell, G. (1988). "Comment." In J. C. Coffee, Jr., L. Lowenstein, and S. Rose-Ackerman (eds.), *Knights, Raiders and Targets: The Impact of Hostile Takeover,* 252–259. New York: Oxford University Press.

Bradley, M., and Wakeman, L. M. (1983). "The Wealth Effects of Targeted Share Repurchases." *Journal of Financial Economics* 11:301–328.

Brealey, R. A., and Myers, S. C. (1991). *Principles of Corporate Finance.* 4th ed. New York: McGraw-Hill.

Bremner, B. (1991). "The Age of Consolidation." *Business Week,* October 14, pp. 86–94.

Breusch, T. S., and Pagan, A. R. (1979). "A Simple Test for Heteroskedasticity and Random Coefficient Variation." *Econometrica* 47:1287–1294.

Brockner, J. (1992). "The Escalation of Commitment to a Failing Course of Action: Toward Theoretical Progress." *Academy of Management Review* 17:39–61.

Brockner, J., and Rubin, J. Z. (1985). *Entrapment in Escalating Conflicts: A Social Psychological Analysis.* New York: Springer-Verlag.

Brodie, J., and Robins, J. M. (1994). "Synergy, Schmynergy." *Variety,* March 21–27.

Bromiley, P. (1991). "Testing a Causal Model of Corporate Risk Taking and Performance." *Academy of Management Journal* 34(1):37–59.

Brown, C., and Medoff, J. L. (1988). "The Impact of Firm Acquisitions on Labor." In A. J. Auerbach, ed., *Takeovers: Causes and Consequences,* 9–31. Chicago: University of Chicago Press.

Brown, L. D. (1983). *Managing Conflict at Organizational Interfaces.* Reading, MA: Addison-Wesley.

Brown, S. J., and Warner, J. B. (1980). "Measuring Security Price Performance." *Journal of Financial Economics* 8:205–258.

Brown, S. J., and Warner, J. B. (1985). "Using Daily Stock Returns: The Case of Event Studies." *Journal of Financial Economics* 14:3–31.

Bruner, R. F., and Paine, L. S. (1988). "Management Buyouts and Managerial Ethics." *California Management Review* 30:89–106.

Brush, T. H. (1996). "Predicted Change in Operational Synergy and Post-Acquisition Performance of Acquired Businesses." *Strategic Management Journal* 17:1–24.

Buffett, W. (1981). *Annual Report to Stockholders 1981*. Berkshire Hathaway Corporation.

Buffett, W. (1982). *Annual Report to Stockholders 1982*. Berkshire Hathaway Corporation.

Buono, A. F., and Bowditch, J. L. (1989). *The Human Side of Mergers and Acquisitions: Managing Collisions Between People and Organizations*. San Francisco: Jossey-Bass.

Buono, A. F., Bowditch, J. L., and Lewis, J. W., III. (1988). "The Cultural Dynamics of Transformation: The Case of a Bank Merger." In R. Kilman, T. Covin, and Associates (Eds.), *Corporate Transformation: Revitalizing Organizations for a Competitive World*, 497–522. San Francisco: Jossey-Bass.

Burns, G. (1996). "Putting the Snap Back in Snapple." *Business Week*, July 22, p. 40.

Burns, J. M. (1978). *Leadership*. New York: Harper & Row.

Byrd, J. W., and Hickman, K. A. (1992). "Do Outside Directors Monitor Managers? Evidence from Tender Offer Bids." *Journal of Financial Economics* 32:195–221.

Cannella, A. A., Jr. (1991). "Executive Departure from Acquired Firms: Antecedents and Performance Implications." Ph.D. dissertation, Columbia University.

Cannella, A. A., Jr., and Hambrick, D. C. (1993). "Effects of Executive Departure on the Performance of Acquired Firms." *Strategic Management Journal* (Special Issue) 14:137–152.

Capen, E. C., Clapp, R. V., and Campbell, W. M. (1971). "Competitive Bidding in High-Risk Situations." *Journal of Petroleum Technology* 23:641–653.

Carter, E. E. (1971). "The Behavioral Theory of the Firm and Top Level Corporate Decisions." *Administrative Science Quarterly* 16:413–428.

Caves, R. E. (1987). "Effect of Mergers and Acquisitions on the Economy: An Industrial Organization Perspective." In L. E. Browne and E. S. Rosengren, eds., *The Merger Boom*, 149–168. Boston: Federal Reserve Bank of Boston.

Caves, R. E. (1989). "Mergers, Takeovers, and Economic Efficiency: Foresight vs. Hindsight." *International Journal of Industrial Organization* 7:151–174.

Caves, R. E., and Barton, D. R. (1990). *Efficiency in U.S. Manufacturing Industries*. Cambridge, MA: MIT Press.

Chakrabarti, A. K., and Souder, W. S. (1987). "Technology, Innovation and Performance in Corporate Mergers: A Managerial Evaluation." *Technovation* 6:103–114.

Chandler, A. D. (1962). *Strategy and Structure: Chapters in the History of the American Industrial Enterprise*. Cambridge: MIT Press.

Chandler, A. D. (1990a). "The Enduring Logic of Industrial Success." *Harvard Business Review* (March–April): 130–140.

Chandler, A. D. (1990b). *Scale and Scope*. Cambridge: Harvard University Press.

Chatterjee, S. (1986). "Types of Synergy and Economic Value: The Impact of Acquisitions on Merging and Rival Firms." *Strategic Management Journal* 7:119–139.

Chatterjee, S. (1990). "The Gains to Acquiring Firms: The Related Principle Revisited." *Academy of Management Best Papers Proceedings*, 12–16.

Chatterjee, S. (1992). "Sources of Value in Takeovers: Synergy of Restructuring— Implications for Target and Bidder Firms." *Strategic Management Journal* 13:267–286.

Chatterjee, S., and Lubatkin, M. (1990). "Corporate Mergers, Stockholder Diversification, and Changes in Systematic Risk." *Strategic Management Journal* 11:255–268.

Chen, M.-J. (1996). "Competitor Analysis and Interfirm Rivalry: Toward a Theoretical Integration." *Academy of Management Review* 21:100–134.

Chen, M.-J., and MacMillan, I. C. (1992). "Nonresponse and Delayed Response to Competitive Moves: The Roles of Competitor Dependence and Action Irreversibility." *Academy of Management Journal* 35:539–570.

Child, J. (1972). "Organization Structure, Environment and Performance: The Role of Strategic Choice." *Sociology* 6:1–22.

Choi, D., and Philippatos, G. C. (1983). "An Examination of Merger Synergism." *Journal of Financial Research* 6:239–256.

Choi, D., and Philippatos, G. C. (1984). "Post-Merger Performance among Homogeneous Firm Samples." *Financial Review* 19:173–194.

Christensen, H. K., and Montgomery, C. A. (1981). "Corporate Economic Performance: Diversification Strategy Versus Market Structure." *Strategic Management Journal* 2:327–343.

Christiansen, E. T. (1985). *Sears, Roebuck & Co. in the 1980's: Renewal and Diversification,* Harvard Case 9-386-029. Boston: Harvard Business School.

Chung, K. S., and Weston, J. F. (1982). "Diversification and Mergers in a Strategic Long-Range Planning Framework." In M. Keenan and L. I. White, eds., *Mergers and Acquisitions,* chap. 13. Lexington, MA: Heath.

Cizik, R., and Sirower, M. L. (1995). "Setting the Record Straight on Acquisition Premiums." Unpublished manuscript, Stern School of Business, New York University.

Coase, R. (1937). "The Nature of the Firm." *Econometrica* 4:386–405.

Cohen, M. D., and March, J. G. (1974). *Leadership and Ambiguity.* Boston: Harvard Business School Press.

Cohen, M. D., March, J. G., and Olsen, P. P. (1972). "A Garbage Can Model of Organizational Choice." *Administrative Science Quarterly* 17:1–25.

Cole, J. (1996). "McDonnell Plans to Shift Its Purchases." *Wall Street Journal,* April 18, p. A3.

Collins, G. (1994). "Quaker Oats to Acquire Snapple." *New York Times,* November 3, p. D1.

Comanor, W. S. (1967). "Vertical Mergers, Market Power, and the Antitrust Laws." *American Economic Review* 57:254–265.

Conn, R. L. (1973). "Performance of Conglomerate Firms: Comment." *Journal of Finance* 28:154–159.

Conover, W. J. (1980). *Practical Nonparametric Statistics.* 2d ed. New York: Wiley.

Cook, R. E. (1987). "What the Economics Literature Has to Say About Takeovers." Working paper no. 106. Center for the Study of American Business, Washington University.

Cooke, T. E., in association with Arthur Young. (1988). *International Mergers and Acquisitions.* Oxford: Blackwell.

Copeland, T., Koller, T., and Murrin, J. (1994). *Valuation: Measuring and Managing the Value of Companies.* 2d ed. New York: Wiley.

Cornell, B., and Shapiro, A. C. (1987). "Corporate Stakeholders and Corporate Finance." *Financial Management* (Spring): 5–14.

Cosier, R. A. (1978). "The Effects of Three Potential Aids for Making Strategic Decisions on Prediction Accuracy." *Organizational Behavior and Human Performance* 22:295–306.

Crudele, J. (1990). "Coming Unglued? Power of 2: Too Good to Be True." *St. Louis Post-Dispatch,* November 12.

Cyert, R. M., and March, J. G. (1963). *A Behavioral Theory of the Firm.* Englewood Cliffs, NJ: Prentice Hall.

Daily, J. E. (1985). "Do Mergers Really Work?" *Business Week,* June 3, pp. 88–100.

Dann, L. (1980). "The Effect of Common Stock Repurchase on Stockholder Returns." Ph.D. dissertation, University of California, Los Angeles.

Dann, L., and DeAngelo, H. (1983). "Standstill Agreements, Privately Negotiated Stock Repurchases and the Market for Corporate Control." *Journal of Financial Economics* 9:113–138.

Datta, D. K., Narayanan, V. K., and Pinches, G. E. (1992). "Factors Influencing Wealth Creation from Mergers and Acquisitions: A Meta-Analysis." *Strategic Management Journal* 13:67–84.

D'Aveni, R. A. (1994). *Hypercompetition.* New York: Free Press.

Davidson, K. M. (1981). "Looking at the Strategic Impact of Mergers." *Journal of Business Strategy* 2:13–22.

Davis, G. F. (1991). "Agents Without Principles? The Spread of the Poison Pill Through the Corporate Network." *Administrative Science Quarterly* 36:583–613.

Davis, G. F., and Thompson, T. A. (1994). "A Social Movement Perspective on Corporate Control." *Administrative Science Quarterly* 39:141–173.

Davis, M. S. (1985). "Two Plus Two Doesn't Equal Five." *Fortune,* December 9, pp. 171–179.

Dearborn, D. C., and Simon, H. A. (1958). "Selective Perceptions: A Note on the Departmental Identifications of Executives." *Sociometry* 21:140–144.

Dennis, D. K., and McConnell, J. J. (1986). "Corporate Mergers and Security Returns." *Journal of Financial Economics* 16:143–187.

DePrano, M. E., and Nugent, J. B. (1969). "Economies as an Antitrust Defense: Comment." *American Economic Review* 59:947–959.

Dierickx, I., and Cool, K. (1989). "Asset Stock Accumulation and the Sustainability of Competitive Advantage." *Management Science* 35:1504–1511.

Dodd, P. (1976). "Corporate Takeovers and the Australian Equity Market." *Australian Journal of Management* 1:15–35.

Dodd, P. (1980). "Merger Proposals, Management Discretion and Shareholder Wealth." *Journal of Financial Economics* 8:105–137.

Dodd, P., and Ruback, R. (1977). "Tender Offers and Stockholder Returns: An Empirical Analysis." *Journal of Financial Economics* 5:351–374.

Dodd, P., and Warner, J. B. (1983). "On Corporate Governance: A Study of Proxy Contests." *Journal of Financial Economics* 5:351–374.

Dodds, J. C., and Quek, J. P. (1985). "Effect of Mergers on the Share Price Movement of the Acquiring Firms: A UK Study." *Journal of Business Finance and Accounting* 12:285–296.

Donaldson, G. (1984). *Managing Corporate Wealth.* New York: Praeger.

Donaldson, G., and Lorsch, J. (1983). *Decision Making at the Top: The Shaping of Strategic Direction.* New York: Basic Books.

Doz, Y. L. (1986). *Strategic Management in Multinational Companies.* Oxford: Pergamon Press.

Doz, Y. L., and Prahalad, C. K. (1987). *The Multinational Mission: Balancing Local Demands and Global Vision.* New York: Free Press.

Drazin, R., and Kazanjian, R. K. (1993). "Applying the Del Technique to the Analysis of Cross-Classification Data: A Test of CEO Succession and the Top Management Team Development." *Academy of Management Journal* 36:1374–1399.

Dubofsky, P., and Varadarajan, P. R. (1987). "Diversification and Measures of Performance: Additional Empirical Evidence." *Academy of Management Journal* 30:597–608.

Duhaime, I. M., and Grant, J. H. (1984). "Factors Influencing Divestment Decision Making: Evidence from a Field Study." *Strategic Management Journal* 5:301–318.

Duhaime, I. M., and Schwenk, C. R. (1985). "Conjectures on Cognitive Simplification in Acquisition and Divestment Decision Making." *Academy of Management Review* 10:287–295.

Dundas, K. N., and Richardson, P. R. (1982). "Implementing the Unrelated Product Strategy." *Management Journal* 3:287–301.

Dutton, J. E., and Jackson S. E. (1987). "Categorizing Strategic Issues: Links to Organizational Action." *Academy of Management Review* 12:76–90.

Dutz, M. A. (1989). "Horizontal Mergers in Declining Industries." *International Journal of Industrial Organization* 7:11–33.

Eccles, R. G., and Crane, D. B. (1988). *Doing Deals: Investment Banks at Work.* Boston: Harvard Business School Press.

Eckbo, B. E. (1983). "Horizontal Mergers, Collusion, and Stockholder Wealth." *Journal of Financial Economics* 11:241–273.

Eckbo, B. E. (1986). "Mergers and the Market for Corporate Control: The Canadian Evidence." *Canadian Journal of Economics* 19:236–260.

Eckbo, B. E., Giammarino, R., and Heinkel, R. (1990). "Asymmetric Information and the Medium of Exchange in Takeovers: Theory and Tests." *Review of Financial Studies* 3:651–676.

Eckbo, B. E., and Langohr, H. (1989). "Information Disclosure, Method of Payment, and Takeover Premiums: Public and Private Tender Offers in France." *Journal of Financial Economics* 24:363–403.

Economist. (1996). "Fatal Attraction." March 23, pp. 73–74.

Eger, C. E. (1983). "An Empirical Test of the Redistribution Effect in Pure Exchange Mergers." *Journal of Financial and Quantitative Analysis* 18:547–572.

Eisenhardt, K. (1989). "Agency Theory: An Assessment and Review." *Strategic Management Review* 14:57–74.

Elgers, P. T., and Clark, J. J. (1980). "Merger Types and Stockholder Returns: Additional Evidence." *Financial Management* 9:66–72.

Elster, J. (1993). "Some Unresolved Problems in the Theory of Rational Behavior." *Acta Sociologica* 36:179–190.

Elwood, J. W. (1987). "The Effects of Mergers and Acquisitions on the Governance of the Modern Corporation." In D. E. Logue, ed., *Handbook of Modern Finance*, 29B1–29B69. Boston: Warren, Gorham, and Lamont.

Fairburn, J. A., and Kay, J. A., eds. (1989). *Mergers and Merger Policy.* New York: Oxford University Press.

Fama, E. F. (1968). "Risk, Return, and Equilibrium—Some Clarifying Comments." *Journal of Finance* 23:29–40.

Fama, E. F. (1980). "Agency Problems and the Theory of the Firm." *Journal of Political Economy* 88:288–307.

Fama, E. F., and French, K. R. (1993). "The Cross-Section of Expected Stock Returns." *Journal of Finance* 7:427–465.

Fama, E. F., and Jensen, M. C. (1983a). "Separation of Ownership and Control." *Journal of Law and Economics* 26:301–325.

Fama, E. F., and Jensen, M. C. (1983b). "Agency Problems and Residual Claims." *Journal of Law and Economics* 26:327–349.

Federal Trade Commission Staff Report. (1972). *Conglomerate Merger Performance: An Empirical Analysis of Nine Corporations.* Washington, D.C.: Government Printing Office.

Feldman, M. S., and March, J. M. (1981). "Information in Organizations as Signal and Symbol." *Administrative Science Quarterly* 26:171–186.

Fiegenbaum, A. (1990). "Prospect Theory and the Risk-Return Association: An Empirical Examination in 85 Industries." *Journal of Economic Behavior and Organization* 14:187–204.

Fiegenbaum, A., and Thomas, H. (1988). "Attitudes Towards Risk and the Risk-Return Paradox: Prospect Theory Explanations." *Academy of Management Journals* 31:85–106.

Finkelstein, S. (1986). "The Acquisition Integration Process." *Academy of Management Best Papers Proceedings.*

Firth, M. (1980). "Takeovers, Shareholder Returns, and the Theory of the Firm." *Quarterly Journal of Economics* 94:315–347.

Firth, M. (1991). "Corporate Takeovers, Stockholder Rewards and Executive Rewards." *Managerial and Decision Economics* 12:421–428.

Fisher, A. B. (1994). "How to Make a Merger Work." *Fortune,* January 24, pp. 66–69.

Fishman, M. (1989). "Preemptive Bidding and the Role of the Medium of Exchange in Acquisitions." *Journal of Finance* 44:41–58.

Fombrun, C. J. (1983). "Attributions of Power Across a Social Network." *Human Relations* 36:493–507.

Fowler, K. L., and Schmidt, D. R. (1988). "Tender Offers, Acquisitions and Subsequent Performance in Manufacturing Firms." *Academy of Management Journal* 31:962–974.

Fowler, K. L., and Schmidt, D. R. (1989). "Determinants of Tender Offer Post-Acquisition Financial Performance." *Strategic Management Journal* 10:339–350.

Franks, J. R., Broyles, J. E., and Hecht, M. J. (1977). "An Industry Study of the Profitability of Mergers in the United Kingdom." *Journal of Finance* 32:1513–1525.

Franks, J. R., and Harris, R. S. (1989). "Shareholder Wealth Effects of Corporate Takeovers." *Journal of Financial Economics* 23:225–249.

Franks, J. R., Harris, R. S., and Mayer, C. (1988). "Means of Payment in Takeovers: Results for the U.K. and U.S." In A. J. Auerbach, ed., *Corporate Takeovers: Causes and Consequences,* 221–258. Chicago: University of Chicago Press.

Franks, J. R., Harris, R. S., and Titman, S. (1991). "The Post-Merger Shareprice Performance of Acquiring Firms." *Journal of Financial Economics* 29:81–96.

Franks, J. R., and Mayer, C. (1990). "Capital Markets and Corporate Control: A Comparison of France, Germany, and the UK." *Economic Policy* 10:1–43.

Frederickson, J. W. (1985). "Effects of Decision Motive and Organizational Performance Level on Strategic Decision Processes." *Academy of Management Journal* 28:821–843.

Frederickson, J. W., and Iaquinto, A. I. (1989). "Inertia and Creeping Rationality in Strategic Decision Processes." *Academy of Management Journal* 32:516–542.

Fromm, D., and Haspeslagh, P. (1987). "The Dutch View of Hostile Takeovers." *Acquisitions Monthly* (September): 51–52.

Gabarro, J. J. (1985). "When a New Manager Takes Charge." *Harvard Business Review* (May–June):110–123.

Gagnon, J. M., Brehain, P., Broquet, C., and Guerra, F. (1982). "Stock Market Behaviour of Merging Firms: The Belgian Experience." *European Economic Review,* 17:187–211.

Geertz, C. (1973). *The Interpretation of Culture.* New York: Basic Books.

Geroski, P. A. (1984). "On the Relationship Between Aggregate Merger Activity and the Stock Market." *European Economic Review* 25:223–233.

Gevurtz, F. A. (1994). "The Business Judgment Rule: Meaningless Verbiage or Misguided Notion?" *Southern California Law Review* 67:287–324.

Ghemawat, P. (1988). "Sustainable Advantage." *Harvard Business Review* (September–October): 53–58.

Ghemawat, P. (1991). *Commitment: The Dynamic of Strategy.* New York: Free Press.

Ghoshal, S. (1987). "Global Strategy: An Organizing Framework." *Strategic Management Journal* 8:425–440.

Gibbs, P. A. (1993). "Determinants of Corporate Restructuring: The Relative Importance of Corporate Governance, Takeover Threat, and Free Cash Flow." *Strategic Management Journal* 14:51–68.

Gilson, R. J., and Black, B. S. (1995). *The Law and Finance of Corporate Acquisitions.* 2d ed. Westbury, NY: Foundation Press.

Gilson, R. J., Scholes, M. S., and Wolfson, M. A. (1988). "Taxation and the Dynamics of Corporate Control: The Uncertain Case for Tax-Motivated Acquisitions." In J. C. Coffee, Jr., L. Lowenstein, and S. Rose-Ackerman, eds., *Knights, Raiders, and Targets: The Impact of Hostile Takeovers,* 271–299. New York: Oxford University Press.

Golbe, D. L., and White L. J. (1988). "A Time Series Analysis of Mergers and Acquisitions in the U.S. Economy." In A. J. Auerbach, ed., *Takeovers: Causes and Consequences,* 265–302. Chicago: University of Chicago Press.

Golbe, D. L., and White L. J. (1978). "It's Good Logic, But Is It Good Business?" *Forbes* November 13, pp. 138–140.

Goldberg, L. G. (1973). "The Effect of Conglomerate Mergers on Competition." *Journal of Law and Economics* 16:137–158.

Goold, M., and Campbell, A. (1987). *Strategies and Styles: The Role of the Centre in Managing Diversified Corporations.* London: Basil Blackwell.

Goold, M., Campbell, A., and Alexander, M. (1994). *Corporate Level Strategy: Creating Value in the Multibusiness Company.* New York: Wiley.

Goold, M., and Luchs, K. (1993). "Why Diversify? Four Decades of Management Thinking." *Academy of Management Executive* 7:7–25.

Gort, M. (1962). *Diversification and Integration in American Industry.* Princeton: Princeton University Press.

Gort, M. (1969). "An Economic Disturbance Theory of Mergers." *Quarterly Journal of Economics* 83:624–642.

Gort, M., and Hogarty, T. F. (1970). "New Evidence on Mergers." *Journal of Law and Economics* 13:167–184.

Granovetter, M. (1985). "Economics Action and Social Structure: The Problem of Embeddedness." *American Journal of Sociology* 91:481–510.

Graves, D. (1981). "Individual Reactions to a Merger of Two Small Firms of Brokers in the Reinsurance Industry: A Total Population Survey." *Journal of Management Studies* 18:89–113.

Greiner, L. (1972). "Evolution and Revolution as Organizations Grow." *Harvard Business Review* (July–August): 37–46.

Grossman, S., and Hart, O. (1980). "Takeover Bids, the Free-Rider Problem, and the Theory of the Corporation." *Bell Journal of Economics* (Spring): 42–64.

Gulliver, F. R. (1987). "Postproject Appraisals Pay." *Harvard Business Review* (March–April): 128–132.

Gupta, A. K., and Govindarajan, V. (1984). "Business Unit Strategy, Managerial Characteristics, and Business Unit Effectiveness at Strategy Implementation." *Academy of Management Journal* 27:25–41.

Guth, W. D., and MacMillan, I. C. (1986). "Strategy Implementation vs. Middle Management Self Interest." *Strategic Management Journal* 7:313–327.

Hall, B. H. (1988). "The Effects of Takeover Activity on Corporate Research and

Development." In A. J. Auerbach, ed., *Takeovers: Causes and Consequences,* 69–96. Chicago: University of Chicago Press.

Hall, E. H., and St. John, C. H. (1994). "A Methodological Note on Diversity Measurement." *Strategic Management Journal* 15:153–168.

Halpern, P. J. (1973). "Empirical Estimates of the Amount and Distribution of Gains to Companies in Mergers." *Journal of Financial Economics* 14:555–579.

Halpern, P. J. (1983). "Corporate Acquisitions: A Theory of Special Cases? A Review of Event Studies Applied to Acquisitions." *Journal of Finance* 38:297–317.

Hamel, G., and Prahalad, C. K. (1989). "Strategic Intent." *Harvard Business Review* (May–June): 63–76.

Hamermesh, R. G. (1986). *Making Strategy Work: How Senior Managers Produce Results.* New York: Wiley.

Hannah, L. (1974). "Mergers in British Manufacturing Industry, 1880–1918." *Oxford Economic Papers* 26:1–20.

Harrigan, K. R. (1985). *Strategic Flexibility: A Management Guide for Changing Times.* Lexington, MA: Lexington Books.

Harrington, D. R., and Wilson, B. D. (1989). *Corporate Financial Analysis.* 3d ed. Homewood, IL: Irwin.

Harris, R. S., Stewart, J. F., and Carleton, W. T. (1982). "Financial Characteristics of Acquired Firms." In M. Keenan and L. J. White, eds., *Mergers and Acquisitions: Current Problems in Perspective,* 223–240. Lexington, MA: Lexington Books.

Haspeslagh, P. C. (1982). "Portfolio Planning: Uses and Limits." *Harvard Business Review* (January–February): 58–73.

Haspeslagh, P. C. (1983). "Portfolio Planning Approaches and the Strategic Management Process in Diversified Industrial Companies." Ph.D. dissertation, Boston: Harvard Business School.

Haspeslagh, P. C. (1985). "Toward a Concept of Corporate Strategy for the Diversified Firm." Research paper no. 816, Graduate School of Business, Stanford University.

Haspeslagh, P. C. (1986). "Making Acquisitions Work." *Acquisitions Monthly* (January): 14–16.

Haspeslagh, P. C. (1990). "Acquisitions as Resource Allocation Decisions: A Multinational Perspective." Working Paper, INSEAD.

Haspeslagh, P. C., and Farquhar, A. (1987). "The Acquisition Integration Process: A Contingent Framework." Paper presented at the Seventh Annual International Conference of the Strategic Management Society, Boston, October 14–17.

Haspeslagh, P. C., and Ghoshal, S. (1990). "The Challenge of Strategic Assembly." Paper presented at the International Conference of the Strategic Management Society, Stockholm, September 24–28.

Haspeslagh, P. C., and Jemison, D. B. (1987). "Acquisitions—Myth and Reality." *Sloan Management Review* 29:53–58.

Haspeslagh, P. C., and Jemison, D. B. (1991). *Managing Acquisitions: Creating Value Through Corporate Renewal.* New York: Free Press.

Haunschild, P. R. (1994). "How Much Is That Company Worth? Interorganizational Relationships, Uncertainty, and Acquisition Premiums." *Administrative Science Quarterly* 39:391–411.

Haunschild, P. R., Davis-Blake, A., and Fichman, M. (1994). "Managerial Overcommitment in Corporate Acquisition Processes." *Organization Science* 5:528–540.

Hax, A. C., and Majluf, N. S. (1984). *Strategic Management: An Integrative Perspective.* Englewood Cliffs, NJ: Prentice Hall.

Hay, G., and Untiet, C. (1981). "Statistical Measurement of the Conglomerate Problem." In R. D. Blair and R. F. Lanzillotti, eds., *The Conglomerate Corporation,* 163–191. Cambridge, MA: Oelgeschlager, Gunn & Hain.

Hayes, R. H. (1979). "The Human Side of Acquisitions." *Management Review* 68:41–46.

Hayes, R. H. (1985). "Strategic Planning-Forward in Reverse?" *Harvard Business Review* (November–December): 111–119.

Hayes, R. H., and Abernathy, W. J. (1980). "Managing Our Way to Economic Decline." *Harvard Business Review* (July–August): 67–77.

Hayes, R. H., and Hoag, G. H. (1974). "Post Acquisition Retention of Top Management." *Mergers and Acquisitions* 9:8–18.

Hayes, S. L., III, Spence, A. M., and Marks, D. V. P. (1983). *Competition in the Investment Banking Industry.* Cambridge: Harvard University Press.

Hays, L., and Bulkeley, W. M. (1995). "If IBM Acquires Lotus, It May Be Years Before It Earns a Respectable Return." *Wall Street Journal,* June 8, p. A3.

Healy, P., Palepu, K., and Ruback, R. S. (1992). "Do Mergers Improve Corporate Performance?" *Journal of Financial Economics* 31:135–175.

Hearth, D., and Zaima, J. K. (1984). "Voluntary Corporate Divestitures and Value." *Financial Management* 13:10–16.

Hennart, J. F. (1988). "A Transaction Cost Approach of Equity Joint Ventures." *Strategic Management Journal* 9:361–374.

Herman, E. S., and Lowenstein, L. (1988). "The Efficiency Effect of Hostile Takeovers." In J. C. Coffee, Jr., L. Lowenstein, and S. Rose-Ackerman, eds., *Knights, Raiders, and Targets,* 211–240. New York: Oxford University Press.

Herzel, L., and Shepro, R. W. (1990). *Bidders and Targets: Mergers and Acquisitions in the U.S.* Cambridge, MA: Basil Blackwell.

Higgins, R. C. (1992). *Analysis for Financial Management.* 3d ed. Homewood, IL: Irwin.

Hindley, B. (1970). "Separation of Ownership and Control in the Modern Corporation." *Journal of Law and Economics* 13:185–221.

Hirsch, P. M., and Andrews, J. A. Y. (1983). "Ambushes, Shootouts and Knights of the Roundtable: The Language of Corporate Takeovers." In L. R. Pondy, P. J. Frost, G. Morgan, and T. C. Dandridge, eds., *Organizational Symbolism,* 145–155. Greenwich, CT: JAI Press.

Hirsch, P. M. (1987). *Pack Your Own Parachute.* Reading, MA: Addison-Wesley.

Hite, G. L. (1989). "Notes on Free Cash Flow Used for Valuation Purposes." (Teaching notes.) Graduate School of Business, Columbia University.

Hite, G. L., and Owers, J. E. (1983). "Security Price Reactions Around Corporate Spin-Off Announcements." *Journal of Financial Economics* 12:409–436.

Hogarty, T. F. (1970). "Profits from Mergers: The Evidence of Fifty Years." *St. John's Law Review,* 44 (special edition): 378–391.

Holderness, C. G., and Sheehan, D. P. (1985). "Raiders or Saviors? The Evidence on Six Controversial Investors." *Journal of Financial Economics* 14:555–579.

Holmstrom, B. (1979). "Moral Hazard and Observability." *Bell Journal of Economics* 10:74–91.

Hout, T., Porter, M. E., and Rudden, E., (1982). "How Global Companies Win Out." *Harvard Business Review* (September–October): 98–108.

Houthakker, H. S. (1950). "Revealed Preference and the Utility Function." *Economica* 17:159–174.

Howell, R. A. (1970). "Plan to Integrate Your Acquisitions." *Harvard Business Review* (November–December): 66–76.

Huang, Y. S., and Walkling, R. A. (1987). "Target Abnormal Returns Associated with Acquisition Announcements: Payment, Acquisition Form and Managerial Resistance." *Journal of Financial Economics* 19:329–349.

Huber, G. P. (1991). "Organizational Learning: An Examination of the Contributing Processes and the Literatures." *Organization Science* 2:46–51.

Hughes, A. (1989). "The Impact of Merger: A Survey of Empirical Evidence for the UK." In J. Fairburn and J. Kay, eds., *Mergers and Merger Policy,* 30–98. Oxford: Oxford University Press.

Hughes, A., and Singh, A. (1980). "Mergers, Concentration, and Competition in Advanced Capitalist Economies: An International Comparison." In D. C. Mueller, ed., *The Determinants and Effects of Mergers: An International Comparison,* 1–26. Cambridge, MA: Oelgeschlager, Gunn & Hain.

Ikeda, K., and Doi, N. (1983). "The Performance of Merging Firms in Japanese Manufacturing Industry: 1964–75." *Journal of Industrial Economics* 31:257–266.

Itami, H. (1987). *Mobilizing Invisible Assets.* Cambridge: Harvard University Press.

Ivancevich, J. M., Schweiger, D. M., and Power, F. R. (1987). "Strategies for Managing Human Resources During Mergers and Acquisitions." *Human Resource Planning* 10:19–35.

Jaccard, J., Turrisi, R., and Wan, C. K. (1984). *Interaction Effects in Multiple Regression.* Newbury Park, CA: Sage.

Jackson, S. E., and Dutton, J. E. (1988). "Discerning Threats and Opportunities." *Administrative Science Quarterly* 33:370–387.

Jacobson, R. (1987). "The Validity of ROI as a Measure of Business Performance." *American Economic Review* 77:470–478.

Jacobson, R. (1992). "The 'Austrian' School of Strategy." *Academy of Management Review* 17:782–807.

Jacquemin, A. P., and Berry, C. H. (1979). "Entropy Measure of Diversification and Corporate Growth." *Journal of Industrial Economics* 27:359–369.

Jacquemin, A., and Slade, M. E. (1989). "Cartels, Collusion, and Horizonal Merger." In R. Schmalensee and R. Willig, eds., *Handbook of Industrial Organization,* 1:415–473. Amsterdam: North Holland.

Janis, I. L. (1972). *Victims of Groupthink.* Boston: Houghton Mifflin.

Janis, I. L. (1982). "Decision Making Under Stress." In L. Goldberg and S. Breznits, eds., *Handbook on Stress: Theoretical and Clinical Aspects.* New York: Free Press.

Janis, I. L. (1989). *Crucial Decisions: Leadership in Policymaking and Crisis Management.* New York: Free Press.

Janis, I. L., and Mann, L. (1977). *Decision Making: A Psychological Analysis of Conflict, Choice, and Commitment.* New York: Free Press.

Jarrell, G. A., Brickley, J. A., and Netter, J. M. (1988). "The Market for Corporate Control: The Empirical Evidence Since 1980." *Journal of Economic Perspectives* 2:21–48.

Jarrell, G. A., and Poulsen, A. (1987). "Shark Repellants and Stockprices: The Effects of Antitakeover Amendments Since 1980." *Journal of Financial Economics* 19:127–168.

Jarrell, G. A., and Poulsen, A. (1989). "The Returns to Acquiring Firms in Tender Offers: Evidence from Three Decades." *Financial Management* 18:12–19.

Jarrell, S. L. (1995). "The Long-Term Performance of Corporate Takeovers: An Improved Benchmark Methodology." Working paper, Graduate School of Business, Columbia University.

Jemison, D. B. (1981a). "Organizational Versus Environmental Sources of Influence in Strategic Decision Making." *Strategic Management Journal* 2:77–89.

Jemison, D. B. (1981b). "The Importance of an Integrative Approach to Strategic Management Research." *Academy of Management Review* 6:601–608.

Jemison, D. B. (1985). "The Role of the Division General Manager in Corporate Strategic Management." In R. Lamb and P. Shrivastava, eds., *Advances in Strategic Management,* 163–179. Greenwich, CT: JAI Press.

Jemison, D. B. (1986). "Strategic Capability Transfer in Acquisition Integration." Research paper series no. 913, Graduate School of Business, Stanford University.

Jemison, D. B. (1988). "Value Creation and Acquisition Integration: The Role of Strategic Capability Transfer." In G. Liebcap, ed., *Corporate Restructuring Through Mergers, Acquisitions and Leveraged Buyouts,* 191–218. Greenwich, CT: JAI Press.

Jemison, D. B., and Sitkin, S. B. (1986a). "Corporate Acquisitions: A Process Perspective." *Academy of Management Journal* 11:145–163.

Jemison, D. B., and Sitkin, S. B. (1986b). "Acquisitions: The Process Can Be a Problem." *Harvard Business Review* 64 (March–April): 107–116.

Jennings, R., and Mazzeo, M. (1991). "Stock Price Movements Around Acquisition Announcements and Management's Response." *Journal of Business* 64:139–163.

Jensen, E., Robichaux, M., and Steinmetz, G. (1994). "Larry-Barry Show: Is CBS in Play Now? If Merger Is 'Strategic,' What Is the Strategy?" *Wall Street Journal,* July 1, p. A1.

Jensen, M. C. (1972). *Studies in the Theory of Capital Markets.* New York: Praeger.

Jensen, M. C. (1983). "Organization Theory and Methodology." *Accounting Review* 58:319–345.

Jensen, M. C. (1984). "Takeovers: Folklore and Science." *Harvard Business Review* 62 (November–December): 109–121.

Jensen, M. C. (1986). "Agency Costs of Free Cash Flow, Corporate Finance, and Takeovers." *American Economic Review* 76:323–329.

Jensen, M. C. (1987a). *Hearing on Impact of Mergers and Acquisitions,* before the U.S. House of Representatives, Committee on Energy and Commerce, Subcommittee on Telecommunications and Finance.

Jensen, M. C. (1987b). "The Free Cash Flow Theory of Takeovers: A Financial Perspective on Mergers and Acquisitions and the Economy." In L. E. Browne and E. S. Rosengren, eds., *The Merger Boom,* 102–143. Boston: Federal Reserve Bank of Boston.

Jensen, M. C. (1988). "The Takeover Controversy: Analysis and Evidence." In J. C. Coffee, Jr., L. Lowenstein, and S. Rose-Ackerman, eds., *Knights, Raiders, and Targets: The Impact of Hostile Takeovers,* 171–193. New York: Oxford University Press.

Jensen, M. C. (1991). "Corporate Control and the Politics of Finance." *Journal of Applied Corporate Finance* 4:13–33.

Jensen, M. C. (1993). "The Modern Industrial Revolution, Exit, and the Failure of Internal Control Systems." *Journal of Finance* 48:831–880.

Jensen, M. C., and Meckling, W. H. (1976). "Theory of the Firm: Managerial Behavior, Agency Costs and Ownership Structure." *Journal of Financial Economics* 3:305–360.

Jensen, M. C., and Ruback, R. S. (1983). "The Market for Corporate Control: The Scientific Evidence." *Journal of Financial Economics* 11:5–50.

Jick, T. (1979). "Process and Impacts of a Merger: Individual and Organizational Perspectives." Ph.D. dissertation, Cornell University.

Jick, T. D. (1988). *Unisys: The Merger of Burroughs and Sperry.* Harvard Case 9-489-055.

Jick, T. D. (1990). *Northwest Airlines Confronts Change.* Harvard Case 9-491-036.

Jones, G., and Hill, C. (1988). "Transaction Cost Analysis of Strategy-Structure Choice." *Strategic Management Journal* 9:159–172.

Kahneman, D., Slovic, P., and Tversky, A. (1982). *Judgment Under Uncertainty: Heuristics and Biases.* Cambridge: Cambridge University Press.

Kahneman, D., and Tversky, A. (1972). "Subjective Probability: A Judgement of Representativeness." *Cognitive Psychology* 3:430–454.

Kahneman, D., and Tversky, A. (1979). "Prospect Theory. An Analysis of Decisions Under Risk." *Econometrica* 47:263–291.

Kalay, A., and Loewenstein, U. (1985). "Predictable Events and Excess Returns: The Case of Dividend Announcements." *Journal of Financial Economics* 18:423–449.

Kaplan, M. R., and Harrison, J. R. (1993). "Defusing the Director Liability Crisis: The Strategic Management of Legal Threats." *Organization Science* 4:412–432.

Kaplan, S. N. (1989a). "Management Buyouts: Evidence on Taxes as a Source of Value." *Journal of Finance* 44:611–632.

Kaplan, S. N. (1989b). "Campeau's Acquisition of Federated." *Journal of Financial Economics* 25:191–212.

Kaplan, S. N., and Weisbach, M. S. (1992). "The Success of Acquisitions: Evidence from Divestitures." *Journal of Finance* 47:107–138.

Keil, P. J. (1966). "Expert Stresses Need for Planning." *California Business,* July 5, pp. 8–10.

Keller, J. J. (1995). "Disconnected Line: Why AT&T Takeover of NCR Hasn't Been a Real Bell Ringer." *Wall Street Journal,* September 19, p. A1.

Kelley, G. (1976). "Seducing the Elites: The Politics of Decision Making and Innovation in Organizational Networks." *Academy of Management Review* 1:66–74.

Kim, E. H., and McConnell, J. J. (1977). "Corporate Mergers and the Co-Insurance of Corporate Debt." *Journal of Finance* 32:349–363.

Kim, E. H., McConnell, J. J., and Greenwood, P. (1977). "Capital Structure Rearrangement and Me-First Rules in an Efficient Capital Market." *Journal of Finance* 32:789–810.

Kim, W. C., Hwang, P., and Burgers, W. P. (1989). "Global Diversification Strategy and Corporate Profit Performance." *Strategic Management Journal* 10:45–57.

Kim, W. C., Hwang, P., and Burgers, W. P. (1993). "Multinationals' Diversification and the Risk-Return Trade-off." *Strategic Management Journal* 14:275–286.

Kimberly, J. R. (1984). *New Futures: The Challenges of Managing Corporate Transitions.* Homewood, IL: Dow Jones–Irwin.

Kitching, J. (1967). "Why Do Mergers Miscarry?" *Harvard Business Review* 45 (November–December): 84–101.

Kitching, J. (1974). "Winning and Losing with European Acquisitions." *Harvard Business Review* (March–April): 124–136.

Klein, A. (1986). "The Timing and Substance of Divestiture Announcement: Individual, Simultaneous, and Cumulative Effects." *Journal of Finance* 41:685–696.

Kmenta, J. (1986). *Elements of Econometrics.* 2d ed. New York: Macmillan.

Kogut, B. (1985). "Designing Global Strategies: Comparative and Competitive Value Added Choices." *Sloan Management Review* 26:15–28.

Kogut, B. (1988). "Joint Ventures: Theoretical and Empirical Perspectives." *Strategic Management Journal* 9:319–322.

Kuehn, D. (1975). *Takeovers and the Theory of the Firm.* London: Macmillan.

Kusewitt, J. B., Jr. (1985). "An Exploratory Study of Strategic Acquisition Factors Relating to Performance." *Strategic Management Journal* 6:151–169.

Lamoreaux, N. R. (1985). *The Great Merger Movement in American Business.* Cambridge: Cambridge University Press.

Lang, L. H. P., and Stulz, R. M. (1994). "Tobin's q, Corporate Diversification and Firm Performance." *Journal of Political Economy* 102:1248–1280.

Lang, L. H. P., Stulz, R. M., and Walkling, R. (1989) "Tobin's Q and the Gains from Successful Tender Offers." *Journal of Financial Economics* 24:137–154.

Lang, L. H. P., Stulz, R. M., and Walkling, R. A. (1991). "The Test of the Free Cash Flow Hypothesis: The Case of Bidder Returns." *Journal of Financial Economics* 29:315–335.

Langetieg, T. C. (1978). "An Application of a Three-Factor Performance Index to Measure Stockholder Gains from Merger." *Journal of Financial Economics* 6:365–384.

Larcker, D. (1983). "Managerial Incentives in Mergers and Their Effects on Shareholder Wealth." *Midland Corporate Finance Journal* 1:29–35.

Lawrence, P. R., and Dyer, D. S. (1983). *Renewing American Industry.* New York: Free Press.

Leamer, E. E. (1978). *Specification Searches.* Wiley: New York.

Leavitt, H. J. (1986). *Corporate Pathfinders: Building Visions and Values into Organizations.* Homewood, IL: Dow Jones–Irwin.

Lehn, K., and Poulsen, A. B. (1988). "Leveraged Buyouts: Wealth Created or Wealth Redistributed?" In L. M. Weidenbaum and K. Chilton, eds., *Public Policy Toward Corporate Takeovers,* 46–62. New Brunswick, NJ: Transaction Publishers.

Leighton, C. M., and Tod, G. R. (1969). "After the Acquisition: Continuing Challenge." *Harvard Business Review* (March–April): 90–102.

Lemelin, A. (1982). "Relatedness in the Patterns of Interindustry Diversification." *Review of Economics and Statistics* 64:646–657.

Lenz, R. T. (1980). "Strategic Capability: A Concept and Framework for Analysis." *Academy of Management Review* 5:225–234.

Levin, D. (1989). *Irreconcilable Differences.* Boston: Little, Brown.

Levinson, H. (1979). "A Psychologist Diagnoses Merger Failures." *Harvard Business Review* (March–April): 139–147.

Levitt, B., and March, J. G. (1988). "Organizational Learning." *Annual Review of Sociology* 14:319–340.

Levy, H., and Sarnat, M., (1970). "Diversification Portfolio Analysis and the Uneasy Case for Conglomerate Mergers." *Journal of Finance* 25:795–802.

Lewellen, W. G. (1971). "A Pure Financial Rationale for the Conglomerate Merger." *Journal of Finance* 16:521–537.

Lewellen, W. G., Loderer, C., and Rosenfeld, A. (1985). "Merger Decisions and Executive Stock Ownership in Acquiring Firms." *Journal of Accounting and Economics* 7:209–231.

Lichtenberg, F. R. (1992). "Industrial De-Diversification and Its Consequences for Productivity." *Journal of Economic Behavior and Organization* 18:427–438.

Lichtenberg, F. R., and Siegel, D. (1989). "Productivity and Changes in Ownership of Manufacturing Plants." *Brookings Papers on Economic Activity: Microeconomics,* 643–673.

Lichtenberg, F. R., and Siegel, D. (1990a). "The Effects of Leveraged Buyouts on Productivity and Related Aspects of Firm Behavior." *Journal of Financial Economics* 27:265–284.

Lichtenberg, F. R., and Siegel, D. (1990b). "The Effect of Ownership Changes in the Employment and Wages of Central Office and Other Personnel." *Journal of Law and Economics* 33:383–408.

Lindgren, U. (1982). *Foreign Acquisitions: Management of the Integration Process.* Stockholm: Business School Press.

Linn, S. C., and Rozeff, M. S. (1985). "The Effect of Voluntary Spin-offs on Stock Prices: The Anergy Hypothesis." In C. F. Lee, ed., *Advances in Financial Planning and Forecasting,* 1:265–291. Greenwich, CT: JAI Press.

Lintner, J. (1965). "The Valuation of Risk Assets and the Selection of Risky Investments in Stock Portfolios and Capital Budgets." *Review of Economics and Statistics* 47:13–37.

Lintner, J. (1971). "Expectations, Mergers and Equilibrium in Purely Competitive Securities Markets." *American Economic Review* 61:101–111.

Lippman, S. A., and Rumelt, R. P. (1982). "Uncertain Imitability: An Analysis of Interfirm Differences in Efficiency Under Competition." *Bell Journal of Economics* 13:418–438.

Loderer, C., and Martin, K. (1990). "Corporate Acquisitions by NYSE and AMEX Firms: The Experience of a Comprehensive Sample." *Financial Management* (Winter): 17–33.

Loderer, C., and Martin, K. (1992). "Postacquisition Performance of Acquiring Firms." *Financial Management* (Autumn): 69–79

Lohr, S. (1989). "Synergy, Redefined, Back in Style." *New York Times,* May 8, p. D3.

Lorange, P. (1980). *Corporate Planning: An Executive Viewpoint.* Englewood Cliffs, NJ: Prentice Hall.

Lorange, P., and Vancil, R. F. (1977). *Strategic Planning Systems.* Englewood Cliffs, NJ: Prentice Hall.

Lowenstein, R. (1991). "After 2 Years, Time Warner Marriage Still Has to Bloom." *Wall Street Journal,* June 18, p. C1.

Lubatkin, M. (1983). "Mergers and the Performance of the Acquiring Firm." *Academy of Management Review* 8:218–225.

Lubatkin, M. (1987). "Merger Strategies and Stockholder Value." *Strategic Management Journal* 8:39–53.

Lubatkin, M., and Lane, P. J. (1996). "Psst . . . The Merger Mavens Still Have It Wrong!" *Academy of Management Executive* 10:21–37.

Lubatkin, M., Merchant, H., and Srinivasan, N. (1993). "Construct Validity of Some Unweighted Product-Count Diversification Measures." *Strategic Management Journal* 14:433–449.

Lubatkin, M., and O'Neill, H. M. (1987). "Merger Strategies and Capital Market Risk." *Academy of Management Journal* 30:665–684.

Lutz, R. A. (1995). "Finding Competitive Advantage in a Changing World: A Difference of Opinions." Address to the Strategic Management Society's 15th Annual International Conference, Mexico City, October 18.

MacCrimmon, K. R., and Wehrung, D. H. (1986). *Taking Risks: The Management of Uncertainty.* New York: Free Press.

MacDonald, J. M. (1985). "R&D and the Directions of Diversification." *Review of Economics and Statistics* 67:583–590.

Mace, M. L., and Montgomery, G. (1962). *Management Problems of Corporate Acquisitions.* Cambridge: Harvard University Press.

Magenheim, E. B., and Mueller, D. C. (1988). "Are Acquiring-Firm Shareholders Better Off After an Acquisition?" In J. C. Coffee, L. Lowenstein, and S. Rose-Ackerman, eds., *Knights, Raiders, and Targets: The Impact of Hostile Takeovers,* 171–193. New York: Oxford University Press.

Mahoney, J. T., and Pandian, J. R. (1992) "The Resource-based View Within the Conversation of Strategic Management." *Strategic Management Journal* 13:363–380.

Malatesta, P. H. (1983). "The Wealth Effect of Merger Activity and the Objective Functions of Merging Firms." *Journal of Financial Economics* 11:155–181.

Mandelker, G. (1974). "Risk and Return: The Case of Merging Firms." *Journal of Financial Economics* 1:303–335.

Manne, H. G. (1965). "Mergers and the Market for Corporate Control." *Journal of Political Economy* 73:110–120.

March, J. G. (1962). "The Business Firm as a Political Coalition." *Journal of Politics* 24:662–678.

March, J. G. (1978). "Bounded Rationality, Ambiguity, and the Engineering of Choice." *Bell Journal of Economics* 9:587–608.

March, J. G., and Shapira, Z. (1987). "Managerial Perspectives on Risk and Risk Taking." *Management Science* 33:1404–1418.

Markham, J. W., (1955). "Survey of the Evidence and Findings on Mergers." In *Business Concentration and Price Policy,* 141–182. New York: National Bureau of Economic Research.

Markides, C. C. (1990). "Corporate Refocusing and Economic Performance." Ph.D. dissertation. Harvard Business School.

Markides, C. C., and Williamson, P. J. (1994). "Related Diversification, Core Competencies and Corporate Performance." *Strategic Management Journal* 15:149–165.

Markowitz, H. (1952). "Portfolio Selection." *Journal of Finance* 7:77–91.

Marks, M. L. (1982). "Merging Human Resources: A Review of Current Research." *Mergers and Acquisitions* 17:38–44.

Marks, M. L., and Mirvis, P. (1985). "Merger Syndrome: Stress and Uncertainty." *Mergers and Acquisitions* (Summer): 50–55.

Marks, M. L., and Mirvis, P. (1991). *Managing the Merger.* Englewood Cliffs, NJ: Prentice Hall.

Marris, R. (1963). "A Model of the 'Managerial' Enterprise." *Quarterly Journal of Economics* 77:185–209.

Marris, R. (1964). *The Economic Theory of Managerial Capitalism.* Glencoe, IL: Free Press.

Marshall, W. J., Yawitz, J. B., and Greenberg, E. (1984). "Incentives for Diversification and the Structure of the Conglomerate Firm." *Southern Economic Journal* 51:1–23.

Martin, J., and Meyerson, D. (1988). "Organizational Cultures and the Denial, Channeling, and Acknowledgement of Ambiguity." In L. R. Pondy, R. J. Boland, and H. Thomas, eds., *Managing Ambiguity and Change,* 93–126. New York: Wiley.

Martin, J., and Siehl, C. (1983). "Organizational Cultures and the Counterculture: An Uneasy Symbiosis." *Organizational Dynamics* (Autumn): 52–64.

Masson, R. T. (1971). "Executive Motivation, Earnings, and Consequent Equity Performance." *Journal of Political Economy* 79:1278–1292.

McCann, J. E., and Gilkey, R. (1988). *Joining Forces: Creating and Managing Successful Mergers and Acquisitions.* Englewood Cliffs, NJ: Prentice Hall.

McCasky, M. B. (1982). *The Executive Challenge: Managing Change and Ambiguity.* Boston: Pitman.

McConnell, J. J., and Muscarella, C. J. (1985). "Corporate Capital Expenditure Decisions and the Market Value of the Firm." *Journal of Financial Economics* 14:399–422.

McGuckin, R. H., Warren-Boulton, F., and Waldstein, P. (1988). *Analysis of Mergers Using Stock Market Returns.* Discussion paper no. 8801. Washington, D.C.: U.S. Department of Justice, Economic Analysis Group.

Meeks, G. (1977). *Disappointing Marriage: A Study of the Gains from Merger.* Cambridge, U.K.: Cambridge University Press.

Meeks, G., and Meeks, J. G. (1981). "Profitability Measures as Indicators of Post-Merger Efficiency." *Journal of Industrial Economics* 29:335–344.

Melcher, R. A. (1996). "How Eagle Became Extinct." *Business Week,* March 4, pp. 68–69.

Melicher, R. W., Ledolter, J., and D'Antonio, L. J. (1983). "A Time Series Analysis of Aggregate Merger Activity." *Review of Economics and Statistics* 65:423–430.

Melicher, R. W., and Rush, D. F. (1974). "Evidence on the Acquisition-Related Performance of Conglomerate Firms." *Journal of Finance* 29:141–149.

Mergerstat Review. (1996). Los Angeles: Houlihan Lokey Howard & Zukin.

Meyer, J. W., and Rowan, B. (1977). "Institutionalized Organizations: Formal Structure as Myth and Ceremony." *American Journal of Sociology* 83:340–363.

Meyer, M. W., and O'Shaughnessy, K. C. (1992). "Organizational Design and the Performance Paradox." Working paper, University of Pennsylvania.

Michel, A., and Shaked, I. (1984). "Does Business Diversification Affect Performance?" *Financial Management* 13:18–25.

Miles, R. H. (1981). "Learning from Diversifying." Harvard Business School Note 9-481-060.

Miles, R. H. (1982). *Coffin Nails and Corporate Strategies.* Englewood Cliffs, NJ: Prentice Hall.

Miles, J. A., and Rosenfeld, J. D. (1983). "The Effect of Voluntary Spin-off Announcements on Shareholder Wealth." *Journal of Finance* 38:1597–1606.

Miller, M. H., and Modigliani, F. (1961). "Dividend Policy, Growth and the Valuation of Shares." *Journal of Business* 34:411–433.

Mintzberg, H. (1973). *The Nature of Managerial Work*. New York: Harper & Row.

Mintzberg, H. (1978). "Patterns in Strategy Formulation." *Management Science* 24:934–948.

Mintzberg, H. (1987). "Crafting Strategy." *Harvard Business Review* (July–August): 66–75.

Mitchell, M. L., and Lehn, K. (1990). "Do Bad Bidders Make Good Targets?" *Journal of Political Economy* 98:372–398.

Modigliani, F., and Miller, M. H. (1958). "The Cost of Capital, Corporation Finance and the Theory of Investment." *American Economic Review* 48:261–297.

Monks, R. A. G., and Minow, N. (1995). *Corporate Governance*. Cambridge, MA: Blackwell.

Montgomery, C. A. (1982). "The Measurement of Firm Diversification: Some New Empirical Evidence." *Academy of Management Journal* 25:299–307.

Montgomery, C. A. (1985). "Product-Market Diversification and Market Power." *Academy of Management Journal* 28:789–798.

Montgomery, C. A. (1991). *Sears, Roebuck and Co. in 1989*. Harvard Case 9-391-147.

Montgomery, C. A., and Singh, H. (1984). "Diversification Strategy and Systematic Risk." *Strategic Management Journal* 5:181–191.

Montgomery, C. A., Thomas, A. R., and Kamath, R. (1984). "Divestiture, Market Valuation, and Strategy." *Academy of Management Journal* 27:830–840.

Morck, R., Shleifer, A., and Vishny, R. W. (1988). "Characteristics of Targets of Hostile and Friendly Takeovers." In A. J. Auerbach, ed., *Takeovers: Causes and Consequences*, 101–129. Chicago: University of Chicago Press.

Morck, R., Shleifer, A., and Vishny, R. (1990). "Do Managerial Objectives Drive Bad Acquisitions?" *Journal of Finance* 45:31–48.

Mueller, D. C. (1969). "A Theory of Conglomerate Mergers." *Quarterly Journal of Economics* 83:643–659.

Mueller, D. C. (1972). "A Life Cycle Theory of the Firm." *Journal of Industrial Economics* 20:199–219.

Mueller, D. C. (1977). "The Effects of Conglomerate Mergers: A Survey of the Empirical Evidence." *Journal of Banking and Finance* 1:315–347.

Mueller, D. C. (1980). *The Determinants and Effects of Mergers: An International Comparison*. Cambridge, MA: Oelgeschlager, Gunn & Hain.

Mueller, D. C. (1985). "Mergers and Market Share." *Review of Economics and Statistics* 67:259–267.

Mueller, D. C. (1986). *Profits in the Long Run*. Cambridge: Cambridge University Press.

Mueller, D. C. (1989). "Mergers: Causes, Effects, and Policies." *International Journal of Industrial Organization* 7:1–10.

Mueller, D. C. (1990). *The Dynamics of Company Profits*. Cambridge: Cambridge University Press.

Mueller, D. C. (1995). "Mergers: Theory and Evidence." In G. Mussati, ed., *Mergers, Markets and Public Policy*, 9–43. Netherlands: Kluwer.

Mueller, D. C., and Sirower, M. L. (1996). "Motives in the Market for Corporate Control: An Empirical Analysis." Working paper, Stern School of Business, New York University.

Muller, J. (1976). "The Impact of Mergers on Concentration: A Study of Eleven West German Industries." *Journal of Industrial Economics* 25:113–132.

Mullins, D. W., Jr. (1982). "Does the Capital Asset Pricing Model Work?" *Harvard Business Review* (January–February): 104–114.

Murphy, K. J. (1985). "Corporate Performance and Managerial Remuneration: An Empirical Analysis." *Journal of Accounting and Economics* 7:11–42.

Muth, J. F. (1960). "Optimal Properties of Exponentially Weighted Forecasts." *Journal of American Statistical Association* 55:299–306.

Muth, J. F. (1961). "Rational Expectations and the Theory of Price Movements." *Econometrica* 29:315–335.

Myers, S., and Majluf, N. S. (1984). "Corporate Financing and Investment Decisions When Firms Have Information That Investors Do Not Have." *Journal of Financial Economics* 13:187–221.

Nahavandi, A., and Malekzadeh, A. R. (1988). "Acculturation in Mergers and Acquisitions." *Academy of Management Review* 13:79–90.

Napier, N. K. (1989). "Mergers and Acquisitions, Human Resource Issues and Outcomes: A Review and Suggested Typology." *Journal of Management Studies* 26:271–289.

Napier, N. K., Simmons, G., and Stratton, K. (1989). "Communication During a Merger: Experience of Two Banks." *Human Resource Planning* 12:105–122.

Nathanson, D. A. (1985). "The Strategic Diversity Classification System: A Framework for Decision Making." In W. D. Guth, ed., *Handbook of Business Strategy*, 1–20. New York: Warren, Gorham and Lamont.

Naylor, T. H. (1979). *Corporate Planning Models.* Reading, MA: Addison-Wesley.

Nees, D. (1981). "Increase Your Divestment Effectiveness." *Strategic Management Journal* 2:119–130.

Nelson, C. A., and Lagges, J. G. (1993). "Corporate Boards and Mergers." *Corporate Board* (May–June): 12–16.

Nelson, R. L. (1959). *Merger Movements in American Industry, 1885–1956.* Princeton: Princeton University Press.

Nelson, R. L. (1966). "Business Cycle Factors in the Choice Between Internal and External Growth." In W. Alberts and J. Segall, eds., *The Corporate Merger.* Chicago: University of Chicago Press.

Nelson, R. R., and Winter, S. G. (1982). *An Evolutionary Theory of Economic Change.* Cambridge: Harvard University Press.

Newbould, G. D. (1970). *Management and Merger Activity.* Liverpool: Guthstead.

Newbould, G. D., Stray, S. J., and Wilson, K. W. (1976). "Shareholders' Interests and Acquisition Activity." *Accounting and Business Research* 23:201–213.

Normann, R. (1977). *Management for Growth.* New York: Wiley.

Norris, F. (1993). "On Wall Street, Love Can Soon Turn to Hate." *New York Times,* October 17, p. D1.

Norris, F. (1994). "In Paramount Battle, the Winners Lost $4.1 Billion." *New York Times,* February 20, p. E1.

Ohlson, J. A., and Penman, S. H. (1985). "Volatility Increases Subsequent to Stock Splits." *Journal of Financial Economics* 14:251–266.

Oneal, M. (1995). "I'm Perfectly Willing to Be Run out of Town." *Business Week,* October 9, pp. 38–39.

O'Reilly, C. (1989). "Corporations, Culture, and Commitment: Motivation and Social Control in Organizations." *California Management Review* 31:9–25.

Palepu, K. (1985). "Diversification Strategy, Profit Performance, and the Entropy Measure." *Strategic Management Journal* 6:239–255.

Palepu, K. (1986). "Predicting Takeover Targets: A Methodological and Empirical Analysis." *Journal of Accounting and Economics* 8:3–35.

Palij, P. (1992). "Primerica Corporation (A)." In N. Capon, ed., *The Marketing of Financial Services: A Book of Cases.* Englewood Cliffs, NJ: Prentice Hall.

Panzar, J. C., and Willig, R. D. (1977). "Economies of Scale and Economies of Scope in Multi-Output Production." *Quarterly Journal of Economics* 91:481–493.

Panzar, J. C., and Willig, R. D. (1981). "Economies of Scope." *American Economic Review* 71:268–272.

Pare, T. P. (1994). "The New Merger Boom." *Fortune,* November 28, pp. 95–106.

Patterson, G. (1994). "Sears to Spin Off Allstate; Brennan to Retire in 1995." *Wall Street Journal,* November 11, p. A3.

Peavy, J. W., III. (1984). "Modern Financial Theory, Corporate Strategy, and Public Policy: Another Perspective." *Academy of Management Review* 9:152–157.

Penn, T. A. (1981). "Premiums: What Do They Really Measure?" *Mergers and Acquisitions* (Fall): 30–34.

Penrose, E. (1959). *The Theory of the Growth of the Firm.* Oxford: Blackwell.

Perry, M. K. (1989). "Vertical Integration: Determinants and Effects." In R. Schmalensee and R. Willig, eds., *Handbook of Industrial Organization* 1:415–473. Amsterdam: North-Holland.

Perry, M. K., and Porter, R. H. (1985). "Oligopoly and the Incentive for Horizontal Merger." *American Economic Review* 75:19–27

Peteraf, M. A. (1993). "The Cornerstones of Competitive Advantage: A Resource-based View." *Strategic Management Journal* 14:179–191.

Peters, T. J., and R. H. Waterman, Jr. (1982). *In Search of Excellence.* New York: Basic Books.

Pettigrew, A. M. (1977). "Strategy Formulation as a Political Process." *International Studies of Management and Organization* 7:78–87.

Pettigrew, A. M. (1979). "On Studying Organizational Cultures." *Administrative Science Quarterly* 24:570–581.

Pfeffer, J. (1981). *Power in Organizations.* Marshfield, MA: Pitman Publishing.

Picini, R. (1970). "Mergers, Diversification and the Growth of Large Firms 1948–1965." *St. John's Law Review* (Spring): 44–64.

Porter, M. E. (1980). *Competitive Strategy.* New York: Free Press.

Porter, M. E. (1985). *Competitive Advantage.* New York: Free Press.

Porter, M. E. (1987). "From Competitive Advantage to Corporate Strategy." *Harvard Business Review* (May–June): 43–59.

Porter, M. E. (1990a). "Japan Isn't Playing by Different Rules." *New York Times,* July 22.

Porter, M. E. (1990b). *The Competitive Advantage of Nations.* New York: Free Press.

Pound, J. (1992). "Beyond Takeovers: Politics Comes to Corporate Finance." *Harvard Business Review* (March–April): 83–93.

Pound, J. (1993). "The Rise of the Political Model of Corporate Governance and Corporate Control." *New York University Law Review* 68:1003–1071.

Pound, J. (1995). "The Promise of the Governed Corporation." *Harvard Business Review* (March–April): 89–98.

Praeger, F. A. (1976). "A Framework for Evaluating Mergers." In S. C. Meyers, ed., *Modern Developments in Financial Management.* Hinsdale, IL: Dryden Press.

Prahalad, C. K., and Bettis, R. A. (1986). "The Dominant Logic: A New Linkage Between Diversity and Performance." *Strategic Management Journal* 7:485–501.

Prahalad, C. K., and Hamel, G. (1990). "The Core Competence of the Corporation." *Harvard Business Review* (May–June): 79–91.

Pritchett, P. (1985). *After the Merger: Managing the Shockwaves.* Homewood, IL: Dow Jones–Irwin.

Pritchett, P. (1987). *Making Mergers Work: A Guide to Managing Mergers and Acquisitions.* Homewood, IL: Dow Jones–Irwin.

Queenan, J. (1995). Comments from the PBS Video roundtable discussion, *Profits and Promises.* New York: Seminars, Inc.

Quinn, J. B. (1980). *Strategies for Change: Logical Incrementalism.* Homewood, IL: Richard D. Irwin.

Ramanujam, V., and Varadarajan, P. (1989). "Research on Corporate Diversification: A Synthesis." *Strategic Management Journal* 10:523–551.

Rappaport, A. (1979). "Strategic Analysis for More Profitable Acquisitions." *Harvard Business Review* 57 (July–August): 99–111.

Rappaport, A. (1986). *Creating Shareholder Value: The New Standard for Business Performance.* New York: Free Press.

Ravenscraft, D. J., and Scherer, F. M. (1987a). "Life After Takeover." *Journal of Industrial Economics* 36:147–156.

Ravenscraft, D. J., and Scherer, F. M. (1987b). *Mergers, Sell-offs, and Economic Efficiency.* Washington, D.C.: Brookings Institution.

Ravenscraft, D. J., and Scherer, F. M. (1988). "Mergers and Managerial Performance." In J. C. Coffee, L. Lowenstein, and S. Rose-Ackerman, eds., *Knights, Raiders, and Targets: The Impact of Hostile Takeovers,* 194–210. New York: Oxford University Press.

Ravenscraft, D. J., and Scherer, F. M. (1989). "The Profitability of Mergers." *International Journal of Industrial Organization* 7:101–116.

Ravenscraft, D. J., and Scherer, F. M. (1991). "Divisional Sell-Off: A Hazard Function Analysis." *Managerial and Decision Economics* 12:429–438.

Reed, R., and Luffman, G. A. (1986). "Diversification: The Growing Confusion." *Strategic Management Journal* 7:29–35.

Reid, S. R. (1968). *Mergers, Managers and the Economy.* New York: McGraw-Hill.

Reid, S. R. (1970). "A Reply to the Weston/Mansinghka Criticisms Dealing with Conglomerate Mergers." *Journal of Finance* 26:937–946.

Rhoades, S. A. (1983). *Power, Empire Building and Mergers.* Lexington, MA: Lexington Books.

Rhoades, S. A. (1987). "The Operating Performances of Acquired Firms in Banking." In R. L. Wills, J. A. Caswell, and J. D. Culbertson, eds., *Issues After a Century of Federal Competition Policy,* 277–292. Lexington, MA: Lexington Books.

Roe, M. J. (1991). "A Political Theory of American Corporate Finance." *Columbia Law Review* 91:10–67.

Roll, R. (1986). "The Hubris Hypothesis of Corporate Takeovers." *Journal of Business* 59:197–216.

Roll, R. (1988). "Empirical Evidence on Takeover Activity and Shareholder Wealth." In J. C. Coffee, L. Lowenstein, and S. Rose-Ackerman, eds., *Knights, Raiders, and Targets: The Impact of Hostile Takeovers,* 241–252. New York: Oxford University Press.

Rosenzweig, P. M., and Pearson, A. E. (1992). *Primerica: Sandy Weill and His Corporate Entrepreneurs.* Harvard Case 9-393-040.

Ross, S. A., Westerfield, R. W. and Jaffe, J. F. (1993) *Corporate Finance.* 2d ed. Boston: Irwin.

Ruback, R. S. (1982). "Conoco Takeover and Stockholders' Returns." *Sloan Management Review* 23:13–33.

Ruback, R. S. (1983). "Assessing Competition in the Market for Corporate Acquisitions." *Journal of Financial Economics* 11:141–153.

Ruback, R. S. (1988a). "An Overview of Takeover Defenses." In A. J. Auerbach, ed., *Mergers and Acquisitions,* 49–67. Chicago: University of Chicago Press.

Ruback, R. S. (1988b). "Comment." In A. J. Auerbach, ed., *Corporate Takeovers: Courses and Consequences,* 260–263. Chicago: University of Chicago Press.

Rubin, P. H. (1973). "The Expansion of Firms." *Journal of Political Economy* 81:936–949.

Ruefli, T. (1990). "Mean-Variance Approaches to Risk-Return Relationships in Strategy: Paradox Lost." *Management Science* 36:368–380.

Rugman, A. M. (1979). *International Diversification and the Multinational Enterprise.* Lexington, MA: Heath.

Rumelt, R. P. (1974). *Strategy, Structure and Economic Performance.* Boston: Harvard University Press.

Rumelt, R. P. (1982). "Diversification Strategy and Profitability." *Strategic Management Journal* 3:359–369.

Salant, S. W., Switzer, S., and Reynolds, R. J. (1983). "Losses from Horizontal Merger: The Effects of an Exogenous Change in Industry Structure on Cournot-Nash Equilibrium." *Quarterly Journal of Economics* 98:185–199.

Sales, A., and Mirvis, P. H. (1985). "When Cultures Collide: Issues in Acquisitions." In J. R. Kimberly and R. E. Quinn, eds., *New Futures: The Challenge of Managing Corporate Transitions,* 107–133. Homewood, IL: Dow Jones–Irwin.

Salinger, M. (1992). "Standard Errors in Event Studies." *Journal of Financial and Quantitative Analysis* 27:39–53.

Salter, M. S., and Weinhold, W. A. (1978). "Diversification via Acquisition: Creating Value." *Harvard Business Review* 56 (July–August): 166–176.

Salter, M. S., and Weinhold. W. A. (1979). *Diversification Through Acquisition: Strategies for Creating Value.* New York: Free Press.

Salter, M. S., and Weinhold, W. A. (1982). "What Lies Ahead for Merger Activities in the 1980's." *Journal of Business Strategy* 2:66–99.

Sametz, A. W., ed. (1991). *The Battle for Corporate Control: Shareholder Rights, Stakeholder Interests, and Managerial Responsibilities,* Homewood IL: Business One Irwin.

Samuelson, Paul A. (1948). *Foundations of Economic Analysis.* Cambridge, MA.: Harvard University Press.

Schelling, T. C. (1960). *The Strategy of Conflict.* Cambridge, MA: Harvard University Press.

Schendel, D. E., and Hofer, C. E. (1979). *Strategic Management.* Boston: Little, Brown.

Scherer, F. M. (1986). "Mergers, Sell-offs, and Managerial Behavior." In L. G. Thomas III, ed., *The Economics of Strategic Planning, Essays in the Honor of Joel Dean,* 43–170. Lexington, MA: Lexington Books.

Scherer, F. M. (1988). "Corporate Takeovers: The Efficiency Arguments." *Journal of Economic Perspectives* 2:69–82.

Scherer, F. M., and Ross, D. (1990). *Industrial Market Structure and Economic Performance.* 3d ed. Boston: Houghton Mifflin.

Schipper, K., and Smith, A. (1983). "Effects of Recontracting on Shareholder Wealth: The Case of Voluntary Spin-Offs." *Journal of Financial Economics* 12:437–467.

Schipper, K., and Thompson, R. (1983). "Evidence on the Capitalized Value of Merger Activity for Acquiring Firms." *Journal of Financial Economics* 11:85–119.

Schmidt, D. R., and Fowler, K. L. (1990). "Post-Acquisition Financial Performance and Executive Compensation." *Strategic Management Journal* 11:559–569.

Schumpeter, J. A. (1934). *The Theory of Economic Development.* Cambridge, MA: Harvard University Press.

Schwartz, S. (1982). "Factors Affecting the Probability of Being Acquired: Evidence for the United States." *Economic Journal* 92:391–398.

Schweiger, D. M., and DeNisi, A. S. (1987). "The Effects of Communication with Employees Following a Merger: A Longitudinal Field Experiment." Paper presented at the Annual Meeting of the Academy of Management, New Orleans.

Schweiger, D. M., and Ivancevich, J. M. (1987a). "The Effects of Mergers and Acquisitions on Organizations and Employees: A Contingency View." Paper presented at the International Conference of the Strategic Management Society, Boston.

Schweiger, D. M., Ivancevich, J. M., and Power, F. R. (1987b). "Executive Actions for Managing Human Resources Before and After Acquisition." *Academy of Management Executive* 1:127–138.

Schweiger, D. M., and Walsh, J. (1990). "Mergers and Acquisitions: An Interdisciplinary View." In K. M. Rowland and G. R. Ferris, eds., *Research in Personnel and Human Resource Management,* 8:41–107. Greenwich, CT: JAI Press.

Scott, J. J. (1982). "Multimarket Contact and Economic Performance." *Review of Economics and Statistics* 64:367–375.

Scott, J. J. (1989). "Purposive Diversification as a Motive for Merger." *International Journal of Industrial Organization* 7:35–47.

Searby, F. W. (1969). "Control Post Merger Change." *Harvard Business Review* (September–October): 4–12.

Selznick, P. (1957). *Leadership in Administration.* Evanston, IL: Row, Peterson.

Servaes, H. (1991). "Tobin's Q and the Gains from Takeovers." *Journal of Finance* 46:409–419.

Seth, A. (1990a). "Value Creation in Acquisitions: A Re-examination of Performance Issues." *Strategic Management Journal* 11:99–115.

Seth, A. (1990b). "Sources of Value Creation in Acquisitions: An Empirical Investigation." *Strategic Management Journal* 11:431–446.

Settle, J. W., Petry, W. H., and Hsia, C. C. (1984). "Synergy, Diversification, and Incentive Effects of Corporate Merger on Bondholder Wealth: Some Evidence." *Journal of Financial Research* 7:329–339.

Seyhun, N. (1990). "Do Bidder Managers Knowingly Pay Too Much for Target Firms?" *Journal of Business* 63:439–464.

Shanley, M. T. (1987). "Post Acquisition Management Approaches: An Exploratory Study." Ph.D. dissertation, Wharton School, University of Pennsylvania.

Shanley, M. T. (1988). "Reconciling the Rock and the Hard Place: Management Control versus Human Resource Accommodation in Acquisition Integration." Working paper. Chicago: Graduate School of Business, University of Chicago.

Shanley, M. T., and Correa, M. E. (1992). "Agreement Between Top Management Teams and Expectations for Post Acquisition Performance." *Strategic Management Journal* 13:245–266.

Sharpe, W. F. (1964). "Capital Assets Prices: A Theory of Market Equilibrium Under Conditions of Risk." *Journal of Finance* 19:425–442.

Shelton, L. M. (1985). "The Role of Strategic Business Fits in Creating Gains to Acquisition." Ph.D. dissertation, Harvard University.

Shelton, L. M. (1988). "Strategic Business Fits and Corporate Acquisition: Empirical Evidence." *Strategic Management Journal* 9:279–287.

Shiller, R. J. (1981). "Do Stock Prices Move Too Much to Be Justified by Subsequent Changes in Dividends?" *American Economic Review* 71:421–436.

Shiller, R. J. (1984). "Stock Prices and Social Dynamics." *Brookings Papers on Economic Activity*, 457–498.

Shirley, R. C. (1977). "The Human Side of Merger Planning." *Long Range Planning* 10:35–39.

Shleifer, A., and Summers, L. H. (1988). "Break of Trust in Hostile Takeovers." In A. J. Auerbach, ed., *Corporate Takeovers: Causes and Consequences,* 333–356. Chicago: University of Chicago Press.

Shleifer, A., and Vishny, R. W. (1986). "Greenmail, White Knights, and Shareholders' Interest." *Rand Journal of Economics* 17:293–309.

Shleifer, A., and Vishny, R. W. (1988). "Value Maximization and the Acquisition Process." *Journal of Economic Perspectives* 2:7–20.

Shleifer, A., and Vishny, R. W. (1989a). "Managerial Entrenchment: The Case of Manager-Specific Investments." *Journal of Financial Economics* 25:123–139.

Shleifer, A., and Vishny, R. W. (1989b). "The Takeover Wave of the 1980's." *Science* 249:745–749.

Shleifer, A., and Vishny, R. W. (1991). "Takeovers in the '60s and '80s: Evidence and Implications." *Strategic Management Journal* 12:51–59.

Shrivastava, P. (1986). "Postmerger Integration." *Journal of Business Strategy* 7:65–76.

Siehl, C., Ledford, G., Silverman, R., and Fay, P. (1988). "Preventing Culture Clashes from Botching a Merger." *Acquisitions Monthly* (March–April): 51–57.

Siehl, C., Smith, D., and Omura, A. (1990). "After the Merger: Should Executives Stay or Go?" *Academy of Management Executive* 4:50–60.

Simon, H. A. (1987). "Making Management Decisions: The Role of Intuition and Emotion." *Academy of Management Executive* 1:57–64.

Simon, H. (1976). *Administrative Behavior.* 3d ed. New York: Free Press.

Sims, C. (1993). "'Synergy': The Unspoken Word." *New York Times,* October 5, p. D1.

Sinetar, M. (1981). "Mergers, Morale and Productivity." *Personnel Journal* (November): 863–867.

Singh, A. (1971). *Takeovers: Their Relevance to the Stock Market and the Theory of the Firm.* Cambridge: Cambridge University Press.

Singh, A. (1975). "Takeovers, Economic Natural Selection and the Theory of the Firm: Evidence from the Post-War United Kingdom Experience." *Economic Journal* 85:497–515.

Singh, H. (1984). "Corporate Acquisitions and Economic Performance." Ph.D. dissertation, University of Michigan.

Singh, H., and Montgomery, C. A. (1987). "Corporate Acquisition Strategies and Economic Performance." *Strategic Management Journal* 8:377–386.

Sirower, M. L. (1991). "Bankruptcy as a Strategic Planning Tool." *Academy of Management Best Papers Proceedings* 46–50.

Sirower, M. L. (1993). "Acquisition Premiums and the Post-Merger Challenge: A New Perspective on Acquirer Performance." Paper presented at the Thirteenth Annual International Conference of the Strategic Management Society, Chicago, September 13–16.

Sirower, M. L. (1994). "Acquisition Behavior, Strategic Resource Commitments and the Acquisition Game: A New Perspective on Performance and Risk in Acquiring Firms." Ph.D. dissertation, Graduate School of Business, Columbia University.

Sirower, M. L. (1995a). "Acquisition Premiums and the Acquisition Game: Testing the Synergy Limitation Model of Acquiring Firm Performance." Working Paper, Stern School of Business, New York University.

Sirower, M. L. (1995b). "Business Strategy and Target Capital Structure." Working Paper, Stern School of Business, New York University.

Sirower, M. L. and Abzug. R. (1996). "Duty of Care and Duty of Loyalty: The Unsettling Case of Fiduciary Liability in Acquiring Firms." Paper presented at the Fifty-sixth Annual Academy of Management Meetings, Cincinnati, August 9–14.

Sirower, M. L., and Auster, E. R. (1992). "An Institutional Perspective on Corporate Mergers and Takeovers: An Alternative to Economic Efficiency Arguments." Paper presented at the Fifty-second Annual Meeting of the Academy of Management, Las Vegas, August 9–12.

Sirower, M. L., and Harrigan, K. R. (1996). "Desperately Seeking Synergy? Toward a Competitive Model of Creating Value in Acquisitions." Paper presented at the Sixteenth Annual International Conference of the Strategic Management Society, Phoenix, November 10–13.

Slater, R. (1987). *The Titans of Takeover.* New York: Prentice Hall.

Slusky, A. R., and Caves, R. E. (1991). "Synergy, Agency, and the Determinants of Premia Paid in Mergers." *Journal of Industrial Economics* 39:277–296.

Smart, T. (1996). "Defying the Law of Gravity," *Business Week,* April 8, pp. 124–127.

Smiley, R. (1976). "Tender Offers, Transactions Costs and the Theory of the Firm." *Review of Economics and Statistics* 48:22–31.

Smirnov, N. V. (1939). "Estimate of Deviation Between Empirical Distribution Functions in Two Independent Samples." *Bulletin Moscow University* 2(2):3–16.

Smith v. Van Gorkom, 488 A.2d 858 (Del. 1985).

Smith, C. (1986). "Investment Banking and the Capital Acquisition Process." *Journal of Financial Economics* 15:3–29.

Souder, W. S., and Chakrabarti, A. K. (1984). "Acquisitions: Do They Really Work Out?" *Interfaces* 14 (July–August): 41–47.

Starbuck, W. H. (1965). "Organizational Growth and Development." In J. G. March, ed., *Handbook of Organizations,* 451–533. Chicago: Rand McNally.

Staw, B. M. (1976). "Knee-Deep in the Big Muddy: A Study of Escalating Commitment to a Chosen Course of Action." *Organizational Behavior and Human Performance* 16:27–44.

Staw, B. M. (1981). "The Escalation of Commitment to a Course of Action." *Academy of Management Review* 6:577–587.

Staw, B. M., and Ross, J. (1978). "Commitment to a Policy Decision: A Multitheoretical Perspective." *Administrative Science Quarterly* 23:40–64.

Staw, B. M., and Ross, J. (1987). "Knowing When to Pull the Plug." *Harvard Business Review* (March–April): 68–74.

Staw, B. M., Sandelands, L. E., and Dutton, J. E. (1981). "Threat-Rigidity Effects in Organizational Behavior: A Multilevel Analysis." *Administrative Science Quarterly* 26:501–524.

Steiner, P. O. (1975). *Mergers: Motives, Effects, Policies.* Ann Arbor: University of Michigan Press.

Sterngold, J. (1994). "Sony, Struggling, Takes a Huge Loss on Movie Studios." *New York Times,* November 18, p. A1.

Stevens, D. L. (1973). "Financial Characteristics of Merged Firms: A Multivariate Analysis." *Journal of Financial and Quantitative Analysis* 8:149–158.

Stewart, G. B. III. (1991). *The Quest for Value.* New York: HarperCollins.

Stewart, J. (1994). "Sony's Bad Dream." *New Yorker,* February 28, pp. 43–51.

Stewart, J. F., Harris, R. S., and Carleton, W. T. (1984). "The Role of Market Structure in Merger Behavior." *Journal of Industrial Economics* 32:293–312.

Stigler, G. J. (1950). "Monopoly and Oligopoly by Merger." *American Economic Review* 40:23–34.

Stillman, R. (1983). "Examining Antitrust Policy Toward Horizontal Mergers." *Journal of Financial Economics* 11:225–240.

Stum, D. L. (1988). "The Transition to Unisys." *Training and Development Journal* 9(August): 41–43.

Summer, C. E. (1980). *Strategic Behavior in Business and Government.* Boston: Little, Brown.

Taggart, R. A., Jr. (1988). "The Growth of the 'Junk' Bond Market and Its Role in Financing Takeovers." In A. J. Auerbach, ed., *Mergers and Acquisitions,* 5–24. Chicago: University of Chicago Press.

Tamburri, R., and Clark, D. (1996). "Corel to Acquire Novell's WordPerfect for $124 Million in Cash and Stock." *Wall Street Journal,* February 1, p. A3.

Tang, M.-J. (1988). "An Economic Perspective on Escalating Commitment." *Strategic Management Journal* 9:79–92.

Teece, D. J. (1980). "Economies of Scope and the Scope of the Enterprise." *Journal of Economic Behavior and Organization* 1:223–247.

Teece, D. J. (1982). "Towards an Economic Theory of the Multiproduct Firm." *Journal of Economic Behavior and Organization* 3:39–63.

Teece, D. J., Pisano, G., and Shuen, A. (1990). "Firm Capabilities, Resources, and the Concept of Strategy: Four Paradigms of Strategic Management." Working paper, University of California at Berkeley.

Tehranian, H., and Waeglian, J. F. (1985). "Market Reaction to Short Term Executive Compensation Plan Adoption." *Journal of Accounting and Economics* 7:131–144.

Thaler, R. (1988). "Anomalies: The Winner's Curse." *Journal of Economic Perspectives* 2:191–201.

Trautwein, F. (1990). "Merger Motives and Merger Prescriptions." *Strategic Management Journal* 11:283–296.

Travlos, N. G. (1987). "Corporate Takeover Bids, Methods of Payment, and Bidding Firms' Stock Return." *Journal of Finance* 42:943–963.

Tregoe, B. B., and Zimmerman, J. W. (1980). *Top Management Strategy: What It Is and How to Make It Work.* New York: Simon & Schuster.

Tushman, M. L., and Katz, R. (1980). "External Communication and Project Performance: An Investigation into the Role of Gatekeepers." *Management of Science* 26:1071–1085.

Tushman, M. L., and Romanelli, E. (1983). "Uncertainty, Social Location and Influence in Decision Making: A Sociometric Analysis." *Management Science* 29:12–23.

Tversky, A., and Kahneman, D. (1979). "The Framing of Divisions and the Rationality of Choice." *Science* 211:453–458.

Useem, M. (1993). *Executive Defense: Shareholder Power and Corporate Reorganization.* Cambridge, MA: Harvard University Press.

Varadarajan, P., and Ramanujam, V. (1987). "Diversification and Performance: A Re-Examination Using a New Two-Dimensional Conceptualization of Diversity in Firms." *Academy of Management Journal* 30:380–393.

Varaiya, N. P. (1986). "An Empirical Investigation of the Bidding Firms' Gains from Corporate Takeovers." In A. Chen, ed., *Research in Finance.* Greenwich, CT: JAI Press.

Varaiya, N. P. (1987). "Determinants of Premiums in Acquisition Transactions." *Managerial and Decision Economics* 8:175–184.

Varaiya, N. P. (1988). "The 'Winner's Curse' Hypothesis and Corporate Takeovers." *Managerial and Decision Economics* 9:209–220.

Varaiya, N. P., and Ferris, K. R. (1987). "Overpaying in Corporate Takeovers: The Winner's Curse." *Financial Analysts' Journal* (May–June): 64–73.

Varaiya, N. P., Kerin, R. A. and Weeks, D. (1987). "The Relationship Between Growth, Profitability, and Firm Value." *Strategic Management Journal* 8:487–497.

von Neumann, J., and Morgenstern, O. (1947). *Theory of Games and Economic Behavior* Princeton: Princeton University Press.

Walkling, R. A., and Long, M. S. (1984). "Agency Theory, Managerial Welfare, and Takeover Bid Resistance." *Rand Journal of Economics* 15:54–68.

Walsh, J. P. (1988). "Top Management Turnover Following Mergers and Acquisitions." *Strategic Management Journal* 9:173–183.

Walsh, J. P. (1989). "Doing a Deal: Merger and Acquisition Negotiations and Their Impact upon Target Company Top Management Turnover." *Strategic Management Journal* 10:307–322.

Walter, G. A. (1985). "Culture Collisions in Mergers and Acquisitions." In B. J. Frost, L. F. Moore, and C. C. Lundberg, eds., *Organizational Culture,* 301–314. Beverly Hills: Sage.

Warner, J. B. (1977). "Bankruptcy Costs: Some Evidence." *Journal of Finance* 32:337–348.

Watts, R. (1986). "Does It Pay to Manipulate EPS?" In J. M. Stern and D. H. Chew, eds., *The Revolution in Corporate Finance.* New York: Basil Blackwell.

Weidenbaum, M., and Vogt. S. (1987). "Takeovers and Stakeholders: Winners and Losers." Working Paper no. 107. Center for the Study of American Business, Washington University.

Weiss, L. (1965). "An Evaluation of Mergers in Six Industries." *Review of Economics and Statistics* 47:172–181.

Wernerfelt, B. (1984). "A Resource-based View of the Firm." *Strategic Management Journal* 5:171–180.

Wernerfelt, B., and Montgomery, C. A. (1988). "Tobin's q and the Importance of Focus to Firm Performance." *American Economic Review* 78:246–250.

Weston, J. F. (1970). "The Nature and Significance of Conglomerate Firms." *St. John's Law Review* 44 (special edition): 66–80.

Weston, J. F., and Chung, K. S. (1983). "Some Aspects of Merger Theory." *Journal of the Midwest Finance Association* 12:1–33.

Weston, J. F., and Mansinghka, S. K. (1970). "Tests of the Efficiency Performance of Conglomerate Firms." *Journal of Finance* 26:919–936.

White, H. (1980). "A Heteroskedasticity-consistent Covariance Matrix Estimator and a Direct Test for Heteroskedasticity." *Econometrica* 48:817–838.

White, L. J. (1982). "Mergers and Aggregate Concentration." In M. Keenan and L. J. White, eds., *Mergers and Acquisitions,* 97–111. Lexington, MA: Lexington Books.

Wicker, A. W., and Kauma, C. E. (1974). "Effects of a Merger of a Small and Large Organization on Members' Behaviors and Experiences." *Journal of Applied Psychology* 59:24–30.

Williamson, O. E. (1964). *The Economics of Discretionary Behavior: Managerial Objectives in a Theory of the Firm.* Englewood Cliffs, NJ: Prentice Hall.

Williamson, O. E. (1965). "Managerial Discretion and Business Behavior." *American Economic Review* 53:1032–1057.

Williamson, O. E. (1970) *Corporate Control and Business Behavior: An Inquiry into the Effects of Organization Form on Enterprise Behavior.* Englewood Cliffs, NJ: Prentice Hall.

Williamson, O. E. (1975). *Markets and Hierarchies: Analysis and Antitrust Implications.* New York: Free Press.

Williamson, O. E. (1979). "Transaction Cost Economics: The Governance of Contractual Relations." *Journal of Law and Economics* 22:233–261.

Wolf Bytes No. 7 (1991). First Boston Equity Research. July 10.

Wrigley, L. (1970). "Divisional Autonomy and Diversification." Ph.D. dissertation, Harvard Business School.

Yip, G. S. (1982). "Diversification Entry: Internal Development Versus Acquisition." *Strategic Management Journal* 3:331–345.

You, V. L., Caves, R. E., Henry, J. S., and Smith, M. M. (1986). "Mergers and Bidders' Wealth: Managerial and Strategic Factors." In L. G. Thomas, ed., *The Economics of Strategic Planning: Essays in Honor of Joel Dean*. 201–220. Lexington, MA: Lexington Books.

Zachary, G. P. (1994). "Novell Pact with WordPerfect Followed a Secret Bidding War Initiated by Lotus." *Wall Street Journal,* March 24, p. A3.

Zajac, E. J., and Bazerman, M. H. (1991). "Blind Spots in Industry and Competitor Analysis: Implications of Interfirm (mis)perceptions for Strategic Decisions." *Academy of Management Review* 16:37–56.

Zangwill, W. I. (1995). "Models for Successful Mergers." *Wall Street Journal,* December 18, p. A19.

Zollo, M. (1996). "An Evolutionary Model of Post-Acquisition Integration and Performance." Paper presented at the Fifty-sixth Annual Academy of Management Meetings, Cincinnati, August 9–14.

Zweig, P. L. (1995). "The Case Against Mergers." *Business Week* Special Report, October 30, pp. 122–130.

Index

A-B. *See* Anheuser-Busch Inc.

A. L. Williams, 34, 41–42

A. T. Kearney, 61

Abzug, R., 164, 231n1

Accounting performance, post-acquisition, 139

Acquiring firms: announcement effects on, 10, 81, 110–11, 174, 229n9; and competitive challenge of synergy, 24–28; conceptual model of acquirer performance and risk taking, 87–88; description of author's research sample, 15–16, 81, 167, 202–23; important considerations for, 45–46; list of, in author's research sample, 202–23; management literature on performance of, 85–86, 114, 151–57, 231–32nn1–2; measurements of performance in author's methodology, 101–104; merger law and shareholders of, 70; previous acquisitions of, as control variable, 108; reduction of value of, by acquisition strategies, 3, 5–6, 11, 18, 81, 88, 123–24, 146–50, 153, 167, 172–74; research results on acquirer performance and risk taking, 126–36, 178–97; risk taking of, following acquisition, 97–99, 109–10, 112–13; size of, as control variable, 108; value creation of, 152–53. *See also* Acquisition premiums; Acquisitions; Research on acquisitions; and specific firms

Acquisition failures: author's hypotheses on, 88–99; in author's sample, 123; examples of, 120, 140; hubris hypothesis of, 11–12, 120, 160–62, 226n20; and hypothesis on managers pursuing own objectives, 11, 12; likelihood of, 19, 141, 143; McKinsey & Company study on, 150; metaphor for, 80; overview of, 3–8; and relative size of acquisition, 96

Acquisition game: description of, 8–10, 115–16; examples similar to, 44–45, 77–78, 80; importance of concept of, 139; introduction to, 3–5; mergers and acquisitions phenomenon, 5–8; and synergy, 17, 19–21, 76–77, 80, 142; tools and lessons for, 75–82. *See also* Acquisition premiums; Acquisitions; Research on acquisitions; Synergy

Acquisition premiums: amount of, 5, 14, 52, 167; assumptions in prior research on, 13–14; author's research on, 81–82, 87–90, 105–106, 124–29, 169–72, 175–89; and cash flows, 48–50; and contested versus uncontested acquisitions, 82, 95, 132–34, 169–70, 192–93; and discount rate, 47–48; economics of, 45–46; and equity market value/book value ratio, 53–56, 106–107; executives' lack of focus on, 142; ex–post and ex–ante interpretation of overpayment, 118; and "failing course of action" environment, 122; as fair values, 13–14; and hubris hypothesis, 161; measurement of, in author's study, 105–106, 234n10; and multiple bidders, 126–27; overpayment and MV/BV ratio, 106; and performance requirements, 52; and predictable

275

About the Author

Mark L. Sirower is a corporate development advisor with The Boston Consulting Group and a visiting professor at New York University's Stern School of Business. He speaks worldwide on creating value through mergers and acquisitions and actively consults with major corporations on M&A decisions.

Dr. Sirower's research on acquisition performance has been featured in major business periodicals including *Business Week, Fortune, The Wall Street Journal, The New York Times, Harvard Business Review, The Economist, Financial Times, CFO,* and *Barron's.* He has been a featured speaker on important business programs such as the Fortune 500 Forum for CEOs and CFOs, and has made numerous appearances on national television and radio including *CBS News,* CNNfn, CNBC, *The Wall Street Journal Business Report, BBC World,* and NPR's *All Things Considered.* He received his Ph.D. from the Columbia University Graduate School of Business and has held faculty positions at The Wharton School, Columbia University, and New York University. He lives in Manhattan.